BUSINESS ENVIRONMENT

BUSINESS ENVIRONMENT

Vishwajeet Prasad

genNEXT Publication

Business Environment

Rs. 890

ISBN: 978-81-908675-6-6

Published in 2010 in India by
Gennext Publication
23 Main Ansari Road, Darya Ganj,
New Delhi-110002
E-Mail:GenNextpublication@hotmail.com
Phone: 23282060

Printed at: Young Art Press, Delhi-110092

Contents

Preface

Business environment refers to all external forces, which have some effect on the functioning of business. Environment factors are generally external and beyond the control of individual industrial enterprises and their managements. Business environment includes factors such as socio-economic, technological, supplier, competitor and the government.

The volume introduces and examines the business environment model and presents methods of appraisal to examine the model, allowing students to view the business environment both internally and externally. It will help students to understand how business organizations operate in political, social, technological, legal, and economic environments.

Due to an increase in globalization of business, chapter has been dedicated to the international business environment, allowing students to connect what they have learnt in a broader global context. The book is planned to provide a logical treatment of the business environment in the Indian as well as international context. The book covers chapters discussing political environment, economic systems, economic growth and development.

It will be a handy tool for the practicing business managers and also those general readers who would like to keep themselves au courant with the contemporary business environment.

This book answers basic questions and offers research tools, research resources, and information sources. The well-written materials ensure that students are able to understand all topics clearly. With its unique approach, generalized frameworks, elaborate research and extensive data analysis, this book will be of immense value to students and professionals of the Indian corporate sector and marketing departments of national and multinational companies in India.

Author is confident that this book will be a handy tool for the students learning business environment. Sincere feedback, suggestions and comments are always welcome.

1

Business and its Environment

Business may be understood as an organized efforts of enterprise to supply consumers with goods and services for profit. Businesses vary in size, as measured by the number of employees or by sales volume. But, all businesses share the same purpose to earn profits.

The purpose of business goes beyond earning profit. They are as follows:

- It is an important institution in society.
- Be it for the supply of goods and services
- Creation of job opportunities
- Offer of better quality of life
- Contributing to the economic growth of the country.

Hence, it is understood that the role of business is crucial. Society cannot do without business. It needs no emphasis that business needs society as much.

BUSINESS TODAY

Modern business is dynamic. If there is any single word that can best describe today's business, it is change. This change makes the companies spend substantially on Research and development (R & D) to survive in the market. Mass production and mass marketing are the norms followed by business enterprises. The number of companies with an annual turnover of Rs.100 crore each was only three in 1969-70.The figure has gone up by hundreds these days. Today's business is characterized by diversification, which may be:

- Concentric Diversification - It refers to the process of adding new, but relates products or services.

- Horizontal Diversification - Adding new, unrelated products or services for present customers is called horizontal Diversification.
- Conglomerate Diversification - It refers to adding new and unrelated products or services.

Going international is yet another trend followed by modern business houses. Business houses are exposed to global competition, which argues well for consumers. Also occupying a major role is science in the global economic scenario.

BUSINESS IN 21ST CENTURY

Large organizations, with a large workforce never exist. They will be 'Mini' organizations. Business during the 21st century will be knowledge-based, tomorrow's manager need not spend his time on file pushing and paper-shuffling. Information technology will take care of most of that work. Organizations will become flat. Linear relationship between the boss and manger and authority flowing downwards and obedience upward will disappear. Employees will have no definite jobs. Most of the jobs will last for two to five years. Remuneration will depend on one's contribution to organization.

Business Goals:

Following are the major goals of business:

- Profit - Making profit is the primary goal of any business enterprise.
- Growth - Business should grow in all directions over a period of time.
- Power - Business houses have vast resources at its command. These resources confer enormous economic and political power.
- Employee satisfaction and development - Business is people. Caring for employee satisfaction and providing for their development has been one of the objectives of enlightened business enterprises.
- Quality Products and Services - Persistent quality of products earns brand loyalty, a vital ingredient of success.
- Market Leadership - To earn a niche for oneself in the market, innovation is the key factor.

- Challenging - Business offers vast scope and poses formidable challenges.
- Joy of creation - It is through business strategies new ideas and innovations are given a shape and are converted into useful products and services.
- Service to society - Business is a part of society and has several obligations towards it.

SCOPE OF BUSINESS ENVIRONMENT

Environment refers to all external forces, which have a bearing on the functioning of business. Environment factors "are largely if not totally, external and beyond the control of individual industrial enterprises and their managements. The business environment poses threats to a firm or offers immense opportunities for potential market exploitation.

TYPES OF ENVIRONMENT

Environment includes such factors as socio-economic, technological, supplier, competitor and the government. There are two more factors, which exercise considerable influence on business. They are physical or natural environment and global environment.

- Technological Environment: Technology is understood as the systematic application of scientific or other organized knowledge to practical tasks. Technology changes fast and to keep pace with it, businessmen should be ever alert to adopt changed technology in their businesses.
- Economic Environment: There is close relationship between business and its economic environment. Business obtains all its needed inputs from the economic environment and it absorbs the output of business units.
- Political Environment: It refers to the influence exerted by the three political institutions viz., legislature executive and the judiciary in shaping, directing, developing and controlling business activities. A stable and dynamic political environment is indispensable for business growth.
- Natural Environment: Business, an economic pursuit of man, continues to be dictated by nature. To what extend business depends on nature and what is the relationship between the two constitutes an interesting study.

- Global or international Environment: Thanks to liberalization, Indian companies are forces to view business issues from a global perspective. Business responses and managerial practices must be fine-tuned to survive in the global environment.
- Social and culture Environment: It refers to people's attitude to work and wealth; role of family, marriage, religion and education; ethical issues and social responsiveness of business.

ENVIRONMENT - BUSINESS RELATIONS

Business is the product of the technological, political-legal, economic, social - cultural, global and natural factors amidst which it functions. Three features are common to this web of relationship between business and its environment.

- There is symbolic relationship between business and its environment and among the environmental factors. In other words, business is influenced by its environment and in turn, to certain degree, it will influence the external forces. Similarly, political-legal environment influences economic environment and vice versa. The same relationship between other environment factors too.
- These environmental forces are dynamic. They keep on changing as years roll by, so does business.
- The third feature is that a particular business firm, by itself, may not be in a position to change its environment. But along with other firms, business will be in a position to mould the environment in its favor.

IMPORTANCE OF ENVIRONMENTAL STUDY

The benefits of environmental study are as follows:

- Development of broad strategies and long-term policies of the firm.
- Development of action plans to deal with technological advancements.
- To foresee the impact of socio-economic changes at the national and international levels on the firm's stability.
- Analysis of competitor's strategies and formulation of effective countermeasures.
- To keep oneself dynamic.

ENVIRONMENTAL ANALYSIS PROCESS

The analysis consists of four sequential steps:

- Scanning: It involves surveillance of all environmental factors and their interactions in order to: same the following.
  — Identify early signals of possible environmental change
  — Detect environmental change already underway
- Monitoring: It involves tracking the environmental trends, sequences of events, or streams of activities. It frequently involves following signals or indicators unearthed during environmental scanning.
- Forecasting: Strategic decision-making requires a future orientation. Naturally, forecasting is an essential element in environmental analysis. Forecasting is concerned with developing plausible projections of the direction, scope, and intensity of environmental change.
- Assessment: In assessment, the frame of reference moves from understanding the environment- the focus of scanning, monitoring and forecasting - to identify what the understanding means for the organization. Assessment, tries to answer questions such as what are the key issues presented by the environment, and what are the implications of such issues for the organization.

CORPORATE GOVERNANCE, SOCIAL RESPONSIBILITY AND BUSINESS ETHICS

Corporate failures and widespread dissatisfaction with the way many corporate functions have led to the realization, globally, of the need to put in place a proper system for corporate governance.

Corporate governance is concerned with holding the balance between economic and social goals and between individual and communal goals. The governance framework is there to encourage the efficient use of resources and equally to require accountability for the stewardship of those resources.

The aim is to align as nearly as possible the interest of individuals, corporations, and society. The incentive to corporations and to those who own and manage them to adopt internationally accepted governance standards is that these standards will help them to achieve their corporate aims and to attract investment.

The incentive for their adoption by states is that these standards will strengthen the economy and discourage fraud and mismanagement.

RELEVANCE

Three reasons have triggered off concern in corporate governance in our country. Which are as follows:

- Since 1991, the country has moved into liberalized economy and one of the victims of the market-based economy is transparent fair business practice. Several instances of mismanagement have been alleged, with some well-known and senior executive being hauled up for non-performance and /or non-compliance with legal requirements.
- Both domestic as well as foreign investors are becoming more demanding in their approach towards the companies in which they have invested their funds. They seek information and want to influence decisions.
- Interests of non-promoter shareholder and those of small investors are increasingly being undermined. Several MNCs have sought to set up 100 percent subsidiaries and transfer their businesses to them .In many cases, there was no thought of consultation with non-promoter shareholders. In this context, some norms of behavior to ensure responsive behavior are of great help. Hence, corporate governance.

FOCUS

Corporate governance is concerned with the values, vision and visibility. It is about the value orientation of the organization, ethical norms for its performance, the direction of development and social accomplishment of the organization and the visibility of its performance and practices. Corporate management is concerned with the efficiency of the resources use, value addition and wealth creation within the broad parameters of the corporate philosophy established by corporate governance.

IMPORTANCE

- Studies of firms in India and abroad have shown that markets and investors take notice of well-managed companies, respond positively to them, and reward such companies, with higher valuations. In other words they have a system of good corporate governance.

- Strong corporate governance is indispensable to resilient and vibrant capital markets and is an important instrument of investor protection.
- Corporate governance prevents insider trading.
- Under corporate governance, corporates are expected to disseminate the material price sensitive information in a timely and proper manner and also ensures that till such information is made public, insiders abstain from transacting in the securities of the company.
- The principle should be 'disclose or desist'. Good corporate governance, besides protecting the interests of shareholders and all other stakeholders, contributes to the efficiency of a business enterprise, to the creation of wealth and to the country's economy.
- Good corporate governance is considered vital from medium and long-term perspectives to enable firms to compete internationally in sustained way and make them, not only to improve standard of living materially but also to enhance social cohesion.

PRE-REQUISITES

A system of good corporate governance requires the following:

- A proper system consisting of clearly defined and adequate structure of roles, authority and responsibility.
- Vision, principles and norms, which indicate development path, normative considerations, and guidelines and norms for performance.
- A proper system for guiding, monitoring, reporting and control.

SOCIAL RESPONSIBILTY

Social responsibility is the obligation of decision-makers to take actions, which protect and improve the welfare of society as a whole along with their own interests. Every decision the businessman takes and every action he contemplates have social implications. Be it deciding on diversification, expansion, opening of a new branch, and closure of an existing branch or replacement of men by machines, the society is affected in one way or the other. Whether the issue is significant or not, the businessman should keep his social obligation in mind before contemplating any action.

Arguments for Social Responsibility:

- Business has to respond to the needs and expectations of society.
- Improvement of the social environment benefits both society and business.
- Social responsibility discourages additional governmental regulation and intervention.
- Business has a great deal of power, which should be accompanied by an equal amount of responsibility.
- Internal activities of the enterprise have an impact on the external environment.
- The concept of social responsibility protects interests of stockholders.
- Social responsibility creates a favorable public image.
- Business has the resources to solve some of society's problems.
- It is better to prevent social problems through business involvement than to cure them.

Arguments Against Social Responsibility:

- Social responsibilities could reduce economic efficiency.
- Social responsibility would create excessive costs for business.
- Weakened international balance of payments
- Business has enough power, and social involvement would further increase its power and influence.
- Business people lack the social skills necessary to deal with the problems of society.
- Business is not really accountable to society.

SOCIAL STAKEHOLDERS

Managers, who are concerned with corporate social responsibility, need to identify various interest groups which may affect the functioning of a business organization and may be affected by its functioning. Business enterprises are primarily responsible to six major groups:

- Shareholders
- Employees
- Customers

- Creditors, suppliers and others
- Society and
- Government.

These groups are called interest groups or social stakeholders. They can be affected for by the business activities of corporations.

Social Responsiveness

Social responsiveness (SR) is "the ability of a corporation to relate it operations and policies to the social environment in ways that are mutually beneficial to the company and to society".

In other words, it refers to the development of organizational decision processes whereby managers anticipate, respond to, and manage areas of social responsibility. The need to measure the social responsiveness of an organization led to the concept of social audit. The social responsiveness of an organization can be measured on the basis of the following criteria:

- Contributions to charitable and civic projects
- Assisting voluntary social organizations in fund-raising
- Employee involvement in civic activities
- Proper reuse of material
- Equal employment opportunity
- Promotion of minorities
- Direct corporate social responsiveness investment
- Fair treatment of employees
- Fair pay and safe working conditions
- Safe and quality products to consumers
- Pollution avoidance and control

BUSINESS ETHICS

The two issues - an organization's social responsibility and responsiveness- ultimately depend on the ethical standards of mangers. The term ethics commonly refers to the rules or principles that define right and wrong conduct. Ethics is defined as the "discipline dealing with what is good and bad and with moral duty and obligation". Business ethics is concerned with truth and justice and has a variety of aspects such as expectations of society, fair competition, advertising, public relations, social responsibilities, consumer autonomy, and corporate behavior in the home country as well as abroad.

Types of Business Ethics

Moral management: Moral management strives to follow ethical principles and precepts, moral mangers strive for success, but never violate the parameters of ethical standards. They seek to succeed only within the ideas of fairness, and justice. Moral managers follow the law not only in letter but also in spirit. The moral management approach is likely to be in the best interests of the organization, long run.

Amoral management: This approach is neither immoral nor moral. It ignores ethical considerations. Amoral management is broadly categorized into two types - intentional and unintentional.

- Intentional amoral managers exclude ethical issues because they think that general ethical standards are not appropriate to business.
- Unintentional amoral managers do not include ethical concerns because they are inattentive or insensitive to the moral implications.

Immoral Management

Immoral management is synonymous with "unethical" practices in business. This kind of management ignores concerns, it is actively opposed to ethical behavior.

Need for Business Ethics:

- Ethics corresponds to the basic human needs. It is a human trait that man desires to be ethical, not only in his private life but also in his business. These basic ethical need compel the organizations to be ethically oriented.
- Values create credibility with public. A company perceived by the public to be ethically and socially responsive will be honored and respected. The management has credibility with its employees precisely because it has credibility with the public.
- An ethical attitude helps the management make better decisions, because ethics will force a management to take various aspects-economic, social, and ethical in making decisions.
- Value driven companies are sure to be successful in the long run, though in the short run, they may lose money.

- Ethics is important because the government, law and lawyers cannot do everything to protect society.

Ethical Guidelines:

- Obeying the law: Obedience to the law, preferably both the letter and spirit of the law.
- Tell the Truth: To build and maintain long-term, trusting and win-win relationships with relevant stockholders.
- Uphold human dignity: Giving due importance to the element of human dignity and treating people with respect.
- Adhere to the golden rule: "Do unto others as you would have others do unto you"
- Premium Non-Nocere: (Above all, do no harm)
- Allow Room for participation: Soliciting the participation of stakeholders rather than paternalism. It emphasizes the significance of learning about the needs of stakeholders.
- Always Act When You Have Responsibility: Managers have the responsibility of taking action whenever they have the capacity or adequate resources to do so.

Tools for Ethical Management:

- Top management commitment: Managers can prove their commitment and dedication for work and by acting as role models through their own behaviors.
- Codes of Ethics: A formal document that states an organization's primary values and the ethical rules it expects employees to follow. The code is helpful in maintaining ethical behavior among employees.
- Ethics committees: Appointment of an ethics committee, consisting of internal and external directors is essential for institutionalizing ethical behavior.
- Ethics Audits: Systematic assessment of conformance to organizational ethical policies, understanding of those policies, and identification of serious deviations requiring remedial action.
- Ethics training: Ethical training enables managers to integrate employee behavior in ethical arena with major organizational goals.
- Ethics Hotline: A special telephone line that enables employees to bypass the normal chain of command in reporting their

experiences, expectations and problem. The line is usually handled by an executive appointed to help resolve the issues that are reported.

ECONOMIC SYSTEMS

MEANING

Economic system is a social organism through which people earn their living. It is constituted of all those individuals, households, farms, firms, factories, banks and government, which act and interact to produce and consume goods and services. Individuals and households put their resources (land, labour, capital and skill) to one or more of their alternative uses and make their living; firms buy factors of production and organize them in the process of production, produce goods and services, and sell them to their users to make projects. Consumers are able to get the goods and services of their requirement; producers are able to produce and sell various kinds of products in appropriate quantities and so on. The system is operated by, What Adam Smith called "invisible hands", the market forces of demand and supply. A modern economic system is enormously complex. Millions of people participate and contribute to its working in different capacities - as producers, traders, workers, consumers and financers and so on. Thousands of people are involved in production and distribution of single commodity. A community, before it reaches its final consumer, passes through a complex process of production and through a number of intermediary hands.

KINDS OF ECONOMIC SYSTEMS

Free Enterprise Economy

This economic system works on the principle of Laissez Faire system, i.e., the least interference by the government or any external force. The primary role of the government, if any, is to ensure free working of the economy by removing obstacles to free competition.

A free Enterprise Economy is characterized as follows:

- Means of production are privately owned by the people who acquire and posses them
- Private gains are the main motivating and guiding force for carrying out economic activities
- Both consumers and firms enjoy the freedom of choice; consumers have the freedom to consume what they want to and firms have the choice to produce what they want to

- The factor owners enjoy the freedom of occupational choice, i.e., they are free to use their resources in any legal business or occupation;
- There exists a high degree of competition in both commodity and factor markets and
- There is least interference by the government in the economic activities of the people; the government is in fact supposed to limit its traditional functions viz., to defence, police, justice, some financial organizations and public utility services.

GOVERNMENT CONTROLLED ECONOMY

The government-controlled economies are also called as Command, Centrally planned or Socialist economies. Such economies are, in contradistinction to the free enterprise economies, controlled, regulated and managed by the government agencies.

The other features of a pure socialist economy are:

- Means of production are owned by the society or by the state in the name of the community - private ownership of factors and property is abolished;
- Social welfare is the guiding factor for economic activities - private gains, motivations and initiatives are absent,
- Freedom of choice for the consumers is curbed to what society can afford for all, and
- The role of market forces and competition is eliminated by law.

MIXED ECONOMY

A mixed economy is one in which there exists both government and private economic systems. It is supposed to be composed of good elements of both free enterprise and socialist economies. A mixed economy is widely known as one, which had both "public sector" (the government economy) and "private sector" (the private economy). The private sector has features of a free enterprise economy and the public sector has features of socialist economy. It is important to note here that most economies in the world today are Mixed Economies.

There are two different forms of the Mixed Economies.

- Mixed Capitalist Economies: A mixed Capitalist economy is a variant of the free enterprise economic system. To this category fall the highly developed nations like the United States, U.K., France, Japan etc. though these economies have a very large government sector, their private sectors work on the principles of the free enterprise system. The government plays a significant role in preserving capitalist mode of production, ensuring a workable competition in factor and product markets, providing infrastructure for promotion of private sector economic activities.

- Mixed Socialist Economies: To the category of the Mixed Socialist Economies belong the countries which have adopted " socialist pattern of society: and economic planning as he means of growth and social justice (e.g. India) and the former communist countries (e.g. Russia and china) which have of late carried out drastic economic reforms and liberalized their economies for private entrepreneurship. The government of these countries takes upon themselves to control and regulate the private sector activities in accordance with the plan objectives.

BASIC PROBLEMS OF AN ECONOMY AND THE ROLE OF GOVERNMENT

Whatever the nature of the economic system, all types of economies have been faced with certain common basic problems. The major economic problems faced by an economy may be classified into two broad groups:

i. Micro-economic problems called basic problems, which are related to the working of the constituents of the economic system; and

ii. Macro-economic problems related to the growth, stability, and management of the economy as a whole. The way the basic problems of an economy are solved depends on the nature of the economy. While in a socialist economy they are solved by the government agencies, like central planning authority, in a free enterprise or mixed capitalist economy this task is performed by the Price Mechanism or Market Mechanism. Though free enterprise system is capable of bringing economic growth, it does not ensure a stable, sustained, and balanced growth. It becomes therefore inevitable for the government to intervene fair competition, and help the economy in achieving its goals - efficiency, stability, growth and economic justice.

Now, the question arises as to what should be the appropriate role of the government in economic management of the country or what should be the form, nature and extent of government's interference with market mechanism. Nevertheless, the economic role of the government can be broadly categorized on the basis of the three economic systems which presently prevail in the world, viz., Capitalist System or Free Enterprise System, Socialist System, and the Mixed-Economy System.

- Capital Society: In this system, the primary role of the government are:
  i. To preserve and promote free market mechanism wherever it is possible to ensure a workable competition,
  ii. To remove all unnecessary restrictions on the free operation of competitive market, and
  iii. To provide playground and rules of the market game through necessary interventions and controls so that free competition can work effectively. It may be inferred that the government's role in a capitalist society is supposed to be limited to (a) restoration and promotion of necessary conditions for efficient working of free market mechanism; and (b) to enter those areas of production and distribution in which private entrepreneurship is lacking or is inefficient.
- Socialist Economy: In contract with the capitalist system, the role of government in a Socialist economy is much more exhaustive. While in the former, the government is supposed to play a limited role in the economic sphere, in the latter, it exercises comprehensive control on almost all economic activities. In the socialist system, not only there is a complete disregard for free enterprise and market mechanism but also these systems are abolished by law. The private ownership of factors of production is replaced by the State ownership. All economic activities are centrally planned, controlled and regulated by the State. All decisions regarding production resources, allocation, employment, pricing etc., are centralized in the hands of government or the Central Planning Authority.
- Mixed Economy: In this system, a major part of the economy, the private sector, is allowed to function on the principles of free enterprise system or free market mechanism within a broad political and economic policy framework. The other part of the economy, the public sector, is organized and managed along

the socialist pattern. The public sector is created by reserving certain industries, trade, services, and activities for the government control and management. The government prevents by an ordinance the entry of private capital into the industries reserved for the public sector.

Another way of creating or expanding the public sector is nationalization of existing industries. The promotion, control and management of the public sector industries is the sole responsibility of the State. Apart from controlling and managing the public sector industries the government controls and regulates the private sector through its industrial, monetary and fiscal policies. If necessary, direct controls are also imposed.

ECONOMIC TRANSITION IN INDIA: PRIVATIZATION AND GLOBALIZATION

Privatization, which has become a universal trend, means transfer of ownership and management of an enterprise from the public sector to the private sector. It also means the withdrawal of the state from an industry or sector, partially or fully.

Another dimension of privatization is opening up of an industry that has been reserved for the public sector to the private sector. Privatization is an inevitable historical reaction to the indiscriminate expansion of the state sector and the associated problems. Even in the 'communist' countries it became a vital measurement of economic rejuvenation.

Objects

The objects are:

- To improve the performance of PSUs so as to lessen the financial burden on taxpayers.
- To increase the size and dynamism of the private sector, distributing ownership more widely in the population at large.
- To encourage and to facilitate private sector investments, from both domestic and foreign sources.
- To generate revenues for the state
- To reduce the administrative burden on the state
- Launching and sustaining the transformation of the economy from a command to a market model.

Privatization Routes

The important ways of privatization are:

- Divestiture, or privatization of ownership, through the sales of equity.
- Denationalization or reprivatization.
- Contracting - under which government contracts out services to other organizations that produce and deliver them.
- Franchising- authorizing the delivery of certain services in designated geographical areas- is common in utilities and urban transport.
- Government withdrawing from the provision of certain goods and services leaving then wholly or partly to the private sector.
- Privatization of management, using leases and management contracts
- Liquidation, which can be either formal or informal. Formal liquidation involves the closure of an enterprise and the sale of its assets. Under informal liquidation, a firm retains its legal status even though some or all of its operations may be suspended.

Benefits

The benefits of privatization may be listed as follows:

- It reduces the fiscal burden of the state by relieving it of the losses of the SOEs and reducing the size of the bureaucracy.
- Privatization of SOEs enables the government to mop up funds.
- Privatization helps the state to trim the size of the administrative machinery.
- It enables the government to concentrate more on the essential state functions
- Privatization helps accelerate the pace of economic developments as it attracts more resources from the private sector for development.
- It may result in better management of the enterprises.
- Privatization may also encourage entrepreneurship.
- Privatization may increase the number of workers and common man who are shareholders. This could make the enterprises subject to more public vigilance.

Criticisms

Some of the important argument againsts privatization are as follows:

- The public sector has been developed with certain noble objectives and privatization means discarding them in one stroke.
- Privatization will encourage concentration of economic power to the common detriment.
- If privatization results in the substitution of the monopoly power of the public enterprises by the monopoly power of private enterprises it will be very dangerous.
- Privatization many a time results in the acquisition of national firms by foreign firms.
- Privatization of profitable enterprises, including potentially profitable, means foregoing future streams of income for the government.
- Privatization of strategic and vital sectors is against national interests.
- There are well managed and ill-managed firms both in the public and private sectors. It is not sector that matters, but the quality and commitment of the management.
- The capital markets of developing countries are not developed enough for efficiently carrying out privatization.
- Privatization in many instances is a half-hearted measure and therefore it is not properly carried out. As a result that the expected results may not be achieved.
- In many instance, there are vested interested behind privatization and it amounts deceiving the nation. In many countries privatization often has been a "garage sale" to favored individuals and groups.

Conditions for Success

- Privatization cannot be sustained unless the political leadership is committed to it, and it reflects a shift in the preferences of the public arising out of dissatisfaction with the performance of other alternatives.
- Replacement of a government monopoly by a private monopoly may not increase public welfare-there must a multiplicity of private suppliers. Freedom of entry to provide goods and services.

- Public services to be provided by the private sector must be specific or have measurable outcome.
- Lack of specificity makes it more difficult to control services provided by the private sector. Service delivery by non-governmental organizational or local governments may be more appropriate under these conditions.
- Consumers should be able to link the benefits they receive from a service to the costs they pay for it, since they will then shop more wisely for difficult services.
- The importance of educating consumers and disseminating information to the public is necessary.
- Privately provided services should be less susceptible to fraud than government services if they are to be effective.
- Equity is an important consideration in the delivery of public services. Broadly speaking, the benefits of privatization can accrue to the capital owner to the consumer and to public at large.

PRIVATIZATION IN INDIA

In India, although there were some isolated cases of privatization, no definite policy decision was taken until the new economic policy has been ushered in .The accumulated loses of many SOEs, including some state transport corporations, are larger than the capital invested in them. Privatization of certain sectors and enterprises are, therefore, necessary to reduce the budgetary burden on the public, to make available more resources for the development activities, to enable the government to concentrate more on the essential and priority areas.

The new industrial policy, which has abolished the public sector monopoly in all but a very few industries is a significant step towards Privatization. The new policy also proposes Privatization of enterprises by selling shares to mutual funds, workers and the public. The central government has been reviewing the existing portfolio of public investment with a view to offloading public investment.

The disinvestments Commission was set up by Government of India in August 1996, for suggesting the modalities for undertaking disinvestments of equities for select PSUs. The commission has recommended disinvestments at varying levels for a number of PSUs.

PRIVATIZATION POLICY

The current direction of Privatization policy is to put national resources and assets to optimal use and in particular to unleash the productive potential inherent in our public sector enterprises. The policy of disinvestments specifically aimed at:

- Modernization and up gradation of Public Sector Enterprises.
- Creation of new assets.
- Generation of Employment
- Retiring of public debt
- To ensure that disinvestments does not result into the alienation of national assets, which through the process of disinvestments, remain where they are. It will also ensure that disinvestment does not result in private monopolies.
- Setting up a Disinvestments Proceeds Fund.
- Formulating the guidelines for the disinvestments of natural assets companies.

Globalization

India's economic integration with the rest of the world was very limited because of the restrictive economic policies followed until 1991. Indian firms confined themselves, by and large, to the home market. Foreign investment by Indian firms was very insignificant. With the new economic policy ushered in 1991, there has, however, been change. Globalization has in fact become a buzzword with Indian firms now and many are expanding their overseas business by different strategies. Globalization may be defined as " the growing economic interdependence of countries worldwide through increasing volume and variety of cross border transactions in goods and services and of international capital flows, and also through the more rapid and widespread diffusion of technology". Globalization may be considered at two levels viz, at the macro level (i.e., globalization of the world economy) and at the micro level (i.e., globalization of the business and the firm). Globalization of the world economy is achieved, quite obviously, by globalising the national economies. Globalization of the economies and globalization of business are very much interdependent.

Reasons for Globalization

The rapid shrinking of time and distance across the globe thanks to faster communication, speedier transportation, growing financial flows and rapid technological changes.

- The domestic markets are no longer adequate rich. It is necessary to search of international markets and to set up overseas production facilities.
- Companies may choose for going international to find political stability, which is relatively good in other countries.
- To get technology and managerial know-how.
- Companies often set up overseas plants to reduce high transportation costs.
- Some companies set up plants overseas so as to be close to their raw materials supply and to the markets for their finished products.
- Other developments also contribute to the increasing international of business.
- The US, Canada and Mexico have signed the North American Free Trade agreement (NAFTA), which will remove all barriers to trade among these countries.
- The creation of the World Trade Organization (WTO) is stimulating increased cross-border trade.

Features

The following are the features of the current phase of globalization:

New markets:

- Growing global markets in services - banking, insurance, transport.
- New financial markets - deregulated, globally linked, working around the clock, with action at a distance in real time, with new instruments such as derivatives.
- Deregulation of anti - trust laws and proliferation of mergers and acquisitions.
- Global consumer markets with global brands.

New actors:

- Multinational corporations integrating their production and marketing, dominating food production
- The World Trade Organization - the first multilateral organization with authority to enforce national governments compliance with rule

- An international criminal court system in the making
- A booming international network of NGOs
- Regional blocs proliferating and gaining importance - European Union, Association of South- East Asian Nations, Mercosur, North American Free Trade Association, Southern African Development Community, among many others
- More policy coordination groups - G-7, G40, G22, G77, OECD

New rules and Norms:

- Market economic policies spreading around the world, with greater privatization and liberalization than in earlier the decades
- Widespread adoption of democracy as the choice of political regime
- Human rights conventions and instruments building up in both coverage and number of signatories - and growing awareness among people around the world
- Consensus goals and action agenda for the development
- Conventions and agreements on the global environment - biodiversity, ozone layer, disposal of hazardous wastes, desertification, climate change
- Multilateral agreements in trade, taking up such new agendas as environmental and social conditions
- New multilateral agreements- for services, intellectual property, communications - more binding on national governments than any previous agreements
- The multilateral agreements on investment under debate

New Tools of Communication:

- Internet and electronic communications linking many people simultaneously
- Cellular phones
- Fax machines
- Faster and cheaper transport by air, rail and road
- Computer-aided design

Stages of Globalization

There are five different stages in the development of a firm into a global corporations.

1. First stage: The first stage is the arm's length service activity of essentially domestic company, which moves into new markets overseas by linking up with local dealers and distributors.
2. Second stage: In the stage two, the company takes over these activities on its own.
3. Third stage: In the next stage, the domestic based company to carry out its own manufacturing, marketing and sales in the foreign markets.
4. Four stage: In the stage four, the company moves to a full insider position in these markets, supported by a complete business system including R & D and engineering. This stage calls on the managers to replicate in a new environment the hardware, systems and operational approaches that have worked so well at home.
5. Fifth stage: In the fifth stage, the company moves toward a genuinely global mode of operation.

Globalization Strategies

The various strategies of transiting a firm into global corporation are as follows:

- Exporting: Exporting, the most traditional mode of entering the foreign market is quite a common one even now.
- Licensing and Franchising: Under international licensing, a firm in one country (the licensor) permits a firm in another country (the licensee) to use its intellectual property (such as patents, trademarks, copyrights, technology, technical know-how, marketing skill or some other specific skill). Franchising is "a form of licensing in which a parent company (the franchiser) grants another independent entity (the franchisee) the right to do business in a prescribed manner.
- Contract manufacturing: A company doing international marketing, contracts with firms in foreign countries to manufacture or assemble the products while retaining the responsibilities of marketing the product.
- Management contracting: In a management contract the supplier brings together a package of skills that will provide an integrated service to the client without incurring the risk and benefit of ownership. The arrangement is especially attractive if the

contracting firm is given an option to purchase some shares in the managed company within a stated period.

- Turnkey contracts: A turnkey operation is an agreement by the seller to supply a buyer with a facility fully equipped and ready to be operated by the buyer's personnel, who will be trained by the seller. Turnkey contracts are common in international business in the supply, erection and commissioning of plants, as in the case of oil refineries, steel mills, cement and fertilizer plants etc.

Wholly Owned Manufacturing Facilities

Companies with long term and substantial interest in the foreign market normally establish fully owned manufacturing facilities there. This method demands sufficient financial and managerial resources on the part of the company.

- Assembly operations: A manufacturer who wants a member of the advantages that are associated with overseas manufacturing facilities and yet does not want to go that far may find it desirable to establish overseas assembly facilities in selected markets. The establishment of an assembly operation represents a cross between exporting and overseas manufacturing.
- Joint Ventures: Any form of association, which implies collaboration for more than a transitory period is a joint venture. Types of joint overseas operations are:
  - Sharing of ownership and management in an enterprise
  - Licensing / franchising agreements
  - Contract manufacturing
  - Management contracts
- Third country location: When there are no commercial transactions between two nations because of political reasons or when direct transactions between two nations are difficult due to political reasons or the like, a firm in one of these nations which wants to enter the other market will have to operate from a third country base. For example, Taiwanese entrepreneurs found it easy to enter People's Republic of china through bases in Hong Kong.
- Mergers and acquisitions: Mergers and acquisitions (M & A) have been a very important market entry strategy as well as

expansion strategy. A number of Indian companies have also used this entry strategy.

- Strategic alliance: This strategy seeks to enhance the long-term competitive advantage of the firm by forming alliance with its competitors, existing or potential in critical areas, instead of competing with each other. Strategic alliance is also sometimes used as a market entry strategy. For example, a firm may enter a foreign market by forming an alliance with a firm in the foreign market.
- Counter trade: Counter trade refers to a variety of unconventional international trade practices which link exchange of goods- directly or indirectly - in an attempt to dispense with currency transactions. Counter trade is a form of international trade in which certain export and import transactions are directly linked with each other and in which import of goods are paid for by export of goods, instead of money payments.

Benefits

The important arguments in favour of globalization are:

- Productivity grows more quickly when countries produce goods and services in which they have comparative advantage.
- Living standards can go up faster.
- Global competition and imports keep a lid on prices, so inflation is less likely to derail economic growth.
- An open economy spurs innovation with fresh ideas from abroad.
- Export jobs often pay more than other jobs.
- Unfettered capital flows give access to foreign investment and keep interest rates low.

Disadvantages

Following are drawback of having the globalization:

- Millions have lost jobs due to imports or production shifts abroad. Most find new jobs that pay less.
- Millions of others fear losing their jobs, especially at those companies operating under competitive pressure.
- Workers face pay cut demands from employers, which often threaten to export jobs.

- Services and white-collar jobs are increasingly vulnerable to operations moving offshore.
- Employees can lose their comparative advantage when companies build advanced factories in low-wage countries, making them as productive as those at home.

Essentials for Globalization

They are some essential conditions to be satisfied on the part of the domestic economy as well as the firm for successful globalization of the business.

- Business freedom: There should not be unnecessary government restrictions like import restriction, restrictions on sourcing finance or other factors from abroad, foreign investments etc. the economic liberalization is regarded as a first step towards facilitating globalization.
- Facilities: The extent to which an enterprise can develop globally from home country base depends on the facilities available like the infrastructural facilities.
- Government support: Government support may take the form of policy and procedural reforms, development of common facilities like infrastructural facilities, R & D support, financial market reforms and so on.
- Resources: Resourceful companies may find it easier to thrust ahead in the global market. Resources include finance, technology, R & D capabilities, managerial expertise, company and brand image, human resource etc.
- Competitiveness: A firm derives competitive advantage from any one or more of the factors such as low costs and price, product quality, product differentiation, technological superiority, after sales services, marketing strength etc.
- Orientation: A global orientation on the part of the business firms and suitable globalization strategies are essential for globalization.

IMPACT OF GLOBALIZATION ON INDIAN ECONOMY

In India, the process of dismantling trade barriers was started in 1991 and subsequently, every year the Government has been announcing reduction in custom duties and removing quantitative restrictions. It is argued that this shall enable free flow of goods, capital and technology and thus globalization becomes a motivating force for nations to develop themselves at a faster rate. For a developing country like India, it opens access to new markets and new technology.

Thus, the import-substitution strategy has been replaced by export led growth during the last decade in India. The recent developments in information and communications technology have further facilitated and accelerated the pace of globalization. International financial markets, transborder production networks and acceleration in capital flows across national frontiers have been the driving forces leading to greater global integration of the economies.

NATURAL RESOURCES AND ECONOMIC DEVELOPMENT

Natural resources include land, water resources, fisheries, mineral resources, forests, marine resources, climate, rainfall and topography. But nature possess more in its bosom and in order to discover what it hides, man is required to develop techniques of knowing the undiscovered resources. Some times the discovery of the use of a resource can immediately increase its use value. When we talk about the natural resources of a country, we have obviously in mind the extent of the known or discovered natural resources with their present uses. With the growth of the knowledge about the unknown resources and their use, the natural endowment of a country will be materially altered.

Another consideration regarding the nature of natural resources is that some resources; e.g., land, water, fisheries and forests are renewable and there are others like minerals and mineral oils which are exhaustible and can be used only once. Consequently, careful use of the exhaustible resources and maintenance of the quality of renewable resources like land are a sine qua non in the process of development.

PRINCIPLES OF RESOURCE DEVELOPMENT

The principal objective of resource development is to maximize Gross Domestic Output (GDP) and for this purpose there should be optimum utilization of resources not only in the short period but, in a sustained manner, over the long period. Various guiding principles for resource development are:

- Economic use of resources to achieve minimum waste
- Sustained use of economic resources through conservation of renewable resources and economic use of exhaustible resources

- Multi-purpose use of resources: if a certain resource has a number of uses, it is necessary to have all the uses
- Integrated planning in the use of natural resources
- Location of industries with a view to reducing transport costs to the minimum
- Abundant supply of energy resources, specially electric power so as to utilize other resources in the best possible manner

Land Resources

The total geographical area of India is about 329 million hectares of which 42 million hectares or 14% of the total reporting area in India is classified as:

- Barren land, such as mountains, deserts, etc. which cannot be brought under cultivation and
- Area under non-agricultural uses, that is, lands occupied by buildings, roads and railways, rivers and canals, and other lands put to uses other than agricultural.
- The rest of the land is put under three major uses, viz., forests, pastures and agriculture.

Forest Resources

Forests are important natural resources of India. They help in controlling floods and thus they protect the soil against erosion. They supply timber, fuel wood, fodder and a wide range of non-wood products. They are the natural habitat for biodiversity and repository of genetic wealth. Forests, thus, play an important role in environmental and economic sustainability. Under land utilization pattern, the Government of India estimated the total area under forests as 68 million hectares or 22 % of the total geographical area. In our country, forests have generally been undervalued in economic and social terms.

The contribution of the forest sector to GDP was put as 1% in 1996 - 97 (measured at 1980 - 81 prices). A recent estimate puts the gross value of goods and services provided by the forest sector at 2.4% GDP. There is concentration of forests in a few states in Assam, Madhya Pradesh, Orissa and a few union territories. Northern India is particularly deficient in forests. There is a need to increase forest areas in the entire country as also to develop them in deficient states.

Forest policy, 1952: Appreciating the necessity of developing forests, the government of India declared its first forest policy in 1952. According to this policy, it was decided to raise steadily the area under forests to 100 million hectares or 33 % for the country as a whole. The target area was to provide green cover over two thirds of the land area in the hills and mountains. The main objectives of forest policy under the Five-Year Plans were:

- To increase the productivity of forests
- To link up forest-development with various forest-based industries and
- To develop forests as a support to rural economy.

New forest policy, 1988: The 1952 forest policy had failed to stop the serious depletion of forest wealth over the years. Accordingly, it became imperative to evolve a new strategy of forest conservation. The government of India announced its new forest policy in December 1988. The important features of this policy are:

- Role of tribal in forests recognized: The new policy enunciates that all agencies responsible for forest management, including forest development corporations should associate tribal people closely in the protection, regeneration and development of forests.
- Depletion of forest area and the target for green cover: The new policy reiterates that green cover should be extended to over two-thirds of that land area in the hills and mountains and that the total forest area in the country should be raised to 100 million hectares or 33 % of the total geographical area in the country.
- Discouragement to forest-based industries: The new forest policy states that no forest based enterprises except at the village or cottage level will be set up in the future, unless it is first cleared, after a careful study of the availability of raw materials.
- End the system of private forest contractors: The new forest policy advocates an end to the system of contractors working the forests. The contractors will be replaced by institutions such as tribal cooperatives, government corporations, etc.
- Forest land not to be diverted to non-forest uses: The forest department used to assign forestland to individuals or nongovernment agencies for the purpose of reforestation.

- Participatory Forest Management System: This new strategy involves rural people, particularly women and tribal community having intimate knowledge of plant species, their growth characteristics, utility and medicinal value, etc.

  They also know the specific requirements of fuel, fodder, timber and other non-food products. The adoption of the new strategy has led to several positive outcomes, such as:

  — Change in the attitude and relationships of local communities and forest officials towards each other and the forests

  — Improvement in the condition of forests

  — Reduction in encroachments

  — Increase in the income of local people and

  — Involvement of non-governmental organizations (NGOs) in forest research, tree planting, promotion of productivity, etc.

Water Resources

India is one of the wettest countries of the world but it is not able to hold all the water it receivers. Because of deforestation and denudation, a large portion of the monsoon water disappears into the sea as surface run-off. Community resources such as ponds, tanks and rivers are misused and continuously neglected.

Rivers are increasingly getting polluted as urban and industrial wastes are dumped into them. India's water policy has concentrated on gigantic river systems and reservoirs and despite huge investments on them, their productivity continues to be low. They have not helped in controlling or moderating floods.

Nor are they cost effective, or ecologically desirable. Ground water table has gone down dramatically in more intensely cropped areas, clearly indicating the need to increase recharges or to regulate pumping. In some areas, there is serious pollution danger to ground water due to industrial wastes.

India continues to be highly flood-prone and drought-prone but neither the government nor the Planning Commission has shown sufficient imagination to appreciate the gravity of the situation and make necessary correction to India's water policy.

Fisheries

India is the sixth largest producer of fish in the world and perhaps, second largest in inland fish production. Fisheries sector plays important role in the socio-economic development of India, generating employment for a large coastal population- about one million fishermen draw their livelihood from fisheries, but they generally live on the verge of extreme poverty. It is not only an important source of direct employment but generates employment in downstream industries. It is estimated that about six million people are employed in the fisheries sector. Fisheries help in raising nutritional levels, augmenting food supply and earning foreign exchange. The contribution of the fisheries sector to Gross Domestic Product (at current prices) has increased from Rs. 1,230 crores to Rs. 32,060 crores between 1980-1981 and 2001-2002. Fisheries contribute about 1.21 % of India's GDP. Broadly, fishery resources of India are either inland or marine. The principal rivers and their tributaries, canals, ponds, lakes, reservoirs comprise the inland fisheries. The five-year plans assign high priority to the development of fisheries because of the necessity to raise the nutritional levels of protein deficient Indian diet and to earn much needed foreign exchange. The fisheries programmes have emphasized family- based Labour intensive inland and brackish water fisheries and improving the harvesting from seas by stimulating the growth of country boats, mechanized boats and deep sea trawlers.

Mineral Resouces

The development and management resources play a vital role in the industrial growth of the nation. Coal and iron, for instance, are the basic minerals needed for the growth of iron and steel industry, which in turn, is vitally necessary for the country's development. Similarly, there are other minerals like mica and manganese, copper, lead and zinc, which are of economic importance.

Then we have mineral fuels like petroleum, coal, thorium and uranium, which are of national importance. Thorium and uranium the atomic energy minerals promise to be tremendous source of power. Besides these, we have a number of minor minerals with varying degrees of utility to the country. The reserves of India in respect of minerals essential for basic industries Viz., coal and iron are ample. But there is a fairly long list of vital minerals like copper, tin, lead, zinc, nickel, cobalt and sulphur and most of all petroleum, in which India is deficient. The Government of India amended the Mines and Minerals (regulated and Development) Act, 1957 in January 1994 and announced a new mineral policy:

- Throwing upon the mining sector to the private sector including direct foreign investment.
- Empowering the states to grant prospecting licenses/mines leases without prior approval of the central Government (except in a few cases).
- Removing the restrictions on equity holding by foreign nationals in a mining company.

The major objectives and the strategies of the new mineral policy are as follows:

- To explore for identification of mineral wealth on land and offshore.
- To develop mineral resources taking into account the national and strategic considerations.
- To minimize adverse effects of mineral development on the forests, environment and ecology through appropriate protective measures.
- To promote foreign trade in minerals.
- To promote research and development in minerals.

HUMAN DEVELOPMENT IN INDIA

Economic growth contributes most to poverty reduction when it expands the employment, productivity and wages of poor people and when public resources are channeled to promoting human development. A virtuous cycle of economic growth and human development arises when growth is labour using and employment generating and when human skills and health improve rapidly.

Income clearly is only one option that people would like to have, though an important one. But it is not the sum total of their lives. Income is also a means, with human development the end. Ever since the publication of the Human Development Report 1990, efforts have been made to devise and further refine measures of human developments. Three measures have been developed. They are Human Development Index (HDI), Gender related Development Index (GDI) and Human Poverty Index (HPI).

Human Development Index

HDI measures the average achievement in three basic dimensions of human development:

- A long and healthy life as measured by life expectancy at birth
- Knowledge as measured by the adult literacy rate (with two third weight) and the combined primary, secondary and tertiary gross enrolment ratio (with one third weight)
- A decent standard of living as measured by GDP per capita (PPP US $)
- Before calculating HDI, an index for each of the three dimensions is created.
- The HDI is calculated as a simple average of the dimension indices. The table indicates Human Development Index for 2002 for selected countries as reported in HDR 2004. Countries have been grouped under three categories:
- Countries in the HDI range 0.8 and above are in the High Human Development group
- Countries in the HDI range 0.5 to 0.8 are in the range of Medium Human Development group
- Countries in the HDI range less than 0.5 are in the Low Human Development group
- The data has been collected for 177 countries. Among them 55 countries were in the High Human Development range, 86 countries were in Medium Human Development range and 36 countries were in Low Human Development range. India, which was at No.138 in HDI in 1994, has improved its position to No.127 in 2002.

Gender Related Development Index (GDI)

While HDI measures average achievement, the GDI adjusts the average achievement to reflect the inequalities between men and women. The three components used for the purpose are:

- Female life expectancy
- Female adult literacy and gross enrolment ratio
- Female per capita income

If gender inequalities were not penalized, the value of GDI and HDI would be the same, but if gender inequalities exists, the value of GDI would be lower than that of HDI. The greater the difference between HDI and GDI, the greater is the gender inequality. From the table (refer GDI column) it may be noted that near gender equality exists in Norway,

Canada, United States, United Kingdom, Japan, Mexico, Russian Federation, Malaysia, Venezuela, Philippines, Sri Lanka, China, Vietnam and Indonesia. Countries s which indicate higher gender inequality are Saudi Arabia, Pakistan, Iran, India, Egypt and Nigeria.

Human Poverty Index (HPI)

Human Development Report 1997 introduced the concept of Human Poverty Index, which concentrates on deprivation in three essential elements of human life already reflected in HDI- longevity, knowledge and a decent living standard. The first deprivation is vulnerability to death at a relatively early age and is represented in the HPI by the percentage of people expected to die before age 40. The second deprivation is related to knowledge and is measured by the percentage of adults who are illiterate. The third deprivation relates to a decent standard of living, in particular, overall provisioning. This is represented by of three variables the combination percentage of people of people with access to:

- Health services
- To safe water
- The percentage of malnourished children under five.

It may be noted that in the case of Nigeria, 70.2 % of the population suffers from income poverty, but HPI index is 35.1 %. However, in the case of Bangladesh, the situation is totally reversed - HPI 42.2, but income poor population is 36 %. In case of India, proportion of population below international income poverty line is 34.7 %, but human poverty Index is 31.4.

Note: Yahoo! (Yahoo) is an internet and media communications company, offering internet services such as search and email. The company provides a range of services to individuals, including search, yellow pages, shopping, information, entertainment and communication. Its major websites include Yahoo! Mail, Yahoo! Jobs, Yahoo! Search, Yahoo! Answers, Yahoo! Videos and Flickr, among others. The company provides services in more than 30 languages and in more than 30 countries, regions, and territories. For detailed information related to this chapter reader can visit www.yahoo.com

2

Labour Environment

INTRODUCTION

Labour and the Environment have long been perceived as an issue vested with highly conflicting interests. Most of the world population relies on natural resources and the environment for wages, if not simply for survival. Many workers share the fear that strengthened environmental policies will lead to job losses. However, perceptions of conflicting interests have evolved over the years. A number of studies, as well as practical experience, have made it clear that changing production and consumption patterns and adopting new techniques and methods - which are among the alternative ways out of the current environmental crisis - will foster job creation. Protecting our natural resource base and the environment will actually contribute to protecting employment and fighting poverty.

As an example, in 2004 there were more than 4.5 million "green power" consumers in Europe, the United States, Canada, Australia and Japan. These consumers purchased power voluntarily at the retail level or used "renewable energy certificates". Direct jobs worldwide from renewable energy manufacturing, operations and maintenance exceeded 1.7 million in the same year, including some 0.9 million jobs related to biofuels production (REN21 2005). Between 2004 and 2005, investment in the renewable energy sector worldwide grew from US$30 billion to US$38 billion; biomass power production grew by 50-100 per cent in several countries; biodiesel production grew by 85 per cent (with nine EU countries becoming producers for the first time); grid-tied solar power grew by 55 per cent (led by Germany, which now has more than 200 000 solar rooftops); and solar hot water capacity grew by 23 per cent in China as well as reaching record levels in Europe (REN21 2006).

These figures demonstrate that moving towards sustainability and creating more jobs are compatible goals. In this context, it is crucial that linkages between Labour and the Environment are adequately addressed in order to build a new economic model - based on global participation, social equity and equality - which will also be environmentally sound and sustainable. Only then will we be able to meet the challenges underlined by the Millennium Development Goals adopted in 2000, reach the targets agreed at the World Summit on Sustainable Development in Johannesburg in 2002 and restore human dignity.

INCREASING PRESSURES ON THE ENVIRONMENT

The human population is expected to reach 6.4 billion in 2005. Estimates are that it will top 8.1 billion in 2030, and that there will be between 8.7 and 11.3 billion people on the earth in 2050 (UNEP 2002 and 2005, WRI 2005). Consumption of both goods and services provide opportunities for a healthy and satisfying life, including employment, mobility, education and adequate nutrition. However, among the factors leading to natural resource depletion and pressures on ecosystems, consumption has had the greatest impact and caused the most direct harm. Much harm has resulted from the overconsumption of animals and plants, mining of soil nutrients, and other forms of biological depletion. Ecosystems have also suffered considerable indirect harm from pollution and wastes originating in agriculture, industry and energy production. Pollution and wastes are, of course, associated with unsustainable patterns and levels of consumption. Pressures on natural resources and the environment - and their unsustainable exploitation - are expected to continue to increase dramatically, despite the efforts made to reverse these trends over a period of more than 30 years. A casual glance at One Planet Many People: Atlas of Our Changing Environment (UNEP 2005) reveals that since the beginning of the 20th century:

- Logging and land use conversion have reduced forest cover by at least 20 per cent, and possibly as much as 50 per cent;
- Nearly 70 per cent of the world's major marine fish stocks have been overfished or are being fished at the biological limit;
- Dams and other engineering works have fragmented 60 per cent of the world's large river systems, and have so impeded water flow that the time it takes for a drop of water to reach the sea has tripled;
- Human activities are significantly altering the basic chemical cycles upon which all ecosystems depend.

The current global economic pattern has exacerbated existing environmental pressures.

Globalization, which is imposing new dynamics on socio-economic development, is of basic importance with respect to the crucial issue of economic development vs. environment and development. Over roughly the past 30 years the environment has been subjected to stresses resulting from an 18-fold increase in world economic output (UNEP 2002).

LABOUR LAWS

Labour law (also known as employment or law) is the body of laws, administrative rulings, and precedents which address the legal rights of, and restrictions on, working people and their organizations. As such, it mediates many aspects of the relationship between trade unions, employers and employees. In Canada, employment laws related to unionized workplaces are differentiated from those relating to particular individuals. In most countries however, no such distinction is made. However, there are two broad categories of labour law. First, collective labour law relates to the tripartite relationship between employee, employer and union. Second, individual labour law concerns employees' rights at work and through the contract for work. The labour movement has been instrumental in the enacting of laws protecting labour rights in the 19th and 20th centuries. Labour rights have been integral to the social and economic development since the industrial revolution.

Labour law arose due to the demands of workers for better conditions, the right to organize, and the simultaneous demands of employers to restrict the powers of workers' many organizations and to keep labour costs low. Employers' costs can increase due to workers organizing to win higher wages, or by laws imposing costly requirements, such as health and safety or equal opportunities conditions. Workers' organizations, such as trade unions, can also transcend purely industrial disputes, and gain political power - which some employers may oppose. The state of labour law at any one time is therefore both the product of, and a component of, struggles between different interests in society.

CONTRACT OF EMPLOYMENT

The basic feature of labour law in almost every country is that the rights and obligations of the worker and the employer among one another are mediated through the contract of employment between the two. This has been the case since the collapse of feudalism and is the core reality of modern economic relations. Many terms and conditions of the contract are however implied by legislation or common law, in such a way as to restrict the freedom of people to agree to certain things in order to protect employees, and facilitate a fluid labour market. One example in many countries is the duty to provide written particulars of employment with the essentialia negotii (Latin for essential terms) to an employee. This aims to allow the employee to know concretely what to expect and is expected; in terms of wages, holiday rights, notice in the event of dismissal, job description and so on. An employer may not legally offer a contract in which the employer pays the worker less than a minimum wage. An employee may not for instance agree to a contract which allows an employer to dismiss them unfairly. There are certain categories that people may simply not agree to because they are deemed categorically unfair. However, this depends entirely on the particular legislation of the country in which the work is.

MINIMUM WAGE

There may be a law stating that the minimum amount that a worker can be paid per hour. Australia, Canada, China, Belgium, France, Greece, Hungary, India, Ireland, Japan, Korea, Luxembourg, the Netherlands, New Zealand, Paraguay, Portugal, Poland, Romania, Spain, Taiwan, the United Kingdom, the United States and others have laws of this kind. The minimum wage is usually different from the lowest wage determined by the forces of supply and demand in a free market, and therefore acts as a price floor. Those unable to command the minimum wage due to a lack of education, experience or opportunity would typically work in the underground economy, if at all. Each country sets its own minimum wage laws and regulations, and while a majority of industrialized countries has a minimum wage, many developing countries have not.

Minimum wage laws were first introduced nationally in the United States in 1938, India in 1948, France in 1950, and in the United Kingdom in 1999. In the European Union, 18 out of 25 member states currently have national minimum wages.

WORKING TIME

Before the Industrial Revolution, the workday varied between 11 and 14 hours. With the growth of industrialism and the introduction of machinery, longer hours became far more common, with 14-15 hours being the norm, and 16 not at all uncommon. Use of child labour was commonplace, often in factories. In England and Scotland in 1788, about two-thirds of persons working in the new water-powered textile factories were children. The eight-hour movement's struggle finally led to the first law on the length of a working day, passed in 1833 in England, limiting miners to 12 hours, and children to 8 hours. The 10-hour day was established in 1848, and shorter hours with the same pay were gradually accepted thereafter. The 1802 Factory Act was the first labour law in the UK.

After England, Germany was the first European country to pass labour laws; Chancellor Bismarck's main goal being to undermine the Social Democratic Party of Germany (SPD). In 1878, Bismarck instituted a variety of anti-socialist measures, but despite this, socialists continued gaining seats in the Reichstag. The Chancellor, then, adopted a different approach to tackling socialism. In order to appease the working class, he enacted a variety of paternalistic social reforms, which became the first type of social security.

The year 1883 saw the passage of the Health Insurance Act, which entitled workers to health insurance; the worker paid two-thirds, and the employer one-third, of the premiums. Accident insurance was provided in 1884, while old age pensions and disability insurance were established in 1889. Other laws restricted the employment of women and children. These efforts, however, were not entirely successful; the working class largely remained unreconciled with Bismarck's conservative government.

In France, the first labour law was voted in 1841. However, it limited only under-age miners' hours, and it was not until the Third Republic that labour law was effectively enforced, in particular after Waldeck-Rousseau 1884 law legalizing trade unions. With the Matignon Accords, the Popular Front (1936-38) enacted the laws mandating 12 days (2 weeks) each year of paid vacations for workers and the law limiting to 40 hours the workweek (outside of overtime).

- Lochner v. New York, 198 U.S. 45 (1905), a notorious, and now defunct case by the US Supreme Court that regulation of working time (for bakeries) to limit workers to a 10 hour day.

HEALTH AND SAFETY

Other labour laws involve safety concerns of workers. The earliest English factory law was drafted in 1802 and dealt with the safety and health of child textile workers.

ANTI-DISCRIMINATION

This clause means that discrimination against employees is morally unacceptable and illegal, on a variety of grounds, in particular racial discrimination or sexist discrimination.

UNFAIR DISMISSAL

Convention no. 158 of the International Labour Organization states that an employee "can't be fired without any legitimate motive" and "before offering him the possibility to defend himself". Thus, on April 28, 2006, after the unofficial repeal of the French First Employment Contract (CPE), the Longjumeau (Essonne) conseil des prud'hommes (labour law court) judged the New Employment Contract (CNE) contrary to international law, and therefore "illegitimate" and "without any juridical value". The court considered that the two-years period of "fire at will" (without any legal motive) was "unreasonable", and contrary to convention no. 158, ratified by France.

CHILD LABOUR

Child labour is the employment of children under an age determined by law or custom. This practice is considered exploitative by many countries and international organizations. Child labour was not seen as a problem throughout most of history, only becoming a disputed issue with the beginning of universal schooling and the concepts of labourers' and children's rights. Child labour can be factory work, mining or quarrying, agriculture, helping in the parents' business, having one's own small business (for example selling food), or doing odd jobs. Some children work as guides for tourists, sometimes combined with bringing in business for shops and restaurants (where they may also work as waiters). Other children are forced to do tedious and repetitive jobs such as assembling boxes, or polishing shoes. However, rather than in factories and sweatshops, most child labour occurs in the informal sector, "selling on the street, at work in agriculture or hidden away in houses - far from the reach of official inspectors and from media scrutiny."

COLLECTIVE LABOUR LAW

Collective labour law concerns the tripartite relationship among the employer, employee and trade unions. Trade unions, sometimes called "labour unions" are the form of workers' organization most commonly defined and legislated on in labour law. However, they are not the only variety. In the United States, for example, workers' centers are associations not bound by all of the laws relating to trade unions.

TRADE UNIONS

The law of some countries place requirements on unions to follow particular procedures before certain courses of action are adopted. For example, the requirement to ballot the membership before a strike, or in order to take a portion of members' dues for political projects. Laws may guarantee the right to join a union (banning employer discrimination), or remain silent in this respect. Some legal codes may allow unions to place a set of obligations on their members, including the requirement to follow a majority decision in a strike vote. Some restrict this, such as the 'right to work' legislation in some of the United States.

STRIKES

Strike action is the weapon of the workers most associated with industrial disputes, and certainly among the most powerful. In most countries, strikes are legal under a circumscribed set of conditions. Among them may be that:

- The strike is decided on by a prescribed democratic process. (Wildcat strikes are illegal).
- Sympathy strikes, against a company by which workers are not directly employed, may be prohibited.
- General strikes may be forbidden by a public order.
- Certain categories of person may be forbidden to strike (airport personnel, health personnel, police or firemen, etc.)
- Strikes may be pursued by people continuing to work, as in Japanese strike actions which increase productivity to disrupt schedules, or in hospitals.

A boycott is a refusal to buy, sell, or otherwise trade with an individual or business who is generally believed by the participants in the boycott to be doing something morally wrong. Throughout history, workers have used tactics such as the go-slow, sabotage or just not turning up en-masse in order to gain more control over the workplace environment, or simply have to work less. Some labour law explicitly bans such activity, none explicitly allows it.

PICKETS

Picketing is a tactic which is often used by workers during their strikes. They may congregate outside the business which they are striking against, in order to make their presence felt, increase worker participation and dissuade (or prevent) strike breakers from entering the place of work. In many countries, this activity will be restricted both by labour law, by more general law restricting demonstrations, or sometimes by injunctions on particular pickets. For example, labour law may restrict secondary picketing (picketing a business not directly connected with the dispute, such as a supplier of materials), or flying pickets (mobile strikers who travel in order to join a picket). There may be laws against obstructing others from going about their lawful business (scabbing, for example, is lawful); making obstructive pickets illegal, and, in some countries, such as Britain, there may be court orders made from time to time against pickets being in particular places or behaving in particular ways (shouting abuse, for example).

WORKPLACE INVOLVEMENT

Workplace consolation statutes exist in many countries, requiring that employers consult their workers on issues that concern their place in the company. Industrial democracy refers to the same idea, but taken much further. Not only that workers should have a voice to be listened to, but that workers have a vote to be counted.

CO-DETERMINATION

Originating in Germany, some form of co-determination (or Mitbestimmung) procedure is practiced in countries across continental Europe, such as Holland and the Czech Republic. This involves the rights of workers to be represented on the boards of companies for whom they work. The German model involves half the board of directors being appointed by the company trade union. However, German company law uses a split board system, with a 'supervisory board' (Aufsichtsrat) which appoints an 'executive board' (Vorstand). Shareholders and unions elect the supervisory board in equal number, except that the head of the supervisory board is, under co-determination law, a shareholder representative. While not gaining complete parity, there has been solid political consensus since the Helmut Schmidt social democrat government introduced the measure in 1976.

In Britain, the similar proposals were drawn up, and a command paper produced named the Bullock Report (Industrial democracy). This was released in 1977 by the James Callaghan Labour government. This proposal involved a similar split on the board, but its effect would have been even more radical. Because U.K. company law requires no split in the boards of directors, unions would have directly elected the management of the company. Furthermore, rather than giving shareholders the slight upper hand as happened in Germany, a debated 'independent' element would be added to the board, reaching the formula 2x + y. However, no action was ever taken as the U.K. slid into the winter of discontent. This tied into the European Commission's proposals for worker participation in the 'fifth company law directive', which was also never implemented.

INTERNATIONAL LABOUR LAW

One of the crucial concerns of workers and those who believe that labour rights are important, is that in a globalizing economy, common social standards ought to support economic development in common markets. However, there is nothing in the way of international enforcement of labour rights, with the notable exception of labour law within the European Union. At the Doha round of trade talks through the World Trade Organization one of the items for discussion was the inclusion of some kind of minimum standard of worker protection. The chief question is whether, with the breaking down of trade barriers in the international economy, while this can benefit consumers it can also make the ability of multinational companies to bargain down wage costs even greater, in wealthier Western countries and developing nations alike. The ability of corporations to shift their supply chains from one country to another with relative ease could be the starting gun for a "regulatory race to the bottom", whereby nation states are forced into a merciless downward spiral, not only slashing tax rates and public services with it but also laws that in the short term cost employers money. Countries are forced to follow suit, on this view, because should they not foreign investment will dry up, move places with lower "burdens" and leave more people jobless and poor. This argument is by no means uncontested. The opposing view suggests that free competition for capital investment between different countries increases the dynamic efficiency of the market place. Faced with the discipline that markets enforce, countries are incentivized to invest in education, training and skills in their workforce in order to obtain a comparative advantage. Government initiative will be spurred, because rational long term investment will be perceived as the better choice to increasing regulation. This theory concludes that an emphasis on deregulation is more beneficial than not. That said, neither the International labour organization, nor the European Union takes this view.

INTERNATIONAL LABOUR ORGANIZATION

The International Labour Organization (ILO), whose headquarter is headquarters are in Geneva, is one of the oldest surving international bodies, and the only surviving international body set up at the time of the League of Nations following the First World War. Its guiding principle is that "labour is not a commodity" to be traded in the same way as goods, services or capital, and that human dignity demands equality of treatment and fairness in dealing within the workplace. The ILO has drawn up numerous conventions on what ought to be the labour standards adopted by countries party to it. Countries are then obliged to ratify the Conventions in their own national law. However, there is no enforcement of this, and in practice most conventions are not agreed to, even if they are adhered to.

EUROPEAN LABOUR LAW

The European Working Time Directive limited the maximum length of a working week to 48 hours in 7 days, and a minimum rest period of 11 hours in each 24 hours. Like all EU Directives, this is an instrument which requires member states to enact its provisions in national legislation. Although the directive applies to all member states, in the UK it is possible to "opt out" of the 48 hour working week in order to work longer hours. In contrast, France has passed more strict legislation, limiting the maximum working week to 35 hours (but optional hours are still possible). The controversial Directive on services in the internal market (aka "Bolkestein Directive") was then passed in 2006.

SOCIAL SECURITY OF LABOUR

The large gaps existing between the rich and the poor and the unorganised workers and the organised workers have led in several countries to attempts at providing social and economic security to the poor and to the unorganised sectors. In Kerala, the introduction of modern techniques of production and the growth of capitalist production relations had important implications for the traditional crafts as well as craftsman in Kerala. One of its implications has been the breakdown of the conventional social security set-up. The search for alternative institutions to fill the gap caused by social transformation was a long-drawn out process. The establishment of Welfare Fund Boards has been a major landmark in this pursuit. Labour welfare legislations, and the institutions constituted under them seem to have had a major impact on the informal labour markets of the State. They are also supposed to have added a new dimension to the social security system of Kerala. Yet, several issues involved in providing social security to workers in informal labour markets appear to have not received the attention they deserve. The present study on construction workers is an attempt to analyse the problems revolving around the Welfare Fund created for them, its impact on the lives of construction workers, and the financial solvency of the Fund in the long run

Social security is one of the pillars on which the structure of a welfare state rests, and it constitutes the hard core of social policy in most countries. It is through social security measures that the state attempts to maintain every citizen at a certain prescribed level below which no one is allowed to fall. It is the security that society furnishes through appropriate organization, against certain risks to which its members are exposed (ILO, 1942). Social security system comprises health and unemployment insurance, family allowances, provident funds, pensions and gratuity schemes, and widows' and survivors' allowances. The essential characteristics of social insurance schemes include their compulsory and contributory nature; the members must first subscribe to a fund from which benefits could be drawn later. On the other hand, social assistance is a method according to which benefits are given to the needy persons, fulfilling the prescribed conditions, by the government out of its own resources. The present section reviews labour welfare activities in India with particular emphasis on the unorganised sector.

Although provisions for workmen's compensation in case of industrial accidents and maternity benefits for women workforce had existed for long, a major breakthrough in the field of social security came only after independence. The Constitution of India (Article 41) laid down that the State shall make effective provision for securing the right to public assistance in case of unemployment, old age, sickness and disablement and in other cases of undeserved want. The Government took several steps in compliance of the constitutional requirements.

The Workmen's Compensation Act (1926) was suitably revised and social insurance programmes were developed for industrial workers. Provident funds and gratuity schemes were introduced in most industries, and maternity legislation was overhauled.

Subsequently, State governments instituted their own social assistance programmes. The provisions for old age comprise pension, provident fund, and gratuity schemes. All the three provisions are different forms of retirement benefits. Gratuity is a lumpsum payment made to a worker or to his/her heirs by the company on termination of his/her service due to retirement, invalidity, retrenchment or death (Bajpayee and Shanker, 1950).

CONCEPT OF LABOUR WELFARE

In its broad connotation, the term welfare refers to a state of living of an individual or a group in a desirable relationship with total environment - ecological, economic, and social. Conceptually as well as operationally, labour welfare is a part of social welfare which, in turn, is closely linked to the concept and the role of the State.

The concept of social welfare, in its narrow contours, has been equated with economic welfare. Pigou defined it as "that part of general welfare which can be brought directly or indirectly into relations with the measuring rod of money" (Pigou, 1962). According to Willensky and Labeaux, social welfare alludes to "those formally organised and socially sponsored institutions, agencies and programmes which function to maintain or improve the economic conditions, health or interpersonal competence of some parts or all of a population"

As these goals may not always be realised by individuals through their efforts alone, the government came into the picture and gradually began to take over the responsibility for the free and full development of human personality of its population.

Labour welfare is an extension of the term Welfare and its application to labour. During the industrialisation process, the stress on labour productivity increased; and brought about changes in the thinking on labour welfare. An early study under the UN observed as follows "in our opinion most underdeveloped countries are in the situation that investment in people is likely to prove as productive, in the purely material sense, as any investment in material resources and in many cases, investment in people would lead to a greater increase of the flow of goods and services than would follow upon any comparable investment in material capital" (UN, 1951). The theory that welfare expenditure, especially expenditure on health and education, is productive investment has led to the view that workers could work more productively if they were given a fair deal both at the work place and in the community.

The concept of labour welfare has received inspiration from the concepts of democracy and welfare state. Democracy does not simply denote a form of government; it is rather a way of life based on certain values such as equal rights and privileges for all. The operation of welfare services, in actual practice, brings to bear on it different reflections representing the broad cultural and social conditions. In short, labour welfare is the voluntary efforts of the employers to establish, within the existing industrial system, working and sometimes living and cultural conditions of the employees beyond what is required by law, the custom of the industry and the conditions of the market.

The constituents of labour welfare included working hours, working conditions, safety, industrial health insurance, workmen's compensation, provident funds, gratuity, pensions, protection against indebtedness, industrial housing, rest rooms, canteens, crèches, wash places, toilet facilities, lunches, cinemas, theatres, music, reading rooms, holiday rooms, workers' education, co-operative stores, excursions, playgrounds, and scholarships and other help for education of employees' children. All labour welfare measures have the following objectives:

- Enabling workers to live richer and more satisfactory lives;
- Contributing to the productivity of labour and efficiency of the enterprise;
- Enhancing the standard of living of workers by indirectly reducing the burden on their purse;
- Enabling workers to live in tune and harmony with services for workers obtaining in the neighbourhood community where similar enterprises are situated;
- Based on an intelligent predictions of the future needs of the industrial workers, designing policies to cushion off and absorb the shocks of industrialisation and urbanisation to workers;
- Fostering administratively viable and essentially developmental outlook among the workforce; and
- Discharging social responsibilities.

PRINCIPLES OF LABOUR WELFARE

Certain fundamental considerations are involved in the concept of labour welfare. The following are the more important among them.

Social responsibility of industry

This principle is based on the social conception of industry and its role in the society that is, the understanding that social responsibility of the state is manifested through industry. It is assumed that labour welfare is an expression of industry's duty towards its employees. Social responsibility means that the obligation of the industry to pursue those policies, to take such decisions, and to follow those lines of action which are desirable in terms of the objectives and values currently obtaining in the society. The values of the Indian community are enshrined in the constitution of the country. Labour welfare is not embroidery on capitalism nor the external dressing of an exploitative management; rather, it is an expression of the assumption by industry of its responsibility for its employees. Industry is expected to win the co-operation of the workers, provide them security of employment, fair wage, and equal opportunity for personal growth and advancement, and make welfare facilities available to them.

DEMOCRATIC VALUES

The principle of democratic values of labour welfare concedes that workers may have certain unmet needs for no fault of their own, that industry has an obligation to render them help in gratifying those needs, and that workers have a right of determining the manner in which these needs can be met and of participating in the administration of the mechanism of need gratification. The underlying assumption to this approach is that the worker is a mature and rational individual who is capable of taking decisions for himself/herself.

ADEQUACY OF WAGES

The third principle of labour welfare is adequacy of wages; it implies that labour welfare measures are not a substitute for wages. It will be wrong to argue that workers are given a variety of labour welfare services, they need be paid only low wages. Right to adequate wage is beyond dispute.

EFFICIENCY

The fourth principle of labour welfare lays stress on the dictum to cultivate welfare is to cultivate efficiency. Even those who deny any social responsibility for industry do accept that an enterprise must introduce all such labour welfare measures which promote efficiency. It has been often mentioned that workers' education and training, housing, and diet are the three most important aspects of labour welfare, which always accentuate labour efficiency.

RE-PERSONALISATION

Since industrial organization is rigid and impersonal, the goal of welfare in industry is the enrichment and growth of human personality. The labour welfare movement seeks to bring cheer, comfort, and warmth in the human relationship by treating man as an individual, with quiet distinct needs and aspirations. Social and cultural programmes, recreation and other measures designed after taking into consideration the workers' interests go a long way in counteracting the effects of monotony, boredom, and cheerlessness.

CO-RESPONSIBILITY

The sixth principle of labour welfare recognises the responsibility for labour welfare lies on both employers and workers and not on employers alone (Moorthy, 1958). Labour welfare measures are likely to be of little success unless mutuality of interest and responsibilities are accepted and understood by both the parties, in particular the quality of responsibility at the attitudinal and organizational level.

TOTALITY OF WELFARE

The final principle of labour welfare is that the concept of labour welfare must permeate throughout the hierarchy of an organization, and accepted by all levels of functionaries in the enterprise.

SOCIAL SECURITY AND UNORGANISED LABOUR

Social security is the protection which society provides for its members, through a series of public measures, against the economic and social distress that otherwise would be caused by the stoppage or substantial reduction in earnings resulting from sickness, maternity, employment injury, unemployment, invalidity, old age and death; provision of medical care, and the provision of subsidies for families with children (ILO, 1989). The system of social security was started with the organised sector. However, owing to pressures brought on the state and the society by the growing awareness within the unorganised sector, concern is increasingly being expressed and attention given to expanding legislative and social security protection to the unorganised sector.

Social security schemes should be linked to economic security, including employment, income, and assets. There should be a convergence of the ways of reaching sustainability and of attaining expanded coverage. The growing demands of the unorganised labour force and their attempts to organise themselves can be met by a decentralised participatory social security system. It will lead to a release of the people's creative energies and a rapid growth of social security for the organised sector. Extending social security to the unorganized sector is not merely a matter of extending existing organised sector schemes to new groups for the following reasons (Getupig, et al, 1992).

1. Unorganised sector is not a homogenous category;
2. Identifying the employer in this sector is difficult;
3. Unlike the organised sector, where steady and regular employment is a given fact, unorganized sector workers need employment security, income security, and social security simultaneously; and
4. Needs of the unorganised sector workers vary from those of the organised sector.

Welfare amenities stipulated in the Factories Act, Mines Act, Plantations Labour Act, etc., are employment-based, in the sense that such Acts are applicable to undertakings employing the minimum prescribed number of workers. Outside the realm of these Acts, there are a large number of small-scale establishments, which have no obligation, statutory or otherwise, to provide welfare amenities to their workers. These establishments are located in both urban and rural areas, and are engaged mostly in processing primary products or in supplementing the existing large-scale industries in transportation, construction, and retail trade. The precise estimate of their employment strength and their wage, welfare and working conditions are not known.

The very nature of industry, the frequent collusion between the employer and his workmen and place of work often being in the backyard of the employers' dwelling are some of the social problems which stand in the way of bringing the real picture of labour conditions to light. In the absence of any reliable data necessary for policy recommendations, one could take stock of the situation only in terms of opinions expressed by knowledgeable sources.

SOCIAL SECURITY MEASURES IN UNORGANISED SECTOR IN INDIA

Social security comprises two types of measures, promotional and protective. Promotional measures consist mainly of employment, training, and nutrition schemes, by which persons are enabled to work and earn a livelihood. On the other hand, protective measures consist of schemes by which the State provides the means of livelihood when a person is not able to work. ILO standards relating to social security are mainly protective and have been designed primarily for workers in the organised sector. Both promotional and protective measures are necessary to provide adequate social security facilities.

MEDICAL CARE

According to ILO recommendation No.69, medical care should be provided either through a social service medical care service, with supplementary provisions by way of social assistance, to meet the requirements of people in need who are not covered by social insurance, or through a public medical service (ILO, 1984). It requires that complete preventive and curative care be available, care which is rationally organised and co-ordinated with general health services. In India, medical care is provided largely by the public medical service, by private doctors and hospitals, and to a limited extent by social insurance schemes, welfare funds, and voluntary health associations. Some of the Welfare Funds in Kerala have adopted the reimbursement of the cost of medical care at standard rates or actuals, whereas the Employees State Insurance Scheme is based on providing the service directly under an integrated arrangement in which the financing and the medical services vest with the same organization. On the other hand, some of the public sector establishments provide service indirectly by entering into contract with doctors, diagnostic centres, and hospitals.

SICKNESS BENEFIT

Sickness benefit is payable when an insured person stops work due to his poor health conditions, and such a stop in work usually entails reduction or stoppage of earnings. Cash benefit is designed to replace in whole, or in part, the lost earnings. In India, there is provision for payment of sickness benefit under the Employees State Insurance Scheme (Government of India, 1996). Employees of Central and State governments and some public and private sector establishments are entitled to medical leave on half-pay.

MATERNITY BENEFIT

One of the earliest conventions adopted by ILO was the Maternity Protection Convention in 1919. The purpose of this Convention was to ensure that a woman worker would be able to sustain herself and her baby during the period immediately before and after her confinement. Maternity benefit is usually provided under a social insurance scheme along with medical care and sickness benefit. In India maternity benefit is provided under the Maternity Benefit Act (as an employers' liability) the Employees State Insurance Act (as a part of the health insurance scheme), the Beedi and Cigar (Conditions of Employment) Act, Beedi and Cigar Labour Welfare Fund Act, and the various State government schemes for social assistance. The National Social Assistance Programme also provides for payment of maternity benefits in lump sum.

EMPLOYMENT INJURY BENEFIT

Employment Injury Benefit is the most widely adopted branch of social security, and is also known as workmen's compensation. According to ILO Recommendation No.67 concerning income security, the contingency for which compensation for employment injury should be paid, is traumatic injury, or disease in the course of employment, and not injury brought about deliberately, or by serious and wilful misconduct of the victim, which results in temporary or permanent disability or death (ILO, 1984). This is a cash benefit but is often associated with medical care. In India, employment injury benefit is provided under the Workmen's Compensation Act and the Employees State Insurance Act. While the former Act is applicable to some employment in the unorganised sector, such as the construction industry, the latter Act is applicable mainly to workers in the organised sector.

OLD-AGE BENEFIT

Old age, invalidity, and survivors' benefits are the main long-term social security benefits, which are of great importance in any social security scheme. ILO conventions stipulate that the pensionable age should not be more than 65 years, unless required by demographic, economic, and social criteria, and that there should be a lower age for persons engaged in arduous occupations. Old age pension may be at a flat rate, or be related to one's past earnings. The current trend appears to be toward building a multi-tiered system consisting of a basic minimum pension and one or more earnings-related pensions. In India old-age benefit is provided as follows (Ministry of Labour, 1996).

a. Government employees: Paid by respective governments on the basis of employers' liability.

b. Employees' pension scheme: Workers covered under the Employees Provident and Miscellaneous Provisions Act.

c. Destitutes and persons below the poverty line: Paid under national old age pension scheme and old age pension schemes of State governments.

There exist no pension schemes for the self-employed, or for workers employed on a casual, temporary or intermittent basis who are not destitute, and who are not covered by the Employees Provident Fund and Miscellaneous Provisions Act.

INVALIDITY BENEFIT

Invalidity benefit is meant for people who have permanently lost their capacity to earn to the extent or the prescribed. According to ILO Recommendation No.67 concerning income security, the contingency in which invalidity benefit is payable is the inability to engage in any substantially gainful activity, because of a chronic condition due to disease or injury, or because of the loss of a member or its proper functioning. The relevant ILO convention specifies 15 years of contribution or employment or 10 years of insurance. But usually one requires only a few years' insurance, say five years, a part of which needs to be immediately preceding the invalidity. In India, the Employees Pension Scheme introduced in 1995 provides for invalidity benefits.

SURVIVORS' BENEFIT

This benefit is meant primarily for widows and children of persons covered by Social Security Schemes who cease to have any financial support on the death of their breadwinner. However, national legislation often recognises claims of other dependents provided there are no primary beneficiaries. A widespread practice is to base the survivors' pension on the rate of the old age pension the deceased was receiving or would have received. In India, survivors' benefit is provided under the Employees State Insurance Act and Workman's Compensation Act in case of death of a person engaged in any employment covered under these Acts. This benefit is provided under the Employees Provident Fund and Miscellaneous Provisions Act in case of the death of a member of the scheme for any reason. Insurance schemes of the Life Insurance Corporation and General Insurance Corporation also provide this benefit. The National Family Benefit Scheme extends this benefit in case of the death of the breadwinner of a family which lies below the poverty line.

UNEMPLOYMENT BENEFIT

The underlying principle of unemployment benefit is that if a person, through no fault of his, is deprived of his income, he has a right to expect income support, at least for the necessities of life while he remains available for work. According to ILO recommendations No.67, the contingency in which unemployment benefit should be paid is loss of earnings due to a state of unemployment of an insured person who is ordinarily employed, a person who is capable of regular employment in some occupation and is searching for suitable employment or due to part time unemployment (Government of India, 1995-'96). Its main purpose is to deal with temporary unemployment of employed persons and not the extensive and prolonged unemployment and under-employment found in many developing countries. The payment of the benefits depends on satisfying the qualifying clause of covered employment, and a waiting period may also be applied.

FAMILY BENEFIT

ILO Recommendation No.67 says that society should co-operate with parents, and give general assistance designed to secure the wellbeing of children. This benefit is intended to assist families in raising their children. Although there are no family benefit schemes in India, which provide for the payment of cash allowances to families for the maintenance of children, there exist many schemes which help families of Scheduled Castes/Tribes, minorities and other weaker sections of society, in the discharge of their responsibilities for education of their children, marriage of their daughters, construction of houses, and meeting funeral expenses.

STRATEGIES FOR SOCIAL SECURITY IN UNORGANISED SECTOR

The majority of the Social security schemes implemented in the country were in the organized sector, keeping large numbers outside the realm of the Social security net. A beginning has been made lately to provide social insurance for workers in the unorganised sector, with the help of the Central and the State governments. These schemes are administered by government agencies, co-operatives or NGOs, and are a combination of social assistance and social insurance.

INSURANCE SCHEMES

The Life Insurance Corporation of India has developed group insurance, which is akin to social insurance based on the large numbers, and has the potential to provide social security to persons in the unorganised industrial and agricultural sectors. There exist now several other group insurance schemes for the unorganised sector workers such as milk producers, handloom weavers, rickshaw pullers, shop assistants, beedi workers, and fish farmers. The schemes of the LIC provide mainly survivor benefits; however, some also provide old-age pensions. The General Insurance Corporation (GIC) of India also administers a few social security schemes for poor families, a Hut Insurance Scheme, and a Solatium Fund. In addition, GIC has introduced a Health Insurance Scheme, and has been administering the comprehensive Group Insurance Scheme for the Central Government. The schemes of the General Insurance Corporation provide invalidity benefits, or health insurance, or protection against loss of property.

NATIONAL SOCIAL ASSISTANCE PROGRAMME

Of the various protective schemes in existence for workers in the unorganised sector, the most important is the National Social Assistance Programme introduced in 1955 (Wadhawan, 1989). It provides social assistance to poor households in the case of old age, death of the breadwinner, and maternity through the National Old Age Pension Scheme, National Family Benefit Scheme, and the National Maternity Benefit Scheme respectively. Under the National Old Age Pension Scheme, Central assistance is provided to States for payment of old age pension to persons who are of the age of 65 years or more. In addition to the National Old Age Pension Scheme, all State governments and Union territories have their own old-age pension schemes.

OTHER PENSION SCHEMES

Apart from the old-age pension schemes which have been already referred to, the States Kerala, Tamil Nadu, Karnataka, Andhra Pradesh, Maharashtra, and Gujarat have pension schemes for agricultural workers. Many states have extended the old-age pension scheme benefits to destitute widows, physically and mentally retarded persons, freedom fighters and indigent artists; and some have also set up homes for destitute widows and deserted /divorced women. Under the Family Benefit scheme assistance is given to families below the poverty line on the death of their breadwinner; under the National Maternity Benefit scheme assistance is given to pregnant women for the first two childbirths.

WELFARE FUNDS

Welfare funds represent one of the models tried in India for providing social security protection to workers in the unorganised sector. There exist broadly two types of welfare funds - contributory and tax-based. The Government of India has set up tax-based welfare funds for mine workers, beedi rollers, cine workers, and workers in the building industry; these funds are financed by cess levied on the production or export of specified goods. They provide mainly medical care, assistance for the education of children, housing and water supply, and recreational facilities. There are nearly 20 Welfare Funds constituted by Government of Kerala for the benefit of different target groups such as agricultural workers, head-load workers, construction workers, coir workers, cashew workers, motor transport workers, autorickshaw workers, toddy workers, and artisans the majority of which are contributory.

EXISTING MODELS OF SOCIAL SECURITY AND LABOUR WELFARE

Since India has committed to the welfare of the marginalised sections of the society the government has taken upon itself the delivery of all types of social services and social security. There are mainly three types of social security models: employers' liability, social insurance, and social assistance. The last category includes welfare funds of Central government, welfare funds of State government, subsidised insurance schemes, and other forms of social assistance. The beneficiaries of the first (employers' liability) are mainly workers in the organised sector, whereas under social assistance the beneficiaries are both workers in the organised sector and workers in the informal sector. The latter belong in generally to the marginalised sectors. In the context of growing privatization of services on the one hand and the growing awareness and organization of the oppressed sections of workers on the other, it is necessary to search for models of effective social security provision to all the unorganised sector workers.

Social security for the unorganised workers cannot be reached by centralising and standardizing schemes; they can be reached by 'letting a hundred flowers bloandencouraging workers themselves to take initiative (Subramanya, 1994). People remain weak and vulnerable partly because they are unorganised and hence isolated and powerless. The provision social security can itself be a means that would lead the unorganised sector workers to organize and become empowered. Security of needs like food, health care, housing and child care, is empowering for vulnerable unorganised sector workers and helps them to alter their bargaining positions in the market. Centralised non-participatory systems tend to be dis-empowering, while participatory and beneficiary-run systems lead the workers to organise themselves.

LABOUR WELFARE IN THE CONSTRUCTION INDUSTRY

The construction industry has several features that distinguish it from most of the other industries so far as the welfare of workers is concerned. The majority of construction sites are of a temporary nature, since most structures require little attention of construction workers once construction is completed. This factor, making for mobility of labour in the construction industry, raises special problems on sites, where temporary arrangements must suffice for the provision of welfare amenities. The desirable and practicable amenities would be different according to the duration of the individual work sites, which may widely vary from one another. Some works may be completed in a matter of days, some may last for weeks or months and a few large sites may last for several years.

Mobility of certain construction work-places may also affect the provision of welfare facility. Some work-places such as house construction sites are stationary, while others such as those for the laying of pipelines, and construction of road ways, canals, railways, and water mains, move as the work progresses, so that the site conditions are even more temporary. It is clear, particularly in cases in which the distance travelled on any one job may be appreciable, that any structures associated with the provision of welfare facilities would have themselves to be mobile so as not to become too far removed from the work place.

Sometimes the nature of construction industry results in many sites being not only far away from workers' homes, but also from the normal social and health amenities associated with community line. In such cases, in addition to temporary housing, a whole range of social amenities are to be arranged, which might require careful planning and expenditure. It means that the presence or absence of social amenities in the immediate neighbourhood would have considerable bearing on welfare requirements at the site itself.

The welfare facilities provided on construction sites would in many cases depend on the number of workers engaged. In many countries the rules themselves specify the requirement of certain standard welfare amenities at the construction site. When a number of different firms employ labour to carry out works on the same site, it may be possible to pool resources in the provision of welfare amenities. Under joint management, collaboration among contractors may greatly facilitate provision of adequate welfare amenities.

When workers do not normally live in the neighbourhood of the works it may be necessary to provide for a whole series of welfare facilities, such as transport, periodic home leave, canteens and social amenities depending on the distance of the homes of the workers from the work place. On sites of long duration it may be desirable and practicable to provide housing and other amenities for the workers' families.

Work in cement production plants and plants associated with manufacture of building materials differs from construction work proper, due to exposure of workers to dust and other pollutants, a menace which calls for special welfare amenities (Thakurtha, 1980). Adequate installations, such as 'Cyclones' or other devices should be provided in order the exhaust dust. Protective clothing, in particular coats and gloves, should also be supplied to them in order to prevent spoliation of their apparel with cement dust, which might 'cake' should the clothing become moist, as during a shower, and also to protect their skin from allergic reactions.

The need for provision of most welfare facilities arises primarily from considerations of safety and hygiene. Thus the provision of protective clothing and facilities for drying cloth may be called for by the particular conditions of the work and the exposure to which workers are subjected. The arrangements for disinfection, first aid and sanitary, dietary and sleeping facilities in hostels for workers must satisfy the hygienic and safety requirements of the situation.

The International Labour Organization (1950) has put forward important guidelines for labour welfare facilities in construction industry. The facilities include shelter, meals, protective clothing, accommodation, sanitary facilities, recreation, transportation, and leave.

WELFARE FUND MODEL OF SOCIAL SECURITY MEASURES

Welfare Funds represent one of the models developed in India for providing social security protection to workers in the unorganised sector. Funds are raised by levying a cess on the production, sale or export of specified goods, or through contributions from various sources including employers, employees, as well as the government; the funds are used for meeting expenditure for the welfare of workers.

The present section reviews the growth and functioning of Welfare Funds in the country.

The major limitations of the Welfare Fund model of social security are reviewed. The need for unification of the different Welfare Funds for the purpose of transparency and adaptation on practical grounds is also discussed.

Historical growth

The need for organised welfare activities for industrial labour was forcefully brought out by the Textile Labour Enquiry Committee, in its report to the Government of Bombay in 1937. As a result, a number of labour welfare activities came into being particularly during the Second World War period. In 1944, the Government of India promulgated through an ordinance the Coal Mines Labour Welfare Fund. A Scheme to set up Labour Welfare Trust Funds formulated by the government was discussed at the eighth meeting of the Standing Labour Committee (SLC) held in March 1946. The Scheme was also considered at the seventh and the ninth sessions of the Labour Ministers' Conference, and again at the twelfth session of SLC. A draft bill was prepared in the light of these discussions and submitted to the Indian Labour Conference (ILC) for consideration at its eleventh session. In 1954, the Government of India wrote directly to several employers' and workers' organizations impressing upon them the need to institute Welfare Funds. Meanwhile, the States also instituted Funds for industrial welfare.

Labour Welfare Funds may be categorised into industry-wise funds, State-level funds, and enterprise-level funds (Giri V.V, 1962). Industry-wise funds exist in coal, mica, iron ore, gold-mining, and sugar industries, plantations, and toddy tapping. State-level funds are framed under the jurisdiction of State-level boundaries. Enterprise-level funds exist in most undertakings of the Central Government, such as Post and Telegraphs, Ordnance Factories, and Railways.

Kerala has set up more than 20 Welfare Funds for the benefit of workers. The include funds for abkari workers, agricultural workers, autorikshaw workers, cashew workers, coir workers, construction workers, and transport workers. A statutory fund was created for financing welfare measures for plantation workers in Assam. Similar funds have been set up also in Gujarat, Maharashtra, Karnataka, and Punjab. The Welfare Funds have been set up by special Acts of Parliament. For example, Beedi workers are covered by the Beedi Workers Welfare Fund Act of 1976, Mine workers by the Iron Ore, Manganese Ore And Chrome Mines Labour Welfare Fund Act, 1976; and building workers by the Building and Other Construction Workers (Regulation of Employment and Conditions of Service) Act of 1996. In addition, separate laws have been enacted for collecting cess. The Welfare funds set up by the Central Government are financed by levying a cess on specified goods (Table 3.1). Wide variations are seen in the rate structure of the cess. The duty on mica is on an ad valorem basis, whereas the duties on other commodities are at specific rates, ranging from Rs 0.50 to Rs 4 per metric tonne.

RELATIONS BETWEEN MANAGEMENT AND LABOUR

The field of industrial relations (also called Management and labour relations) looks at the relationship between management and workers, particularly groups of workers represented by a union. Labor relations is an important factor in analyzing "varieties of capitalism", such as neocorporatism (or corporatism), social democracy, and neoliberalism (or liberalism).

Labor relations can take place at many levels, such as the "shop-floor", the regional level, and the national level. The distribution of power amongst these levels can greatly shape the way an economy functions. Another key question when considering systems of labor relations is their ability to adapt to change. This change can be technological (e.g., "What do we do when an industry employing half the population becomes obsolete?"), economic (e.g., "How do we respond to globalization?"), or political (e.g., "How dependent is the system on a certain party or coalition holding power?").

Governments set the framework for labor relations through legislation and regulation. In Australia industrial relations is the commonly used term, though in recent years the term workplace relations has also become common. The academic discipline of labour studies is closely related to and often studied and taught in conjunction with the study industrial and labor relations in English language universities.

PERSPECTIVE THEORIES

When studying the theories of industrial relations, there are three major perspectives that contrast in their approach to the nature of workplace relations. The three views are generally described as the unitary, pluralist and Marxist perspectives. The Marxist perspective is sometimes referred to as the Conflict Model. Each offers a particular perception of workplace relations and will therefore interpret such events as workplace conflict, the role of trade unions and job regulation very differently.

Unitary perspective

In Unitarianism, the organization is perceived as an integrated and harmonious whole with the ideal of "one happy family", where management and other members of the staff all share a common purpose, emphasizing mutual cooperation. Furthermore, unitarism has a paternalistic approach where it demands loyalty of all employees, being predoominantly managerial in its emphasis and application.

Consequently, trade unions are deemed as unnecessary since the loyalty between employees and organizations are considered mutually exclusive, where there can't be two sides of industry. Conflict is perceived as disruptive and the pathological result of agitators, interpersonal friction and communication breakdown.

Pluralistic perspective

In pluralism the organization is perceived as being made up of powerful and divergent sub-groups, each with its own legitimate loyalties and with their own set of objectives and leaders. In particular, the two predominant sub-groups in the pluralistic perspective are the management and trade unions.

Consequently, the role of management would lean less towards enforcing and controlling and more toward persuasion and co-ordination. Trade unions are deemed as legitimate representatives of employees, conflict is dealt by collective bargaining and is viewed not necessarily as a bad thing and, if managed, could in fact be channeled towards evolution and positive change.

Marxist/Radical Perspective

This view of industrial relations looks at the nature of the capitalist society, where there is a fundamental division of interest between capital and labour, and sees workplace relations against this history. This perspective sees inequalities of power and economic wealth as having their roots in the nature of the capitalist economic system. Conflict is therefore seen as inevitable and trade unions are a natural response of workers to their exploitation by capital. Whilst there may be periods of acquiescence, the Marxist view would be that institutions of joint regulation would enhance rather than limit management's position as they presume the continuation of capitalism rather than challenge it.

WORKERS PARTICIPATION

The term participation is generally understood by involved parties. For management it is a joint consultation prior to decision making, for workers it means co determination, while for government it is an association of labour with management without the final authority or responsibility in decision making.

Participation is generally conceived of as a way of reducing power difference and, therefore, equality is stressed. Participation as a means to reduce power inequity however, seems difficult to accept because of the obvious difference in formal power positions between the labourer and the director.

The more precise conceptual properties of participation are not very clear although the following elements seem to be involved

1. The amount of verbal interaction between a supervisor and his subordinates.
2. The degree to which a supervisor perform is role in a group-centred way.
3. The degree to which a supervisors is active in making decisions and setting goals for his work units.

Despite the variations in interpretation there seems to be a consensus that participation means sharing, in an appropriate manage, the decision-making power with the lower ranks of the organization. The general assumption is that by using such a process workers would be able to contribute to the overall effectiveness of the organization. Mhetras has suggested five levels of participation in decision making which range on a scale from minimum to maximum. Since these levels of participation can indicate the extent of co-determination in an organization, they deserve attention. We have tried to highlight these levels briefly, ranking them from eh minimum to the maximum degree of participation.

Informative participation refers to information sharing concerning balance sheet, production, economic condition of the plan, etc. Here the workers have no right of close scrutiny of the information provided. Consultative participation in which the council is consulted on such matters as welfare programmes, and methods of work and safety. However, the final decision is always that of management, the council only works as an advisory body. Associative participation in which the council's role is not purely advisory unlike consultative participation. The management is under a moral obligation to accept and implement the unanimous decision of the council. Administrative participation in which a decision already taken comes tote council with alternatives for it to select from for implementation. Here the degree of sharing authority and responsibility is definitely more than in the others.

The following factors seems to account for the relative failure of workers' participation in India and in some of the other countries where it has been tired out.

1. Workers' participation has suffered largely at the hands of employers who felt, and probably still feel, that such a move will take away form them their right to manage. To some extent this is supported by large-scale Government interference, issuing decrees, enticing acts, and formulating legislative bodies. Voluntary implementation of the concept of participation by employers has been rare, except may be in Sweden where the concept of workers' participation has been relatively successful.
2. Because of this attitude of employers, information -sharing has not been liberal. Workers' representatives have often not been informed about manpower an production schedules, creating an attitude of indifference and even hostility among the representatives.

3. Many studies have pointed out the role conflict the most of the representatives have faced in mixed boards and committees. The conflicts arose because very often representatives were forced to adopt the company view on some matter that contrasted with the wider interest of workers. This not only created a conflict of interest among these representatives but very often generated a crisis of confidence among electors.
4. Unlike the stated aims of participation, in most cases, joint boards, councils, etc., find themselves dealing with personnel and welfare matter rather than with production and efficiency. This, to a large extent, ha been responsible for the dissatisfaction of employers whose concerns rests relatively more with production and efficiency.
5. In some cases, studies have beenfound very little evidence of active communication and feedback between the electors and their representatives. Part of the blame can be assigned to the representatives themselves ill-equipped to judge what should be communicated and partly to the multiplicity of unions, especially in the Indian context.
6. Finally, it has been found that the level at which workers' participation is operationalized influences its cusses or failure. For example, the democratic sharing of power at lower grades of industrial workers has been found to be effective because it furthers the ends of both employers an employees. While applying the aforementioned factors to judge the success or failure of he experiment in industrial democracy, it should be remembered that each country and each organization has a unique culture of its own. Self-determination, so much valued by Americans, is not shared by workers in South America. In some ways, Germans cohere in groups only if they are led by a leader, while the informal group is the norm in USA. Thus there seems to be no reason to expect that the consequences of participation will be universal, although cross-cultural work is scarce, evidence form theoretical studies supports the point.

Decisive participation where decisions are taken jointly on matters related to production, welfare, etc. The level up to which the company will allow the council to participate will depend on the philosophy followed by the company on the one hand and the personality of the council on the other. Participation has been termed one of the most prominent constructs in group dynamics literature. Several empirical findings conducted in the laboratory and otherwise show that significant change, participate in deciding what the change shall be and how it shall be made.

It utilized meaningfully, workers' participation can serve a number of purposes, all geared to archive organizational effectiveness and the satisfaction of the employees. It is a method designed to generate a "we" feeling among workers and thus helps in motivating employees to achieve organizational goals. It ensures joint responsibility and cooperation to optimally utilize the limited resources available to the organization.

The Indian experiment in workers' participation has been far form satisfactory. In a study covering six industrial units, three private and three public sector undertakings, data were collected through interviews with various cadres of management, labour and union.

It was concluded that the functioning of the Joint Management Council had not been entirely satisfactory.

Of the several reasons for failure some are highlighted below:

1. If the Joint Management Council is imposed form above or accepted after hard persuasion it may not be effective.
2. It has been found to be effective only when perceived to meet the needs of the concerned people at the level of organization.
3. It has not been clearly demarcated form other consultative committees like workers committee and production committee, etc.

In an earlier study of five companies, Mhetras found management hesitant to share with workers the right to manage, and also workers reluctant to accept the implied responsibility of participating in managerial action. He concluded that in addition to the attitude and outlook of concerned parties, the Joint management Council's similarity with other consultative bodies endangered its effectiveness.

Table: Indication: of Organization's Efficiency in Production

Area of performance	year	Weldon (%)	Harwood (%)
Return on capital invested	1962	-15	+17
	1964	+17	+21
Make-up pay	1962	12	2
	1964	4	2

Production efficiency	1962	-11	6
	1964	+4	16
Earnings above minimum(piece-rate and other incentives, employees only)	1962	None	17
	1964	16	22
Operator turnover rates (monthly basis)	1962	10	3-4
	1964	4	3-4
Absence from work (daily rate production employees only)	1962	6	3
	1964	3	3

Note: Chevron Corporation (Chevron) is one of the largest integrated energy companies in the world. The company is engaged in every aspect of the oil and natural gas industry, including exploration and production, refining, marketing and transportation, chemicals manufacturing and sales, geothermal, mining operations, and power generation. It has operations in more than 100 countries including the US. Chevron is headquartered in San Ramon, California and employs about 67,000 people. Reader can visit their site www.chevron.com1. For a detailed study of connected to this chapter.

3

Global Trends in Business and Management

INTERNATIONAL RELATIONS

In modern times no state can afford to live in isolation. It has to build relations with others states of the world out of sheer necessity. Just as no individual can live outside the society similarly no state can live outside the international community. Therefore, international relationship is as much a product of necessity as social existence itself. With the industrial revolution the world shrank and the distances were reduced.

As a result the regional and local problems began to assume world character. With this regional - relations were transformed into international relations. The term international relations has been interpreted and defined in two senses- Narrow and Broad. In the narrow sense it is confined to the study of "Official relations conducted by authorized leaders of the state".

By emphasizing official relations, the relations between businessmen, scientists, etc., of the various countries are excluded from the scope of international relations. In the broader sense international relations include "all intercourse among states and all movements of people, goods and ideas across national frontiers".

Types of Relations

Usually two types of relations exist between states - cooperative and oppositional.

- Cooperative relations - They are usually non-political and involve no power.
- Oppositional relations - The oppositional relations imply conflict among groups and demand use of power.

International relations include study of both. At initial stages international relations studied only diplomatic history as conditioned by the happening of the past, but soon even to study of international law was included in its scope. With establishment of the League of Nations, the study of international institutions was also included in its fold. Thus after World War I it came to study the diplomatic history, international law and the league organization. After World War II, its field was further widened and study of military science and regional areas was also included in it. The psychological study through personality and background analysis also gained prominence. Thus at present international relations have become very extensive.

INTERNATIONAL RELATIONS APPROACHES

Broadly speaking there are two approaches for the study of international relations.

- The classical approach considers the substance more important
- Scientific approach attaches more importance to method and technique.

Types of Classical Approach

The prominent amongst the classical approach are:

- Historical approach: Under this approach diplomacy and interrelations of a particular period are studied. This approach is not possible in modern world, though it had the advantage of giving the students a deep understanding of the problems in their correct prescriptive.
- International organization approach: It studies the behavior of various states in the international organization to determine the attitude of a particular power. This theory does not take into account the activities of a state outside the international organization.
- International law approach: It considers the international law as a key to the interpretation of international relations. This approach however ignored the internal politics as a factor in determining the attitude of a power in the international sphere.

Types of Scientific Approach

The prominent scientific or modern approaches are

- Behavior approach is based on psychology and tries to analyze international relations as strife between various national characters.

- Karl detsch developed Quantitative theory and developed certain measurable indices of community development.
- Decision-making approach of Richar C. Synder emphasized the need of probing the minds of the decision makers. While probing their minds both internal and external settings were to be taken into account.
- The systems theory developed by Kapalan holds that a theory of international politics normally cannot predict individual actions because the interaction problem is very complex.
- Equilibrium theory of International relations and institutions was developed by Liska. He holds that the states seek to secure the best attainable position of equilibrium, and this is desirable.
- Power approach or realist theory It tries to understand international relations in term of state interests and holds that the statesmen are guided by interests rather than ideology, or motives.

MULTINATIONAL CORPORATIONS

The dynamics of the business environment fostered by the drastic political changes in the erstwhile communist and socialist countries and the economic liberalization across the world has enormously expanded the opportunities for the multinational corporations, also known by such names as international corporation, transnational corporation, global corporation (or firm, company or enterprise) etc.

The rapidity with which the MNC's are growing is indicated by the fact that while according to the World Investment Report 1997 there were about 45000 MNC's with some 280000 affiliates. According to the World Investment Report 2001 there were over 63,000 of them with about 822,000 affiliates. Only less than 12 % of these affiliates were in the developed countries. China was host to about 3.64 lakh of the affiliates (i.e., more than 44% of the total) compared to more than 1400 in India. The MNC's account for a significant share of the world's industrial investment, production, employment and trade.

DEFINITION AND MEANING

"A corporation that controls production facilities in more than one country, such facilities having been acquired through the process of foreign direct investment. Firms that participate in international business, however large they may be, solely by exporting or by licensing technology are not multinational enterprises."

The various benchmarks sometimes used to define " multi nationality" are that the company must:

- Produce (rather than just distribute) abroad as well as in the headquarters country
- Operate in a certain minimum number of nations (six for example)
- Derive some minimum percentage of its income from foreign operations (e.g., 25%)
- Have a certain minimum ratio of foreign to total number of employees, or of foreign total value of assets
- Possess a management team with geocentric orientations.
- Directly control foreign investments (as opposed simply to holding shares in foreign companies).

Merits

The important arguments in favor of the MNCs are mentioned below:

- MNCs help increase the Investment level and thereby the income and employment in host country.
- The transnational corporation has become vehicles for the transfer technology, especially to the developing countries.
- They also kindle a managerial revolution in the host countries through professional management and the employment of highly sophisticated management techniques.
- The MNCs enable the host countries to increase their exports and decrease their import requirements.
- They work to equalize the cost of factors of production around the world.
- MNCs provide an efficient means of integrating national economies.
- The enormous resources of the multinational enterprises enable them to have very efficient research and development systems. Thus, they make a commendable contribution to inventions and innovations.
- MNCs also stimulate domestic enterprise because to support their own operations, the MNCs may encourage and assist domestic suppliers.
- MNCs help increase competition and break monopolies.

Demerits

The various cases against MNCs are:

- The MNCs technology is designed for the worldwide maximization of profit not the development needs of poor countries.
- Through their power and flexibility, MNCs can evade or undermine national economic autonomy and control, and their activities may be inimical to the national interests
- MNCs may destroy competition and acquire monopoly powers.
- The tremendous power of the global corporations poses the risk that they may threaten the sovereignty of the nations in which they do business.
- MNCs retard growth of employment in the home country.
- The transnational corporations cause fast depletion of some of the nonrenewable natural resources in the host country. They have also been accused of the environmental problems.
- The transfer pricing enables MNCs to avoid taxes by manipulating prices on intra company transactions
- The MNCs undermine local culture and traditions; change the consumption habits for their benefits against the long-term interests of the local community.

Prespective

Future holds out an enormous scope for the growth of MNCs. The changes in the economic environment in a large number of countries indicate this. A united Nation's report described several developments that points to a rapidly changing context for economic growth, along with a growing role transnational corporations in that process. These include:

- Increasing emphasis on the market forces and a growing role for the private sector in nearly all developing countries.
- Rapidly changing technologies that are transforming the nature of organization and location of international production.
- The globalization of firms and industries.
- The rise of services to constitute the largest single sector in the world economy and

- Regional economic integration, which involve both the world' largest economies as well as selected developing countries.

MULTINATIONALS IN INDIA

The inflow of foreign funds through MNCs in India is showing an upward trend in recent years. 1991 onwards, the Government of India has taken several steps to attract foreign investments and entry of the MNCs, such as:

- Abolition of industrial licensing.
- Removal of restriction on investment under the MRTP Act.
- Liberalization of policy and procedure for transfer of technology, import off capital goods, etc.
- Existing companies are allowed to raise foreign equity up to 51%.
- Provisions of the FERA have been relaxed. As a result, companies with more than 40% foreign equity can operate like any other Indian company.
- Foreign companies are permitted to use their trade in domestic markets.
- During the nineties, there has been an increasing trend of foreign investments in India. The government approved 666 foreign collaborations in 1990. This number has become more than double to 1520 by 1992. At present, the USA is the largest invêstor in India, followed by Switzerland, Japan and UK. Foreign investment has largely been concentrated in sector such as fuel and oil refineries, power chemicals and electrical equipments and electronics.

THE RISE OF INDIAN MULTINATIONALS

After liberalization of Indian market in 1991 and in its due course, India INC. is flying high not only over the Indian sky but globally. Though it took almost a decade when many Indian firms have slowly and surly embarked on the global path and lead to the emergence of the Indian Multinational Companies. With each passing day, Indian businesses are acquiring companies abroad, becoming worldwide popular suppliers and are recruiting staff across national boundaries. While an Asian Paints is painting the world red, Tata is rolling out indicas from Birmingham and Sundaram Fasteners nails home the fat that the Indian company is an entity to be reckoned with.

Some facts:

- TATA Motors sells its passenger - car Indica in the UK through a marketing alliance with Rover and has acquired a Daewoo Commercial Vehicles unit giving it access to markets in Korea and China.
- INFOSYS has 25,634 employees including 600 from 33 nationalities other than Indian. It has 30 marketing offices across the world and 26 global software development centers in the US, Canada, Australia, the UK and Japan.
- Ranbaxy is the ninth largest generics company in the world. An impressive 76 % of its revenues come from overseas.
- Dr. Reddy's Laboratories became the first Asia Pacific pharmaceutical company outside Japan to list on the New York Stock Exchange in 2001
- Asian paints are among the 10 largest decorative paints makers in the world and has manufacturing facilities across 24 countries.
- Small auto components company Bharat Forge is now the world's second largest forging maker. It became the world's second largest forgings manufacturer after acquiring Carl Dan Peddinghaus a German forgings company last year. Its workforce includes Japanese, German, American and Chinese people. It has 31 customers across the world and only 31 percent of its turnover comes from India.
- About 80% of revenues for Tata Consultancy Services come from outside India. It raised in Asia's second -biggest tech IPO this year and India's largest IPO ever.
- Sundaram Fasteners is not merely a nuts and bolts company. It believes in thinking out of the box. Probably that is why it decided to acquire a plant in China. The plant in Jiaxin city in the Haiyan economic zone has ensures one fact; that its customers who were earlier buying Sundaram products in Europe and the US, did not have to go far from home to access the product.

FOREIGN CAPITAL AND COLLABORATION

FOREIGN CAPITAL

Most countries of the world which embarked on the road to economic development had to depend on foreign capital to some extent.

The degree of dependence however, varied with the extent to which domestic resources could be mobilized, the state of the domestic economy in respect of technical progress, the attitude of the respective governments, etc. But the fact cannot be denied that foreign capital contributes in many important ways to the process of economic growth and industrialization.

NEED FOR FOREIGN CAPITAL

The need for foreign capital for a developing country like India can arise on account of the following reasons:

- Domestic capital is inadequate for purposes of economic growth.
- For want of experience, domestic capital and entrepreneurship may not flow into certain lines of production.
- There may be potential savings in a developing economy like India but this may come forward only at a higher level of economic activity.
- It may be difficult to mobilize domestic savings for the financing of projects that are badly needed for economic development.
- Foreign capital brings with it other scarce productive factor, such as technical know-how, business experience and knowledge.

FORMS OF FOREIGN CAPITAL

The different forms of foreign investments are as follows:

- Direct Foreign Investment - Foreign capital can enter India in the form of direct investments.
- Foreign Collaboration- Joint participation of foreign and domestic capital. There are three types of foreign collaborations- joint participation between private parties, between foreign firms and Indian government and between foreign governments and Indian government.
- Inter-Government Loans- Since the Second World War, there has been a growing tendency towards direct inter-government loans and grants.
- Loans from International Institutions- International Monetary Fund (IMF), Aid India Consortium, Asian Development Bank (ADB) and the World Bank have been the major sources of external assistance to India.

- External Commercial Borrowing (ECB)- Export credit agencies like the US Exim bank, the Japanese Exim Bank, and ECGC of the UK etc. to obtain commercial borrowing from the capital market.

The Government of India liberalized its policy towards foreign investment in 1991 to permit automatic approval for foreign investment up to 51 percent equity in 34 industries. The Foreign Investment Promotion Board (FIPB) was also set up to process applications in cases not covered by automatic approval. During 1992-93 several additional measures were taken to encourage direct foreign investment, portfolio investment, NRI investment etc.

FOREIGN COLLABORATION

During the early phase of the planning era, the national policy towards foreign capital did recognize the need for foreign capital, but decide not to permit it a dominant position. Consequently foreign collaborations had to keep their equity within the ceiling of 49 % and allow the Indian counterpart a majority stake. Moreover, foreign collaborations were to be permitted in priority areas, more especially those in which we had not developed our capabilities. But in an overall sense, our policy towards foreign collaborations remained restrictive and selective. Consequently, during 1961-70 a total of 2,475 foreign collaborations were approved and during the next decade (1971 - 80) another 3, 041 collaborations were sanctioned.

It was only during the eighties that government relaxed its policy towards foreign collaborations. This was done specifically in respect of investors from Oil Exporting Developing countries with well- defined package exemptions. This was followed by Technology Policy Statement (TPS) in January 1983.The objective of the policy was to acquire imported technology and ensure that it was of the latest type appropriate to the requirements and resources of the country.

FOREIGN INVESTMENTS BY COUNTRIES

Technical collaborations were allowed on financial criteria i.e. royalty or lumpsum payment or a combination of both. These relaxations resulted in a larger inflow of foreign direct investment and consequently, the number of approvals during the decade (1981 - 90) reached a record figure of 7,436 involving a total investment of Rs1, 274 crores.

Country wise analysis of foreign collaboration reveals that USA was at the top accounting for nearly Rs.322.7 crores of investment. This was one fourth of the total foreign collaboration approvals. This was followed by Federal Republic of Germany (17.2%), Japan, UK, Italy, France and Switzerland. Five countries USA, West Germany, Japan, UK and Italy accounted for nearly 63% of total approved foreign investment. Even Non-Resident Indians (NRIs) contributed about Rs.113 crores accounted for 8.9 % of total investment.

FOREIGN INVESTMENT BY INDUSTRIES

An industry wise analysis of foreign collaboration approvals reveals that Electrical and electronic (including telecommunications) accounted for 22% of the total approval, indicating highest priority to this sector, followed by industrial machinery 15.5%. Foreign collaboration in chemicals (other than fertilizers) was third in importance. By and large it may be stated that the priority sector accounted for about 70% of total approvals. It implies that foreign collaborations approvals were more or less in conformity with the general climate towards foreign capital in the country at that time.

FINANCIAL AND TECHNICAL COLLABORATIONS

Foreign collaborations are of two types:

- Technical approvals: That involves the payments for technology
- Financial approvals: That involves equity capital of an existing or new undertaking.
- Upto Rs.600 crores the Industry Ministry accords approval on the advice of Foreign Investment Promotion Board (FIPB), but larger projects over this limits are approved by Cabinet Committee on Foreign Investment (CCFI).

Sources Reveal:

- Financial collaborations were just 20.1% during 1981- 1985, their share improved to 28.8 % during 1985-90 but rose sharply to 72 % during 1991- 1997.
- The amount of approved investment also increased sharply from Rs.899 crores during 1985-90 to Rs.1, 73,510 crores in august 1998.

Obviously there is a shift from technical approvals to financial approvals during the post liberalization phase. However Government has been successful in attracting more foreign investment in the post liberalization phase as compared to the earlier period.

Takeovers and Implementation of Foreign Collaborations

Indian entrepreneur seems to have lost it bargaining power and well known Indian brands have been taken over by TNCs. It needs to be emphasized that takeovers do not add to new production capacities. On the contra, there are likely to add to higher outflow of foreign exchange. In foreign collaborations, transfer of superior technology has not been the main consideration.

Some Recent Takeovers:

- ICI (UK) attempted to take over Asian paints.
- Hindustan lever took over Tomco.
- Premier automobiles transferred two of its plants to Peugeot.
- Transfer of Lakme's brand to a 50:50 joint venture with the Levers.
- TVS Suzuki takes up Hero Honda.
- Whirlpool took over TVS Whirlpool.
- Suzuki's attempted to gain majority control in Maruti Udyog.
- Bridgestone increasing its stake from 51% to 74 % in joint venture with ACC.
- Bausch & Lomb increasing its share in Indian venture to 69%.
- Henkel increasing its share to 70%.
- Blue star edged out of Motorola Blue Star and Hewlett Packard India.
- Shriram's share got reduced in Shriram Honda Power.

Once the Indian partners transferred the units, they neither had the money nor the marketing network with them.

FDI and the Indian Stock Market

- Stock market is an ideal form of organization, which by providing easy liquidity encourages the public to invest, and this brings out the latent surplus in the economy.
- For this purpose, the shares of good promising companies should be listed on the market. During the 70's and 80's, a good number of blue chip TNC scripts got listed. Notable among them were: Abbot labs, Burroughs Wellcome, E.Merck, Eskayef, Fulford, Hoechst, May & Baker, Organon, Parke Davis and Wyeth.

- The chief objective of offering shares to the public by the affiliates could not be to raise fresh capital from the public, but was only a strategy of diluting foreign equity without reducing their foreign parent's quantum of investment.
- In the post-liberalization period, the policy was reversed. At the first available opportunity, many foreign affiliates raised foreign equity to majority levels.
- While raising share of foreign equity to majority level, most TNCs indicate a tendency to avoid the stock market. TNCs are side - stepping the stock market and they sell off the existing units to locals and promote Wholly - Owned -Subsidiaries (WOS) or transfer certain divisions / products to wholly owned subsidiaries of the parent company.
- The number of technical collaborations declined from 629 in 1997 - 1928 to only 299 in 2003-2004. There was a tendency to convert purely technology transfer arrangements later into financial collaboration by buying the equity share of the concerns.

Foreign Capital and Collaboration - A Critical Assessment

- Transfer of technology can be effected with more investment being made by technologically advanced MNCs. But, there are aspects of foreign direct investment which seriously impinge on people's welfare and national sovereignty.
- Nearly half of the Foreign Investment is in the nature of portfolio investment, which only strengthens speculative trading in shares. This is only underlines the fact that MNCs are able to manipulate the stock market to suit their goals.
- Foreign direct investment is catering to the needs of the upper middle and affluent classes. Consequently, there is an utter neglect of the wage goods sector.
- Portfolio investment made in India is in the nature of hot money, which may take to flight if the market signals indicate any adverse trends. Thus, it would be a mistake to treat portfolio investment as a stable factor in our growth.
- A larger inflow of foreign direct investment, more so in the financial sector, will lead to building of reserves, which in turn will expand domestic money supply. Consequently, inflationary trend of prices gets strengthened in the process.

- MNCs after their entry are rapidly increasing their shareholding in Indian companies. This has resulted in a number of takeovers by the MNCs and thus, the process of Indianisation of the corporate sector has been totally reversed.

INTERNATIONAL REGULATORY BODIES

Since its inception in 1995, the World Trade Organization (WTO) has regularly been in the news. There have been optimistic stories of expanding WTO membership that emphasize that freer trade generates numerous benefits for consumers. Newspapers report on the details of WTO entry negotiations for important countries like China and remind us of the gains from trade. At other times, media reports might lead us to believe that disputes among WTO members are about to tear the organization apart. Disagreements between the U.S. and the European Union (EU) over everything from U.S. corporate taxation, to genetically modified organisms, to special steel tariffs make headlines worldwide.

Finally, some groups seem unconvinced by and resentful of claims that free trade makes the entire world better off. Huge numbers of people from environmental and labor groups gather at various international meetings of heads of state and government ministers to protest globalization in general and the WTO in particular. Some representatives of developing countries are concerned that they have liberalized their trade and agreed to intellectual property protection for developed country products but have received almost no additional access to agricultural markets in the industrialized world.

What are we to make of all this? What is the WTO? What is it trying to accomplish and why? How does the world trading system function? Why are there so many disputes among countries that belong to the WTO? Here we are giving an overview of the General Agreement on Tariffs and Trade, better known as GATT, and the WTO system. In the first section, we will present a brief history of GATT and the WTO.

In the following section, we will discuss the fundamental principles underline underlie the post-WWII world trading system and explain how these principles work to increase welfare. In the third section, we will describe the numerous exceptions to GATT's requirement of nondiscrimination, or equal treatment, and review the economics literature that seeks to explain the rationale for and consequences of these exceptions. Then, we will present a short summary of dispute resolution within the WTO.

A BRIEF HISTORY OF THE WTO AND GATT

The World Trade Organization (WTO) and its predecessor, the General Agreement on Tariffs and Trade (GATT) have been enormously successful over the last 50 years at reducing tariff and other trade barriers among an ever-increasing number of countries. The predecessor to the WTO began in 1947 with only 23 members; today it has 146 members, comprising approximately 97 percent of world trade. Although the WTO, established in 1995, is relatively young for an international institution, it has its origins in the Bretton Woods Conference at the end of World War II. At this conference, finance ministers from the Allied nations gathered to discuss the failings of World War I's Versailles Treaty and the creation of a new international monetary system that would support postwar reconstruction, economic stability, and peace. The Bretton Woods Conference produced two of the most important international economic institutions of the postwar period: the International Monetary Fund (IMF) and the International Bank for Reconstruction and Development (the World Bank). Recognizing that the beggar-thy-neighbor tariff policies of the 1930s had contributed to the environment that led to war, ministers discussed the need for a third postwar institution, the International Trade Organization (ITO), but left the problem of designing it to their colleagues in government ministries with responsibility for trade.

By the late 1940s, representatives of the American government had met several times with representatives of other major nations to design a postwar international trading system that would parallel the international monetary system. These meetings had two objectives: (1) to draft a charter for the ITO and (2) to negotiate the substance of an ITO agreement, specifically, rules governing international trade and reductions in tariffs. Although a charter was drafted, the ITO never came into being. By 1948, support for yet another international organization had waned in the U.S. Congress. Without American participation, the institution would have been greatly weakened and, in the event, the effort to create an organization to manage problems relating to international trade was abandoned. However, although the U.S. Congress would not support another international institution, in 1945 it had given the U.S. president the authority to negotiate a treaty governing international trade by extending the 1934 Reciprocal Trade Agreements Act. This led to the establishment of the General Agreement on Tariffs and Trade (GATT) in 1947-a treaty whereby 23 member countries agreed to a set of rules to govern trade with one another and maintained reduced import tariffs for other members.4 The GATT treaty did not provide for a formal institution, but a small GATT

Secretariat, with a limited institutional apparatus, was eventually headquartered in Geneva to administer various problems and complaints that might arise among members.

Over the next 40 years, GATT grew in membership and in its success at reducing barriers to trade. GATT members regularly met in what came to be known as negotiating rounds. These rounds were primarily focused on negotiating further reductions in the maximum tariffs that countries could impose on imports from other GATT members. The success of these rounds is evident. Tariffs on manufactured products fell from a trade-weighted average of roughly 35 percent before the creation of GATT in 1947 to about 6.4 percent at the start of the Uruguay Round in 1986.5 Over the same time period, the volume of trade among GATT members surged: In 2000 the volume of trade among WTO members stood at 25 times its 1950 volume. This growth in the volume of trade is impressive and appears to have accelerated in recent decades. Comparing the growth of world GDP, expressed as an index number, to the growth of the volume of trade among GATT/ WTO members, also expressed as an index number. Despite this success, by the 1980s several problems had surfaced with the GATT apparatus. Firstly, the dispute resolution mechanism of GATT was not functioning as effectively as had been hoped. Countries with longstanding disagreements were unable to reach any sort of resolution on a number of issues, ranging from government subsidies for exports to regulations regarding foreign direct investment. Secondly, a number of commodities, most importantly, agricultural products and textiles, were widely exempt from GATT disciplines. Thirdly, it was widely believed that certain forms of administered trade protection-antidumping duties, voluntary export restraints, and countervailing duties-were restricting trade and distorting trade patterns in many important sectors. Fourthly, trade in services was expanding rapidly and GATT had no rules regarding trade in services. Fifthly, countries that produced intellectual property- movies, computer programs, patented pharmaceuticals-were becoming increasingly frustrated by the lack of intellectual property protection in many developing nations. Lastly, the rules regarding trade-related investment measures- for example, domestic purchase requirements for plants built from foreign direct investment-were hotly disputed. To address these problems, a new round of trade negotiations-the Uruguay Round-was launched in 1986. The goals of the Uruguay Round were far more ambitious than in previous rounds. It sought to introduce major reforms into how the world trading system would function. The treaty negotiated during the Uruguay Round, the GATT treaty of 1994, established the WTO-the international institution to govern trade that was first visualized by the attendees of the Bretton Woods Conference 50 years earlier. The new GATT treaty provided for an entirely new and different dispute resolution mechanism to eliminate the gridlock of the old system. Furthermore, the Uruguay Round expanded GATT's authority to new areas-agreements regarding trade in textiles, agriculture, services, and intellectual property were major achievements. Finally, new sets of rules regarding administered protection came into effect with the creation of the WTO in 1995.

FUTURE PERSPECTIVE OF INDIAN INDUSTRY AND MANAGEMENT

INDUSTRIALIZATION

Industrialization has a major role to play in the economic development of the underdeveloped countries. The gap in per capita incomes between the developed and underdeveloped countries is largely reflected in the disparity in the structure of their economies; the former are largely industrial economies, while in the later production is confined predominantly to agriculture. The pattern of "growth though trade" in primary commodities was, however, realized in the nineteenth century when industrialization was closely linked with international trade. In general, the net value of the output per person is higher in industry than in agriculture. In industry, the scope for internal as well as external economies is greater than in agriculture.

Besides, the process of industrialization is associated with the development of mechanical knowledge, attitudes and skills of industrial work, with the experience of industrial management and with other attributes of a modern society which in turn, are beneficial to the growth of productivity in agriculture, trade, distribution and other related sectors of the economy. As a consequence of these factors, any successful transfer of labour from agriculture to industry contributes to economic development.

THE PATTERN OF INDUSTRIALIZATION

While there is now almost universal agreement on the importance of industrialization, there is still much debate regarding the proper pattern of industrial development. Industrial development depends upon the rate of capital formation. Supply of capital goods can be augmented either through imports or through domestic production. Increase in the imports of capital goods depends upon the rate of growth of exports.

Since the scope for the expansion of the exports of primary commodities is limited, export promoting manufacturing industries may be developed or alternatively, certain import substituting domestic industries may be developed, the effect of which will be to release foreign exchange for the imports of capital goods.

In addition, within the current volume of imports, capital goods may be substituted in place of consumer goods. Thus, export-promoting industries, import-substituting industries and domestic capital goods industries are not mutually exclusive alternatives.

Simultaneously development of all the three classes of industries will approve to be the most effective strategy of industrialization. The relative role of each is likely to vary with the particular economic circumstances of individual countries as well as with their current phase of industrialization.

REVIEW OF INDUSTRIAL GROWTH

The progress of industrialization during the last 50 years since 1951 has been a striking feature of Indian economic development. The process of industrialization, launched as a conscious and deliberate policy under Industrial Policy Resolution of 1956 and vigorously implemented under five year plans, involved heavy investments in building up capacity over a wide spectrum of industries. As a result, over the last nearly 50 years, industrial production went up by about five times, making India the tenth most industrial country of world.

Rate of Industrial Growth- Industrial growth has not been uniform since 1951. After a steady growth of about 8 % during the initial period of 14 years (1951-1965), there was a fluctuating trend since then. In the sixties (1961-70) the average growth of Industrial output was put at 5.5 % and in the seventies (1971-80) the average growth rate was about 4 % per annum. During the 7th plan (1985-90), the growth rate had picked up to an average of over 8% per annum and in the eight plan, it had declined to 7.3 % per annum.

Strategy of Industrial Development- The development strategy adopted by the Indian planners consisted of accelerated industrialization with a base of heavy industry and to generate expanding foreign exchange earnings.

GROWING IMPORTANCE OF BASIC AND CAPITAL GOODS

The structure of Indian industries had changed in favor of basic and capital goods sector. On the other hand the share of consumer goods industries such as textiles, sugar, paper, tobacco, etc., declined.

- Structure of Effective Demand and Pattern of Industrial Development- An unduly large share of resources is absorbed in production, which relates directly or indirectly to maintaining or improving the living standards of the higher income groups. Consumer durables like refrigerators, air-conditioners, TVs, cars and scooters, etc., go to satisfy the wants of the richer sections of the community while the consumer non-durables like sugar, tea, coffee, cloth, vanaspati, matches, etc., enter into mass consumption.
- Relative Roles of Public and Private- The growth of the public sector in a big way in the heavy and basic industries, the machine goods sector, engineering industries etc., Public sector units accounted for 7 % of the number of factories in the country but they employed 32 % of the productive capital. Only 56% of the productive capital is employed by the private sector units, which account for 91 % of the total number of factories.
- Growth of Infrastructure- The rapid pace of industrial growth and the development of productive capacity have been marked by remarkable, though still inadequate, expansion of infrastructural facilities in the country.
- Science and Technology- Significant progress has been recorded in the field of science and technology. India now ranks third in the world in respect of technological talent and manpower. Indian scientists and technologists are working in many areas on the frontiers of today's knowledge, as in agriculture and industry, in the development of nuclear power and the use of space technology for communication and resource development.

INDIAN INDUSTRIES-STRUCTURAL TRANSFORMATION

The industrial structure has been widely diversified covering the entire range of consumer, intermediate and capital goods. The progress India has made in the field of Industrialization is clearly reflected in the commodity composition of India's foreign-trade in which the share of imports of manufactured goods has steadily declined; on the other hand, industrial products, particularly engineering goods have become a growing component of India's exports.

Finally, the rapid stride in industrialization has been accompanied by a corresponding growth in technological and managerial skills for efficient operation of the most sophisticated industries and also planning, designing and construction of such industries.

TOTAL QUALITY MANAGEMENT

Total Quality Management (TQM), a buzzword phrase of the 1980's, though simple seem to be creeping back into existence by "bits and pieces" through the evolution of the ISO 9001 Management Quality System Standard.

Companies who have implemented TQM include Ford Motor Company, Philips Semiconductor, SGL Carbon, Motorola and Toyota Motor Company. The latest changes coming up for the ISO 9001:2000 standard's "Process Model" seem to complete the embodiment.

TQM is the concept that quality can be managed and that it is a process. Total Quality Management (TQM) is a participative management style that stresses total staff commitment to "customer" satisfaction. It is a holistic approach to managing complex organizations and replaces top-down management with decentralized customer-driven decision-making.

Total Quality Management is an integrated management system for creating and implementing a continuous improvement process eventually producing results that exceed customer expectations. It is based on the assumption that 90 % of problems are a result of process, not employees.

TQM-CONCEPT & OBJECTIVES

TQM is a process and strategy that in can improve an organization's effectiveness and efficiency. TQM places responsibilities for quality problems with management rather than on the workers. A principal concept of TQM is the management of process variation which seeks to identify special and common needs.

The objective of TQM is the continual improvement of processes, achieved through a shift in focus from outcomes (or products) to the processes that produce them. TQM achieves its objective through data collection and analysis, flow charts, cause and effect diagrams, and other tools, which are used to understand and improve processes.

PRINCIPLES OF TQM

The principles of TQM are as follows:

- Quality can and must be managed.
- Everyone has a customer and is a supplier.
- Processes, not people are the problem.
- Every employee is responsible for quality.
- Problems must be prevented, not just fixed.
- Quality must be measured.
- Quality improvements must be continuous.
- The quality standard is defect free.
- Goals are based on requirements, not negotiated.
- Life cycle costs, not front end costs.
- Management must be involved and lead.
- Plan and organize for Quality improvement.

KEY ELEMENTS OF TQM

The key elements of TQM are as follows:

- Pursue New strategic Thinking
- Know your customers
- Set True customer requirements
- Concentrate on prevention, not correction
- Reduce chronic Waste
- Pursue a continuous Improvement strategy
- Use structured methodology for process improvement
- Reduce Variation
- Use a Balanced Approach
- Apply to all functions

TQM-PROCESS IMPROVEMENT AND PROBLEM SOLVING SEQUENCE

This consists of the following 5 stages:

I. Plan (Plan a change)

This stage consists of three parts:

a. Define the problem
   1. Recognize that what you are doing is a "PROCESS".
   2. Identify the commodity being processed - Process inference.
   3. Define some measurable characteristics of value to the commodity.
   4. Describe the "PROCESS".
   5. Identify the "BIG" problem.

b. - Identify possible causes
   1. "BRAINSTORM" what is causing the problem.
   2. Determine what past data shows.

c. Evaluate possible causes
   1. Determine the relationship between cause and effect.
   2. Determine what the process is doing now.

II. Implement (Implement the change)
   1. Determine what change would help.
   2. Then make the change.

III. Monitor (Observe the effects)
   1. Test the change.
   2. Determine what change worked (Confirmation)

IV. Action (Take permanent action)
   1. Ensure the fix is embedded in the process and that the resulting process is used.
   2. Continue to monitor the process to ensure the problem is fixed for good and the process is good enough.

V. Follow Up (To ensure continuous improvement)
   1. Return to "step 5".

POLITICAL GEOGRAPHY

In the early 1990s the threat of superpower nuclear war faded as an omnipresent nightmare in international relations. Yet new threats and dangers quickly emerged to take the place of those imagined during the cold war. Fears about terrorism also grew with a series of bombings from Paris, London, and Moscow to Oklahoma City, New York and Atlanta. U.S troops and embassies in Saudi Arabia, Tanzania, Kenya and Yemen were the targets of terrorist attacks. But it was only after the disruption, shock and panic of the devastating terrorist attacks of

September 11, 2001 and subsequent incidents of bioterrorism that would politics was given new definition and clarity by the world's most powerful state. The new meta-narrative of geopolitics is the "war against terror".

Beyond the high dramas of geopolitics, already existing trends in everyday economic and political life deepened in the last decade and a half. New social movements have forced questions concerning the politics of identity and lifestyles onto the political agenda.

The globalization of financial markets, telecommunication systems, and the internet further re-arranged governing notions of " here" and "there", " inside" and " outside ", "near" and "far". With global media networks broadcasting news 24 hours a day and the Internet spreading a world wide web, the 'real' geographies of everyday life were becoming strikingly virtual as well as actual.

Political geographic research during this intense decade and a half of transformation has been triangulated between these multi-scalar geopolitical transformations, the emergence of new intellectual discourses within academia, and the legacy of political-geographic research traditions.

Many of the problematics defining the late twentieth and early twenty first century are inescapably political - geographic questions, from murderous spatial practices like 'ethnic cleansing' or hyperbolic spatial narratives about ' borderlessness' and 'the end of distance' to generalized concern about the changing status of key human geographic notions like 'territory', 'community', 'scale', 'place' and 'democracy'. In simple, an extra ordinary geopolitical transformations and change throughout the country.

Contemporary research on political - geographic questions is located within the mainstream of contemporary social science. It spans the study of global economic transformations, geopolitical re-structuring, the politics of identity, technological change and territoriality, politics of the household and interpersonal relations, and the politics of the environment. With its inherited discourses on place and politics, technological transformations and geopolitical space, nature and the contested politics of human-environment relations, political geographers are well positioned to contribute to the larger social science conversation about the human condition in the 21st century.

LAW OF CONTRACT (INDIAN CONTRACT ACT 1872)

Most of the business transactions are based on promises to be performed at a later date. These promises whether made by businessmen or by others create certain rights and obligations and if these rights and obligations are not enforceable, the business world would be paralysed. It is with the enforcement of these promises that the law of contract is concerned. The contract Act does not lay down the list of obligations that would be enforceable by law but lays down the rules subject to which rights or duties created by the parties would be enforced. The parties to the contract can make whatever rules they want, if these rules are not inconsistent with the provisions of the Act, they would be enforced by courts of law.

1. Meaning: Sec. 2(h) "An agreement enforceable by law is a contract." Therefore, a contract has two important elements, one is the agreement, and the other is the obligation which is enforceable by law. Agreement: Agreement is the outcome of the consensus between the parties who enter into a contract, i.e., the promise made between them, represents concurrence of their minds. (Sec.13). These would not be an agreement if the parties do agree but not on the same thing in the same sense, i.e., consensus is not sufficient. There has to be consensus ad idem. Sec. 2(e) defines an agreement as "Every promise or every set of promises forming consideration for each other". A proposal when accepted becomes a promise. Example: A received Rs.10,000 from B and promises to supply him 10 bags of rice after 10 days. It is a promise. It shall be a set of promises if A promises to supply 10 bags of rice after 10 days and B promises to pay him Rs.10,000 after the rice is supplied. Thus, Agreement = Offer + Acceptance.
2. Offer (Proposal): Offer [(proposal) (Sec. 2(a)] "When one person signifies to another his willingness to do or to abstain from doing anything with a view to obtaining the assent of the other to such act or abstinence, he is said to make a proposal".
3. Acceptance: Acceptance has been defined u/s(Sec.2(b)) as " When the person to whom the proposal is made, signifies his assent thereto, the proposal is said to be accepted. A proposal when accepted becomes a promise".

Example: A lost his Cell Phone and announced that anybody who brought his cell phone back home would receive Rs.500 as reward. B heard the announcement and brought the Cell Phone back home. He is said to have accepted the proposal by doing the act required by A and hence he can recover the reward.

- Promisor: A person who makes the promise is called the 'Promisor' or 'Offeror'. And the person to whom the proposal is made is known as 'Promisee' or 'Offereee'.In case an agreement is a set of promises, then a person becomes a promisor and promisee. Thus if there is an offer, acceptance and consensus ad idem between the parties, there is an agreement. However, this agreement does not become a contract unless there is a corresponding obligation, i.e., enforceability at law.
- Obligation (Sec.10): It is the legal duty of a person to carry out what he has promised to do or not to do. All agreements are contracts if they are made by the free consent of the parties competent to enter into contract, for a lawful consideration and with a lawful object and not hereby expressly declared to be void. Therefore, a person becomes legally bound to do what he has promised to do only if the following conditions are fulfilled.

1. Capacity of the Parties: Only those persons who are competent to enter into a contract can create valid obligations. A minor, a lunatic, a drunkard etc., suffer from flaw in capacity to Contract and therefore the contract made with them can't be enforced against them.
2. Free Consent: Absence of consent does not create a legal obligation. For an agreement to become a contract the parties to an agreement should give their consent to the agreement out of their own free will. It should not be induced by coercion, undue influence, fraud, misrepresentation, etc.
4. Lawful Consideration and Object: Consideration means something in return, i.e., 'quid pro quo' Example. A promises to give his bike to B for no money, here, there is no consideration, hence no obligation. Without consideration a promise can't be enforceable by law. However, consideration need not be in money or in kind. It may be of an act, abstinence, a promise to do, or not to do something. But consideration should be lawful. Example: A promises to pay a sum of money to B if B smuggles the object proposed by A. In this case, there is no lawful object.

5. Intention to create Legal Relationship: Social obligation can't bring legal relationship. For example: Father promised his son to pay Rs.100 per day for pocket `expenses, however later on did not pay the said amount. Therefore, if the parties do not intend to be bound by law at the time they make promises, nothing can bound them to their promises, later on.
6. Possibility of Performance: Example: A promised B that he would make The Sun raises in the West if B pays him Rs.1 lakh., and B agreed to it, this agreement does not create any legal obligation as it would not be enforceable by law.
7. Meaning should be certain: Example: A agrees to sell B's horse. There is nothing whatever to show which horse is intended. The agreement is void for uncertainty.
8. Legal Formalities (If required): An agreement to make a gift for natural love and affection should not only be in writing but registered also (Sec. 25). In the absence of any such specific requirement an oral agreement is as enforceable as a written agreement.
9. Agreements not Declared Void: Indian Contract Act has specifically declared some agreements to be not enforceable at law e.g. Agreements in restraint of trade, Agreements in restraint of marriage, wagering agreements etc. Thus the law of Contract is not the whole law of Agreements. It is the law of those agreements which create obligations.

THE LAW OF CONTRACT IS NOT THE WHOLE LAW OF OBLIGATIONS

There may be certain duties (obligations) which the law may enforce though they were not agreed to by the parties. Such obligations do not create a contract between them. These obligations may arise in the following ways:

1. Torts and Civil Wrong: Where a tort is committed by one person against another the former is bound to compensate the latter even though there is no agreement between the two.
2. Judgments of Courts: These obligation are imposed by the Court by their verdict.

3. Quasi Contracts: Where law creates and enforces an obligation between two persons, it is known as Quasi Contract.
4. Status Obligation: It is the duty of the husband to provide necessities of life to his wife, and if the husband fails to do so, the wife can enforce this obligation at the courts of law and can seek maintenance from her husband.

Kinds of Contracts

1. Valid Contract: It is an agreement which fulfils all the essentials of enforceability and can be enforced by either of the parties at the courts of law.
2. Voidable contract: Sec 2(i) lays down that "An agreement which is enforceable by law at the option of one or more of the parties thereto, but not at the option of the other or others, is a Voidable Contract." This arises where the consent of one of the parties to the contract is not free. Ex., A, at the point of pistol makes B agree to sell his bicycle for Rs.500. Here B's consent is not free.

   Circumstances in which a contract is voidable are:

a. At the conception
   - Consent caused by fraud (Sec.14, 17 and 19)
   - Consent caused by coercion (Sec. 14, 15 and 19)
   - Consent caused by misrepresentation (Sec. 14, 18 and 19)
   - Consent caused by undue influence (Sec. 14, 16 and 19A)
   - When one party induces another to enter into an agreement the object of which is unlawful though it is not known to the other party.

b. By Subsequent Default
   - Where offer of performance is not accepted (Sec. 38)
   - When one party prevents performance of reciprocal promise (Sec. 53)
   - When a party fails to perform at the time fixed, if time is the essence of the contract (Sec. 55)

Consequences of Recession of Voidable Contract

When a voidable contract is rescinded ?

a. As regards the party at whose option the contract is voidable, if he has received any benefit from another party to such contract, he must restore such benefit so far as may be, to the person from whom it has been received. The benefit must have been received under the contract and not otherwise. Security for performance is not the benefit received under the contract.

b. As regards the other party, he need not perform his promise.

3. Void Contract: [Sec 2(j)] "A contract which ceases to be enforceable by law becomes void when it ceases to be enforceable" e.g. A agrees to sell his car to B for Rs.10,000. All essentials of a contract are fulfilled. If A refuses to sell his car, B can go to the court and the court would enforce A's promise. But if, before the delivery the car is destroyed by Tsunami, the court cannot enforce anything and hence this contract becomes unenforceable i.e., void. Thus, void contract is one which was a valid contract when it was made but becomes void later on. Those agreements which are void ab initio (from the very beginning) are called Void Agreements and those which become void later on are called Void Contracts. Following circumstances will transform a valid contract into a void contract.

- Contingent contract: A contingent contract to do or not to do something on the happening of an uncertain future event, becomes void, when the event becomes impossible (Sec 32).
- Repudiation of a voidable contract: When a voidable contract is rescinded by the party at whose option it is voidable, the contract becomes void.
- Subsequent impossibility (Sec. 56): A contract which becomes impossible to perform, after it is made, becomes void.
- Subsequent illegality (Sec. 56): A contract becomes void if it becomes illegal after it is made.

Consequences of a Void Contract: Sec. 65 lays down that when a contract becomes void, the party who has received any advantage under such agreement, should restore it or make compensation for it to the party from whom he received it.

4. Void Agreement: An agreement that is not enforceable by law is called a void agreement. If any of the essentials of obligations

(enforceability), other than free consent, is missing the agreement cannot be enforced at Courts of Law.

Invalidating Causes

In the following circumstances an agreement is void ab initio.

- If a party to the contract is incompetent to contract (Sec.10, 11 & 12)
- If the agreement is without consideration (Sec. 10, 25) barring certain exceptions.
- If the consideration or object is unlawful (Sec. 23)
- If the meaning of the contract is uncertain (Sec. 29)
- If the agreement is to do an impossible act (Sec. 56)
- If both the parties enter into an agreement under a mistake as to the essential matter of fact (Sec. 20). There is no consensus ad idem.
- If both the parties are under a mistake as to foreign law (Sec. 21)
- If the agreement is in restraint of marriage of a person other than a minor (Sec. 26)
- If the agreement is in restraint of trade (Sec. 27) barring certain exceptions.
- If the agreements is in restraint of legal proceedings (Sec. 28)
- If the agreement is by way of wager (Sec. 30)

5. Illegal Agreement: An illegal agreement is one which is forbidden by law i.e. it is entered into with the intention of violating the law. Example: A agrees to steal furniture for B for a consideration of Rs. 1,00,000. It is illegal and therefore it is void. It also attracts the penal provisions of the law it is violating. While all illegal agreements are void, all void agreements are not illegal. Parties to an illegal agreement cannot get any help or protection from law courts.
6. Unlawful Agreements: (Sec. 23). In simple words an agreement may be unlawful because it is:
   - Immoral -i.e. contrary to sound and positive morality as recognized by law, e.g. cohabitation.
   - Opposed Public Policy -i.e. contrary to the welfare of the State as tending to interfere with the civil or judicial

administration, or with individual liberty of citizens, e.g. bribing a public servant.

- Illegal -i.e. contrary to positive law, being forbidden either by statutes law or common law; Hence a line of demarcation needs to be drawn between illegal and unlawful agreements.

7. Unenforceable Contract: Contracts which have all the essentials of enforceability but cannot be enforced due to certain technicalities like insufficiency of stamp, etc. are termed as unenforceable contracts.

8. Express Contract: It is one where the intention of parties are stated in words either written or spoken. Example: A goes to B's shop and asks him to supply 10 boxes @ Rs.20per box. B tells him that he is ready to supply the boxes at the mentioned rate. This is an Express Contract. The same intention of the parties may be expressed in writing signed by both the parties.

9. Implied Contract: The evidence of an implied contract is to be deduced from the acts or conduct of the parties. No exchange of words either written or spoken takes place, but the manifestation of their intentions is inferred from their respective acts or conduct.

10. Quasi Contracts: These are those obligations which are imposed by the Contract Act and do not arise from a consensus between the parties. Example: A, a tradesman, leaves goods at B's house by mistake. B treats the goods as his own. B is bound to pay A for them, the obligation is imposed by law.

11. An Executed Contract: It is one where both the parties to a contract have discharged their respective responsibilities by performing them. All transactions of Cash sales are the examples of Executed Contracts.

12. An Executory Contract: It is one where one or both the parties are yet to perform their respective promises. It is partly Executed and partly Executory.

13. Unilateral Contract: It is one where at the time when the contract is made one party has already performed his obligation and the obligation on the part of the other party only, is outstanding. Example: A goes to a bus stand ticketcounter and buys a ticket for journey. A has performed his duty under the contract i.e., to pay the scheduled fare. But the bus authority is yet to perform

his promise i.e., of carrying him from one point to another. This is a Unilateral Contract.

14. Bilateral Contract: As against Unilateral Contract, a Bilateral Contract is one where at the time of entering into the contract both the parties to the contract are yet to perform their respective promises.

Offer and Acceptance: As seen earlier the first step in making a contract starts with making an offer. We shall, therefore, discuss as to what constitutes a 'lawful offer'.

Offer or Proposal: 'Offer' and 'Proposal' are synonymous terms. According to sec. 2(a), "when one person signifies to another his willingness to do or to abstain from doing anything with a view to obtaining the assent of that other to such act or abstinence, he is said to make a proposal". The person making the proposal is called the "Promisor" and the person to whom the offer is made is called the "Promisee" [Sec.2 (c)] Example: A offers to pay Rs.100 to B if B washes his cloths. A is the promisor and B is the promisee for the promise to pay Rs.100. A is the promisee and B is the promisor for washing his clothes. It is important to note that the offer must be made with the object of obtaining the assent of the other party.

Rules Regarding a Lawful Offer

A valid offer must be in conformity with the following rules:

1. Terms of an offer should be definite or should be capable of being made definite.
2. Offer should be made with an intention to create legal relationship: In the absence of such intention no obligation can arise. Absence of such intention may be express or implied.

   Example: Where A proposes to sell his 'Television' to B for Rs.10000 but tells him that the breach of promise by either party would not create legal rights, no binding contract would arise in that case even if the agreement is in writing.
3. There is no valid offer where:

- It is mere statement of intention:

Example: A gives an advertisement in the television that he would dispose of his building by auction on 5th June at 8 a.m. in the lawns of his bungalow. B, who saw this advertisement, travels a distance of 200 kilometers and reaches A's bungalow at the given time and date and finds that auction has been cancelled. A cannot be held liable because his advertisement to hold auction did not constitute an offer, it was merely an intention to hold an auction where bids would be received.

- It is an invitation to offer: Where A puts his building to public auction he is inviting offers from the bidders and he accepts the offer by falling the hammer or by any other customary method. The actual offer is the bid made at the auction and the auctioneer accepts it.

4. Offer must be communicated: The offer must be brought to the knowledge of the person to whom it is made. If an offer is not communicated to the offeree, the latter cannot accept it.

5. Offer should not contain a term the non-compliance of which would amount to acceptance.

   Example: A writes to B "I shall buy your furniture for Rs, 10,000, if you do not reply I shall assume that you have accepted my offer. This is not a valid offer.

6. Offer may be express or implied: An offer is express when it is stated in words, written or spoken.

7. An offer may be general or specific: When an offer is made to a specific person it is called a specific offer and it can be accepted only by that person but when an offer is addressed to an uncertain body of individuals i.e. the world at large, it is a general offer and can be accepted by any member of the general public by fulfilling the condition laid down in the offer.

Lapse of an Offer

An offer once made cannot be continued for ever. Liability of the party making the proposal cannot be continued for all times to come. An offer becomes invalid i.e. comes to an end in the following circumstances.

1. When the stipulated or reasonable time has expired: Example: A offers to sell his Modern table to B for Rs. 5000 and tells him that B must communicate his acceptance within three days. On fourth day B brings Rs.5000 to buy the table. A refuses. A is not bound because the offer has lapsed on the third day.

2. Where the offer becomes illegal after it is made: Example: X of Mumbai offers to buy Peanuts from Y of Chennai. Next day Central Government prohibits inter-state transfer of Peanuts. The offer lapses by subsequent illegality.

3. Where the offerer or offeree dies or becomes insane before the offer is accepted: Example: A offers to sell his cow to B. Before B could accept the offer, A dies. B cannot accept the offer.
4. Where the offeree does not accept the offer in the mode the offerer had prescribed: Example: A writes to B that he wants to sell his furniture to B for Rs.10000. He also writes to B that if B wants to buy the furniture, he (B) should send him (A) a telegram accepting the offer. B writes a letter to A accepting the offer. If A keeps silence over it, this is a valid acceptance. But if A informs B that he is not treating this letter as acceptance because the offer has not been accepted by a telegram, then this letter would not result in acceptance.
5. An offer lapses by counter offer by the offeree: Example: A tells B, "I want to buy your land for Rs. 10,000". B says, "I shall sell my land for Rs.15,000." A refuses to buy it for Rs. 15,000. Then B insists that A should buy it for Rs. 10,000. A refuses to do so. A is not bound by his offer because the statement of B that 'I shall sell my land for Rs. 15,000' is not acceptance of A's offer but a counter offer. When a counter offer is made the original offer lapses and there is nothing for the offeree to accept. But an enquiry should not be mistaken for a counter offer.
6. An offer comes to an end when the offerer revokes his offer before it is accepted. Tender (standing offer): A tender is an offer made in response to an invitation to offer. The party inviting tenders may require a definite quantity of goods or services to be supplied, in that event the person who responds to that invitation is said to have made a definite offer and would become bound by it if it is accepted.

Acceptance: "When the person to whom the proposal is made signifies his assent thereto the proposal is said to be accepted. A proposal once accepted becomes a contract." Where two parties make offers to each other with identical terms, without knowing each other's offer. These offers are called 'CROSS OFFERS".

Who can accept?: Where an offer is made to a specified person, only that specified person can accept it and nobody else. But where the offer is made to an uncertain body of persons, anybody can accept the offer.

Rules Regarding Acceptance

- Acceptance must be absolute and unqualified: The offeree must accept unconditionally all the terms of the offer without any change in any of them.
- The Acceptance must be expressed in some usual and reasonable manner, unless the proposal prescribes a manner in which it is to be accepted
- Acceptance by performing Conditions or receiving Consideration:

Example: A offers to pay Rs. 100 to B if B throws the ring ball into the basket in first attempt. B immediately throws the ball into the basket in first attempt. By the performance of this condition B is said to have accepted the offer."

- Acceptance must be communicated: Unless acceptance is communicated it would not turn the offer into a contract. However, if the offeree posts the acceptance but it does not reach the offerer, it would be deemed to be communicated. But the offerer cannot frame his offer in such a way that the silence of the offeree would become his acceptance.
- Acceptance should be given within stipulated time and before the offer is revoked: If the offer lapses before acceptance is given the acceptance would not result into a contract. But where no time limit is stipulated the offer should be accepted within a reasonable time.
- Where an offeree accepts an offer knowing that it has been made by the offeror under a mistake, the contract is not binding upon the offeror.

Consensus ad Idem

According to sec. 13, "Two or more persons are said to consent when they agree upon the same thing in the same sense". But where the circumstances lead one party to believe that the other would have understood the terms of the agreement, law may imply unenforceable agreement. Because it is not what a party thinks in his mind but what he expresses or does that binds him to the contract.

Communication of Offer and Acceptance: Problem of communication arises when the parties to the contract are not face to face with each other. It arises in the following cases:

A. Contracts through Telephones:

B. Contracts through Post: Offer and acceptance are generally made through letters and telegrams. Advertisements, notices, circulars, etc., are also used to make an offer. The rules of communication regarding them are as follows:

1. "The communication of a proposal is complete: When it comes to the knowledge of the person to whom it is made..." (sec. 4)
2. "....The communication of an acceptance is complete (i) as against the proposer, when it is put in a course of transmission to him, so as to be out of the power of acceptor; and (ii) as against the acceptor, when it comes to the knowledge of the proposer..." (Sec.4)

From the above it is clear that an offer may be revoked at any time before the acceptance is put in course of transmission to the proposer.

- Revocation of Proposal and Acceptance: "A proposal may be revoked at any time before that communication of its acceptance is complete as against the proposer, but not afterwards."
- Communication of Revocation: "The communication of a revocation is complete... As against the person who makes it, when it is put into a course of transmission to the person to whom it is made, so as to be out of the power of the person who makes it as against the person to whom it is made, when it comes to his knowledge."
- Agreement to Agree in Future: Agreement to enter into an agreement upon terms to be settled afterwards between the parties is a contradiction in terms. It is absurd to say that a man enters into an agreement till the terms of agreement are settled; until those terms are settled, he is perfectly at liberty to retire from the bargain".

CONSIDERATION AND COMPETENCE TO CONTRACT

Consideration is one of the elements of obligation. An agreement becomes enforceable only if it is supported by consideration. (Sec. 10) "All agreements are contracts if they are made... for a lawful consideration..." It clearly shows that consideration is an important prerequisite of a valid contract. (Sec.25) "An agreement made without consideration is void..." Hence the rule is "No Consideration, No Contract.

Essentials of Consideration

A. Based on Definition

An analysis of the above definition reveals the following essentials of consideration.

1. Consideration must move at the desire of the promisor
2. It may move from promisee or from any other person on behalf of promisee.
3. Consideration may be past, present or future
4. Consideration must be real and not illusory
5. Consideration may consist of an act, abstinence or promise

B. Based on other provisions

In addition to the above essentials of consideration that emerge from the definition, the others are as follows:

1. Consideration must be lawful: (Sec. 10) "All agreements are contracts if they are made for a lawful consideration" The consideration of an agreement is unlawful, if:
   - It is forbidden by law, or
   - It is of such a nature that, if permitted, it would defeat the provisions of any law, or
   - It is fraudulent or
   - It involves or implies injury to the person or property of another or
   - The court regards it as immoral or opposed to public policy (Sec. 23).
2. Consideration need not be adequate to the value of the promise: (Sec. 25) "An agreement to which the consent of the promisor is freely given is not void merely because the consideration is inadequate, but the inadequacy of the consideration may be taken into account by the Court in determining the question whether the consent of the promisor was freely given."

Exceptions to the Rule of Consideration

(Sec. 25) In the following cases the agreement would be enforceable even though they are made without consideration.

1. Love and affection:
   1. An agreement without consideration is enforceable if

a. It is made up of love and affection;
b. The love and affection is natural because the parties are so related to each other;
c. The agreement is in writing;
d. The agreement is registered under the law.

2. Compensation for voluntary services: "If it is a promise to compensate, wholly or in part, a person who has already voluntarily done something for the promisor, or something which the promisor was legally compellable to do."
3. Promise to pay a time barred debt: If it is a promise, made in writing and signed by the debtor or his agent to pay wholly or in part a debt which is barred by the limitation.
4. Contract of Agency: Sec. 185 provides "No consideration is necessary to create an agency."
5. Gift already Made: (Sec. 25) "Nothing in this Section shall affect the validity, as between the donor and donee, of any gift actually made."

Unlawful Agreements

According to the Indian Contract Act (Sec. 23), "The consideration or object of an agreement is lawful, unless it is forbidden by law; or is of such a nature that, if permitted, it would defeat the provisions of any law; or is fraudulent; or involves or implies injury to the person or property of another; or the court regards it as immoral, or opposed to public policy.

Let us see the provisions of Sec. 23 which make an agreement unlawful.

- Forbidden by law: If the object of the agreement or the consideration of the agreement is the doing of an act which is forbidden by law, the agreement is void.
- If it is of such a nature that, if permitted, it would defeat the provisions of any law: i.e. it would indirectly lead to a violation of the law.
- If it is fraudulent: Any agreement whose object is to defraud others is void.
- If it involves or implies injury to the person or property of another:
- If the Court regards it as immoral.

- If the Court regards it as opposed to public policy: The following agreements have been held to be against public policy:
- Trading with Enemy:
- Agreements for stifling prosecution: An agreement to suppress criminal charge is void because if a person has committed a crime, public policy requires that he should be prosecuted.
- Agreements interfering with the Course of Justice: An agreement entered into with the object of exercising improper influence on judges or officers of justice is bad in law as opposed to public policy.
- Agreements tending to an abuse of legal process: There may be two types of agreements under this head, one is Maintenance and the other is Champerty.
- Agreement to vary the period of limitation: An agreement that reduces or increases the period of limitation as laid down by the law of limitation is opposed to public policy.
- Traffic in Public Offices: An agreement whereby an appointment to a public office is procured for monetary consideration is against public policy because it would cause corruption in administration of the State.
- Agreement creating an interest opposed to duty
- Agreements restraining personal freedom
- Agreements opposed to parental rights and duties: Father is supposed to be the guardian of his children and in the absence of the father their mother acquires this right as well as responsibility and this right cannot be bartered away.
- Marriage Brokerage Agreements: Agreement to pay reward to a person for negotiating marriage is opposed to public policy.

The following agreements are also opposed to public policy.

i. Agreements in restraint of marriage.

ii. Agreements in restraint of trade.

iii. Agreements in restraint of legal proceedings.

Competence to Contract

Competence to contract is one of the most essential elements of enforceability of an agreement. According to Sec. 10 'All agreements are contracts if they are made by... the parties competent to Contract.....As regards the meaning of competence, Sec.11 of the Contract Act states that "Every person is competent to contract who is of the age of majority according to the law to which he is subject, and who is of sound mind, and is not disqualified from contracting by any law to which he is subject. The following persons are incapable of entering into a contract:

1. A person who has not attained the age of majority i.e. a person who is still a minor.
2. A Person who is not of sound mind.
3. A Person who is disqualified by any other law to which he is subject.

Minor: A minor is a person who has not completed 18 years of age on the date of the contract. But in the following two cases the minority would continue up to the completion of 21 years of age:

a. Where a guardian to the person or property of a minor is appointed by the court.
b. When the minor is under the guardianship of the court of Wards, i.e. minor's property is looked after by the Court of Wards.

Rules Relating to an Agreement with a Minor:

- Agreement is void ab initio: According to Sec. 10, an agreement made by a person incompetent to contract is void. Hence an agreement made by a minor is void. The agreement is void ab initio i.e. void from the very beginning. However, Sec. 68 of the Contract Act lays down "if a person, incapable of entering into a contract or any one whom he is legally bound to support, is supplied by another person with necessaries suited to his condition in life, the person who has furnished such supplies is entitled to be reimbursed from the property of such incapable person.
- Minor can be a promisee: An agreement is void as against a minor but a minor can derive benefit under a contract. The privilege of minority is available to the minor only. Other person cannot avoid the contract because the promisee is a minor. Thus the minor can enforce the agreement against the other party.
- A Minor's Agreement cannot be ratified: Since an agreement with a minor is void ab initio, i.e. it does not exist in the eyes of law, it cannot be ratified by a minor after completing the age of majority.

- No Compensation is payable by a minor: Though an agreement with a minor is void, the minor would not be called upon to refund any benefit which he has received, under such an agreement (i.e. Sec. 64 and Sec. 65 would not apply to a minor).
- The rule of estoppel does not apply to a minor i.e. a minor can misrepresent his age and enter into an agreement and can still plead infancy to avoid that agreement.
- No recovering back the money paid: Where an infant has paid money under a void or voidable contract he cannot recover it unless there has been a total failure of consideration.
- A minor can be sued in tort. If what the infant has done lies right outside the terms of the contract, the infant can be made liable.
- Agency. A minor acting as an agent cannot be held liable even for those acts for which other agents would incur personal liability.
- Negotiable Instrument: A minor can also make and deliver negotiable instruments and can negotiate them making all other persons except himself liable on them.
- Partnership: An agreement with a minor is void. But a minor can be admitted into the benefits of partnership with the consent of all the partners (Partnership Act). This means that the losses of the firm can be recovered only from his share in the firm but unlike other partners his personal property would not be liable for firm's losses.
- Insolvency: A minor cannot be adjudicated insolvent.
- Joint Agreement: Where a minor and another person make a joint promise, the promisee cannot enforce the agreement against the minor but he can enforce it against the other person.
- Guardianship: Though an agreement made by a minor is void but an agreement made by the guardian of a minor is binding on the minor if it is for the benefit of the minor.
- Minor's Parents: Agreements made by a minor are not enforceable against his parents, even through they are for the necessaries supplied to the minor.

Persons of Unsound Mind: According to Sec.11 only a person of sound mind can make a contract. Sec. 12 further defines the term sound mind in these words, "A person is said to be of sound mind for the purpose of making a contract if, at the time when he makes it, he is capable of understanding it and of forming a rational judgment as to its effect upon his interest...". Thus two essentials of 'Sound Mind' emerge from this definition:

(1) Capacity to understand: and Capacity to make a rational judgment

There must be free and full consent of the parties so as to bind them to the contract. Consent is an act of reason accompanied by deliberations. It is due to the absence of rational and deliberate consent that conveyance and contracts of persons of unsound mind are deemed to be invalid. A person of unsound mind may be divided into two broad categories:

- Idiots: An Idiot is one who has lost mental powers completely, i.e., his brain has not developed enough to enable him, at all to understand the contract or of forming a rational judgment of its effects upon his interest. Hence an agreement with him is always void. However, he can be sued for necessaries of life supplied to him or to anybody dependent upon him.
- Lunatic: Lunacy arises from the illness of the brain or mental or bodies distress. The essential element of lunacy is that the mental powers of the lunatic are so deranged that he cannot make a rational judgment of any subject the period of lunacy.

  Effects of agreements made by persons of unsound mind: An agreement made with a person who is suffering from lunacy at the time of entering into the contract, is void (Sec. 10).

Other Disqualifications:

- Alien Enemy: A citizen of a foreign country is known as an alien.
- Foreign sovereigns and their Ambassadors. Foreign sovereigns and their Ambassadors in India can enter into contracts with Indian citizens and can sue them in Indian courts but no suit can be filed against them in local courts unless the permission of the Central Government to this effect has been obtained.
- Corporation: A corporation is an artificial person created by law. Being a legal person only, it cannot act by itself. It has to act through some agent. Its contractual capacity suffers from the following limitations:
- Natural Limitation:

- Legal Limitation:
  - — Insolvents: When a person is adjudged insolvent, he loses contractual powers over his property.
  - — Convicts: A person against whom a sentence of imprisonment is passed loses the capacity to contract.
  - — Married women: A married woman used to suffer from certain disabilities with regard to making of contracts under English Law before 1935. A woman, married or single, in Indian Law, is under no disability as regard, entering into contracts with regard to the property that belongs to her (e.g. stridhan of a married women). Her contracts can be enforced against her husband's property if he has failed to provide necessaries of life to her and the contract relates to necessaries of life.

Free Consent: "The term free consent consists of two requirements viz.:

i. There should be consent: and

ii. That consent should be free.

Consent: The term consent is defined by Sec. 13 as "Two or more persons are said to consent when they agree upon the same thing in the same sense"

Free Consent: "Consent is said to be free when it is not caused by the follwoing:

1. Coercion, as defined in section 15, or:
2. Undue influence as defined in section 16, or:
3. Fraud, as defined in section 17, or:
4. Misrepresentation, as defined in section 18, or:
5. Mistake subject to the provisions of sections 20, 21 and 22.

Consent is said to be so caused when it would not have been given but for the existence of such coercion, undue influence, fraud, misrepresentation or mistake." (Sec.14)

Coercion: "Coercion is the committing or threatening to commit any act, forbidden by the Indian Penal Code or the unlawful detaining or threatening to detain any property, to the prejudice of any person whatever, with the intention of causing any person to enter into agreement."(Sec.15)

A. Coercion is committing any act forbidden by the Indian Penal Code with the intention of causing any person to enter into an agreement.

B. Coercion is the threatening to commit any act forbidden by the Indian Penal Code, with the intention of causing any person to enter into an agreement.

C. Coercion is the Unlawful detaining of any property to the prejudice or any person, whatever, with the intention of causing any person to enter into an agreement.

D. Coercion is the threatening to detain, unlawfully, any property, to the prejudice of any person whatever, with the intention of causing any person to enter into an agreement.

Effect of Coercion: Sec, 19 states "When consent to an agreement is caused by coercion... the agreement is a contract voidable at the option of the party whose consent was so caused" i.e. the aggrieved party at its option, may set aside the contract or may insist that the contract shall performed. Sec. 72 further states, "A person to whom money has been paid, or anything delivered... under coercion, must repay or return it."

Undue Influence: [Sec. 16 (1)] "A Contract is said to be induced by 'undue influence' where the relations subsisting between the parties are such that one of the parties is in a position to dominate the will of the other and uses that position to obtain an unfair advantage over the other." Three conditions should be fulfilled:

- The relation between the contracting parties should be such that one party is in a position to dominate the will of the other; and
- Such party has used that dominant position to enter into a contract with the latter; and
- Such party has obtained an unfair advantage over the other.

Effect of Undue Influence: [Sec. 19 (A)] "When consent to an agreement is caused by undue influence the agreement is a contract voidable at the option of the party whose consent was so caused. Pardanashin Women: A pardanashin woman is susceptible to undue influence and therefore, the law throws around her a "Special cloak of protection" i.e. where such a woman signs a sale, mortgage, gift or release, the person obtaining her signatures has to prove that the transaction was not only explained to her but also that she had understood the transaction and that no undue influence was exercised on her.

Difference between Coercion and Undue Influence:

- Type of pressure: Physical or crude force; Mental pressure.

- Burden of Proof: Prove how the coercion was exercised; Prove that the other party was in a position to dominate his will and that the transaction is unconscionable.
- Nature of Transaction: The party uses that position to obtain an unfair advantage over the other; A transaction, though fair but induced by coercion can still be avoided.

Fraud: Fraud includes any of the following acts committed by a party to a contract, or with his connivance or by his agent with intent to deceive another party thereto or his agent or to induce him to enter into the contract:

- The suggestion, as a fact, of that which is not true by one who does not believe it to be true;
- The active concealment of a fact by one, having knowledge and belief of the fact;
- A promise made without any intention of performing it;
- Any other act fitted to deceive;
- Any such act or omission as the law specially declares to be fraudulent (Sec. 17)

Can silence be Fraudulent? (Sec. 17) "silence as to facts likely to affect the willingness of a person to enter into a contract is not fraud unless the circumstances of the case are such that regard being had to them it is the duty of the person keeping silence to speak or unless his silence is in itself equivalent to speech."

Exception: Silence would amount to Fraud if (a) It is the duty of the person keeping silence to speak. These are called uberrimae fidei contracts: (b) His silence is, in itself, equivalent to speech:

Effect of Fraud:

- Where Fraud is the cause of the contract:(i) Voidable Contract:(ii) Damages
- Where Fraud is not the cause of contract: An attempt at deceit, which does not deceive, is not a fraud.

Misrepresentation

Misrepresentation, better known as 'Innocent misrepresentation' has been defined by Sec. 18 as: "Misrepresentation means and includes-

- The positive assertion in a manner not warranted by the information of the person making it, of that which is not true, though he believes it to be true;

- Any breach of duty which, without an intent to deceive, gains an advantage to the person committing it, or any one claiming under him, by misleading another to his prejudice or to the prejudice of any one claiming under him;
- Causing, however innocently, a party to an agreement to make a mistake as to the substance of the thing which is the subject of the agreement".

Effect of Misrepresentation

"When consent to an agreement is caused by... misrepresentation, the agreement is a contract voidable at the option of the party whose consent is so caused.

Distinction between Fraud and Misrepresentation Fraud: Intention to deceive there is no intention to deceive, fraud to recover damages not available in case of misrepresentation.

Misrepresentation: the aggrieved party loses the right to rescind the contract if it could discover the truth with ordinary diligence. In Fraud, this exception does not apply.

Mistake

Salmond has described these contracts as "error in Causa". As "error in consensus" i.e. there is no 'consensus ad idem'; because of some misunderstanding, called 'Mistake', parties do not agree upon the same thing in the same sense. According to Indian Contract Act, Mistake is of two types, (1) Mistake as to law and (2) Mistake as to fact.

Mistake of Law (Sec. 21): "A contract is not voidable because it was caused by a mistake as to any law in force in India, but a mistake as to a law not in force in India has the same effect as mistake of fact." The reason of this rule lies in the legal maxim " Ignorance of law is no excuse".

Mistake of Fact: (Sec 20:) "Where both the parties to an agreement are under a mistake as to a matter of fact, essential to the agreement, the agreement is void".

Essentials:

1. Mistake must be mutual;
2. Mistake must relate to a fact;
3. Fact should be essential:

Type of Mistakes: Mistake in fact can be divided into the following categories:

A. Bilateral Mistakes:

1. Mistake as to the subject Matter:
   - Mistake regarding existence of subject matter:
   - Mistake regarding identity of the subject matter i.e. the two parties understand different things to be the subject matter:
   - Mistake regarding quantity of subject matter:
   - Mistake regarding title of the subject matter: Where both the parties believe that the seller has the right to sell the goods but unknown to both, the seller has no title to the goods.
   - Mistake regarding the price of the subject matter.
   - Mistake regarding the quality of the subject matter.
2. Mistake as to the possibility of performance of the agreement: if both the parties to the agreement believe that the agreement is capable of being performed though it is not, the agreement is void.

B. Unilateral Mistake: In the following circumstances, even unilateral mistake will make the contract voidable.

- Mistake as to the nature of transaction: This is an exception to the rule that mistake must be mutual. When one of the parties to a contract, without any fault of his own, is made to commit a mistake as to the nature of transaction the agreement would be void.
- Mistake as to the person contracted with: When the identity of the person is essential to the contract and a mistake is committed regarding that,. the contract can be avoided.

VOID AGREEMENTS

Following are those contracts, which may not lack any of the essentials, discussed so far, still the law has specifically declared them void, they are:

1. Agreement in Restraint of Marriage
2. Agreement in Restraint of Trade

Following agreements are not in Restraint of Trade

1. Restraint during the term of service
2. Agreements which promote business and do not restrain it

3. Trade Combinations
4. Agreement in Restraint of Legal Proceedings

(Sec. 28) "Every agreement, by which any party thereto is restricted absolutely from enforcing his rights under or in respect of any contract by the usual legal proceedings in the ordinary tribunals, or which limits the time within which he may thus enforce his rights, is void to that extent".

Exceptions-Arbitration Agreements: An agreement to refer all future as well as present disputes in connection with a contract, to arbitration is valid.

- Uncertain Agreements: (Sec. 29) "Agreements the meaning of which is not certain or capable of being made certain, are void."
- Agreement by Way of Wager:(Sec. 30) "Agreements by way of wager are void, and no suit shall be brought for recovering anything alleged to be won on any wager, or entrusted to any person to abide by the result of any game or other uncertain event on which any wager is made.

Agreements Collateral to Wagering Agreements

However transactions collateral or incidental to a wagering agreement are not void as per Sec. 30.

Lotteries: A lottery is a game of chance and is a wagering agreement.

Cross-word Puzzles: Cross-word puzzles are of two types:

a. One in which any person solving the puzzle would be awarded, therefore it is a game of skill and not of chance and is not a wagering agreement.
b. The other type of cross-word puzzle is one in which the prize would be awarded to that competitor whose solution corresponds to the solution kept with the editor of the newspaper.

Contingent Contracts

(Selection 31) "A contingent contract is a contract to do or not to do something, if some event, collateral to such contract does or does not happen". Thus it is a contract, the performance of which is dependent upon, the happening or non-happening of an uncertain event, collateral to such contract.

Example: X contracts to pay Y Rs.30,000, in consideration of Y paying Rs. 100 monthly premium, if Y's factory is burnt. This is a contingent contract.

Example: A agrees to pay B a sum of money if B marries C. Contracts of insurance and contracts of indemnity and guarantee are popular instances of contingent contracts.

Rules Relating to Contingent Contracts:

- Contingent on the act of party to the contract: If the performance of the promise is contingent upon the pleasure and will of the promisor it is not a contract at all.
- Contingent upon the act of a third party: where the performance of a contract is conditional upon the act of a third party it is a valid contract.
- Contingent on the happening of an event: (Sec.32) "Contingent contracts to do or not to do anything if an uncertain future event happens cannot be enforced by law unless and until that event has happened".
- Contracts contingent on the non-happening of an event: (Sec.33) "Contingent contracts to do or not to do anything if an uncertain future event does not happen, can be enforced when the happening of that event becomes impossible, and not before".
- Contracts contingent on the happening or not happening of a specified event within fixed time (Sec.35). "Contingent contracts to do or not to do anything if a specified uncertain event happens within a fixed time, becomes void if at the expiration of the time fixed, such event has not happened or if, before the time fixed, such event becomes impossible".
- Contracts contingent on impossible event: (Sec. 36-)"Contingent agreement to do or not to do anything if an impossible event happens, are void, whether the impossibility is known or not to the parties to the agreement at the time when it is made."

Difference between a Contingent Contract and Wagering Agreement

The main points of distinction between the two are as under:

1. A contingent contract is a valid contract but wagering agreement is absolutely void.

2. Parties have real interest in the occurrence but or non-occurrence of the event e.g., insurable interest in the property insured. Parties are not interested in the occurrence of the event except for the winning or losing the bet amount.
3. Future uncertain event is merely collateral: uncertain event is the sole determining factor of the agreement.

QUASI CONTRACTS

A quasi contract is an obligation or a right created by law. A quasi contract is based on the principle that no person can enrich himself unjustly, at the expense of another. If he obtains a benefit which under the circumstances he ought, equitably to pay for it, the law would compel him to make the payment even though there is no contract requiring payment. Following relations created by law resemble those created by contract:

- Necessaries Supplied to a Person Incapable of Contracting: Example: X supplies Y, a lunatic, with necessaries suitable to his conditions in life. X is entitled to be reimbursed from Y's property.
- Payment of Money due by Another: (Sec.69) "A person who is interested in the payment of money which another is bound by law to pay, and who therefore pays it, is entitled to be reimbursed by the other."
- Non-gratuitous Act for Another's Bencfit: (Sec.70) "Where a person lawfully does anything for another person or delivers anything to him not to do so gratuitously and such other person enjoys the benefits thereof the latter is bound to make compensation to the former in respect of, or to restore the thing so due or delivered".
- Example: A Businessman leaves goods at B's house with the intention of persuading B to buy them. B treats the goods as his own. He is bound to pay A, for them.
- Finder of Lost Goods: (Sec. 71) "A person who finds goods belonging to another and takes them into his custody is subject to the same responsibility as a bailee."
- Money Paid by Mistake or Under Coercion: (Sec.72) "A person to whom money has been paid or anything delivered by mistake or under coercion must repay or return it". Example:X and Y jointly owe Rs. 1000 to Z. X alone pays the amount to Z and

Y, not knowing the fact pays Rs.1000 over again to Z. Z is bound to repay the amount to Y

- Suit upon Quantum Meruit: The phrase 'Quantum Meruit' means as much as earned or 'in proportion to the work done'. This is a general rule, usually invoked where there is no agreement to pay for the work done. (Sec. 70)

PERFORMANCE AND DISCHARGE OF CONTRACTS

'Performance of Contracts' refers to the fulfillment of their respective legal obligations, created under the contract, by both the parties. It is a natural and normal mode of discharging a contract. The various aspects related to performance are discussed below:

A. Actual Performance: "The parties to a contract must either perform, or offer to perform their respective promises, unless such performance is dispensed with or excused under the provisions of this Act of any other law...".

   Example: X bought goods from Y and promised to pay Rs.1000 to Y on 10th June. X went to Y on 10th June to give Rs.1000 in cash but Y did not accept it. Though X may not be discharged from the payment of Rs.1000 but he would not be liable to pay interest thereon from 10th June onwards. For a tender to become legally valid it must fulfill the following conditions:

   - It should be unconditional (Sec. 38): The promisor while offering to perform his promise must do it unconditionally.
   - Offer must not be of a part only (Sec. 38): The offer must be of whole payment or performance. A creditor is not bound to accept less than what is actually due and would not lose his right to interest on that portion.
   - Proper time and place (Sec. 38): The offer must be made at a proper time and place.
   - Able and willing (Sec. 38): "It must be made... under such circumstances that the person to whom it is made may have a reasonable opportunity of ascertaining that the person by whom it is made is able and willing there and then to do the whole of what he is bound by his promise to do."
   - Reasonable opportunity (Sec. 38): "...If the offer is an offer to deliver anything to the promisee, the prmisee

must have a reasonable opportunity of seeing that thing offered is the thing which the promisor is bound by this promise to deliver. Thus buyer must have reasonable opportunity to ascertain that the goods offered are contracted for.

- Tender of money: A tender of money must be in legal tender money, and not in any foreign currency, promissory note or cheque' (vii) Joint Promisees: (Sec. 38) "An offer to one of several joint promises has the same legal consequences as an offer to all of them."

B. Refusal to Perform (SEC.39): "When a party to a contract has refused to perform, or disabled himself from performing, his promise in its entirely, the promisee may put an end to the contract, unless he has signified, by words or conduct, his acquiescence in its continuance."

C. Who Can Demand Performance?: It is only the promisee who can demand performance of the promise under a contract, for the general rule is that "a person cannot acquire rights under a contract in which he is not a party."

D. By Whom Contracts Must be Performed: (1) By the promisor himself: (Sec. 40) "If it appears from the nature of the case that it was the intention of the parties to any contract that any promise contained in it, should be performed by the promisor himself, such promise must be performed by the promisor..." Generally where personal skill, taste etc. are involved, it is presumed that the promisor would himself perform the contract. (2) By promises representative: (Sec. 37) "...Promises bind the representatives of the promisors in the case of death of such promisors before performance, unless a contrary intention appears from the contract". Example: A promises to deliver goods to B on a certain day on payment of Rs.10,000. A dies before that day . A's representatives are bound to deliver the goods to B, and B is bound to pay Rs.10,000 to A's representatives.

E. Offer to Perform (Tender): (Sec 37) "A party who has not already performed his obligation must offer to perform the same. (Sec. 38) "Where a promisor has made an offer of performance to the promisee, and the offer has not been accepted, the promisor is not responsible for non-performance, nor does he thereby lose his rights under the contract". Example:

A promises to paint a wall for B. A must perform this promise personally.

F. Devolution of Joint Rights and Joint Liabilities (Joint Promises): When two or more persons make a joint promise to other or others, they are known as joint promisors e.g. A and B sign a promissory note, they are joint promisors. When a promise is made to two or more persons, they are Joint Promises. Following rules govern such promises: (1) All promisors must jointly fulfill the promise: (2) Any one of the joint promisors may be compelled to perform: (3) Right of contribution between joint promisors: (4) Effect of release of one joint promisor: Example: A, B and C Jointly promise to pay D Rs. 5000. D may compel either A or B or C to pay him Rs. 5000.

G. Time and Place for Performance:

- Within a reasonable time: (Sec 46)"Where a promisor is to perform his promise without application by the promisee, and no time for performance is specified, the engagement must be performed within a reasonable time." "The question what is a reasonable time is, in each particular case, a question of fact."
- During usual hours of business: (Sec.47) "When a promise is to be performed on a certain day, and the promisor has undertaken to perform it without application by the promisee, the promisor may perform it at any time during the usual hours of business on such day and at the place at which the promise ought to be performed."
- Promisee's duty to apply for performance: (Sec. 46) "When a promise is to be performed on a certain day, and the promisor has not undertaken to perform it without application by the promisee, it is the duty of the promisee to apply for performance at proper place and within the usual hours of business."
- Promisor should apply for fixing a reasonable place: (Sec.49) "When a promise is to be performed with application by the promisor and no place is fixed for the performance of it, it is the duty of the promisor to apply to the promisee to appoint a reasonable place for the performance of the promise, and to perform it at such place."

- In the manner prescribed by promisee: (Sec. 50) "The performance of any promise may be made in any manner, or at any time which the promisee prescribes."

H. Performance of Reciprocal Promises: [Sec. 2 (f)] "Promises which form the consideration or part of the consideration for each other are called reciprocal promises." Rules regarding the performance of reciprocal promises are:
   - When promises are to be performed simultaneously: "When a contract consists of reciprocal promises to be simultaneously performed no promisor need perform his promise unless the promisee is ready and willing to perform his reciprocal promise."
   - In the order, which the nature of transaction requires: (Sec. 52) "Where the order in which reciprocal promises are to be performed is expressly fixed by the contract, they shall be performed in that order; and where the order is not expressly fixed by the contract, they shall be performed in that order which the nature of the transaction requires."
   - When the performance of a promise is dependent upon other: (Sec. 54) "When the contract consists of reciprocal promises, such that one of them can not be performed or that its performance cannot be claimed till the other has been performed and the promisor of the promise last mentioned fails to perform it, such promisor cannot claim the performance of the reciprocal promise, and must make compensation to the other party for any loss which such other party may sustain by the non-performance of the contract." These are known as mutual and dependent promises.
   - When one party prevents the other from performing his promise: (Sec.53) " When a contract contains reciprocal promises, and one party to the contract prevents the other from performing his promise the contract becomes voidable at the option of the party so prevented.
   - Where the promise is partly legal and partly illegal: (Sec.57) "Where persons reciprocally promise, firstly, to do certain things which are legal, and secondly, under specified circumstances, to do certain other things which are illegal the first set of promises is a contract, but the second is a void agreement."

I. Time of Performance:

- When time is the essence of the contract: (Sec.55) "When a party to a contract promises to do certain thing at or before a specified time, or certain things at or before specified times, and fails to do any such thing at or before the specified time, the contract, or so much of it as has not been performed, becomes voidable to the option of the promisee, if the intention of the parties was that time should be the essence of the contract."
- When time is not the essence of the contract: If it was not the intention of the parties that time should be the essence of the contract, the contract does not become voidable by the failure to do such thing at or before the specified time, but the promisee is entitled to compensation from the promisor for any loss occasioned to him by such failure.
- Condition for compensation when contract is voidable and goods are accepted: "If in case of a contract voidable on account of the promisor's failure to perform his promise at the time agreed, the promisee accepts performance of such promise at any time other than that agreed, the promisee cannot claim compensation for any loss occasioned by the nonperformance of promise at the time agreed unless, at the time of such acceptance, he gives notice to the promisor of his intention to do so." (Sec.55)

DISCHARGE OF A CONTRACT

A contract is discharged, terminated when the rights and obligations created by it to an end. A contract is terminated in the following ways:

I. By Performance (Sec. 37): When the parties to a contract perform their respective promises, the contract comes to an end. Nothing remains to be performed.

II. By Tender (Attempted Performance): When a promisor makes an offer of performance tender and the offer is not accepted, the promisor is not responsible for non-performance, i.e. he is discharged from his obligations under the contract. But he does not lose his rights under the contract i.e. the promisee is not discharged from his obligations.

III. By Supervening Impossibility: Impossibility is of two types:

A. Impossibility at the Time of Contract: (Sec.56) "An agreement to do an act impossible in itself is void.": Example A agrees with B to discover gold by magic. The agreement is void.

B. Subsequent or Supervening Impossibility: Where a contract originates as one capable of performance but later due to change of circumstances its performance becomes impossible, it becomes void by subsequent or supervening impossibility (section 56). In English law this is called "Doctrine of Frustration".

Example: A and B contract to marry each other. Before the time fixed for marriage, B becomes mad. The contract becomes void. Supervening impossibility may arise in any of the following ways:

1. Destruction of the subject matter: The contract becomes void when the subject matter is destructed.

2. When the foundation of the contract ceases to exist: If in a contract, it is deemed that the parties had assumed certain state of things to continue and that state of things ceases to exist, the contract can come to an end.

3. Change of Law: A contract which becomes illegal after it is made, becomes void and the parties to the contract will be discharged from their respective obligations.

4. Death or personal incapacity: Where the contract is of personal nature the death or incapacity of the promisor may discharge the contract.

5. Declaration of war: A contract entered into with an alien enemy before the war breaks out is either suspended or discharged after the declaration of war if it does not aid the enemy in the pursuit of war, it is suspended and would be performed after the war is over, otherwise it is terminated and the parties to the contract are discharged from their respective obligations.

IV. Exceptions to the Principle of Supervening Impossibility:

Impossibility as a rule is no excuse for non-performance: Following are some of the circumstances in which non-performance of a contract was held not to be excused.

i. Difficulty of performance: If a contract becomes difficult to perform but not impossible the promisor would not be discharged on that account.

Commercial Impossibility would not discharge of a contract. A contract would not be deemed to be impossible because it does not remain profitable to the promisor or would make the promisor to incur losses.

- Action of a third party: If a man chooses to answer for the voluntary act of a third person there is no reason in law or justice why he should not be held for his inability to procure that act.
- Strikes, lock-outs, civil disturbances and riots do not discharge a contract unless there is a clause in the contract to that effect.
- Partial impossibility: Where a contract is entered into for more than one purpose, the contract would not become impossible if one of the objects has become impossible to achieve.

Consequences of Supervening Impossibility

Supervening impossibility makes a contract void. The parties are discharged from their respective obligations under the contract (Sec. 65). The party who has received same advantages under it should restore it to the other party.

V. Mutual Agreement: A contract is created by the parties to it, therefore, it can also come to an end by their mutual agreement. Termination by mutual agreement may occur in any one of the following ways.

1. Novation: When a new contract is substituted for an existing contract, either between the same parties or between different parties, it is called novation.
2. Alteration: When one or more of the terms of a contract are changed it is called alteration. In case of alteration, parties to the contract do not change. Example: A agrees to supply to B 20 readymade pants, 10 of the size 32 and 10 of the size 34. Later on B requests A to supply all 20 pants of the size 32 only. A agrees to it. The old contract comes to an end.
3. Rescission: When both the parties to a contract agree to put an end to the contract, without performing it, the contract is said to be rescinded by mutual agreement. Example: A promises to supply to B 20 shirts on 15th January and B promises to pay Rs 5000 on the same day after delivery, On 10th January. both the parties agree that the contract would not be performed. Parties are said to have rescinded the contract.

4. Remission: When a party to a contract accepts, from the other party, a performance lesser than what he had contracted for, he is deemed to have remitted the remaining performance, and the contract is discharged. Example: A owes B Rs.500 rupees but pays on by Rs. 200, and B accepts at in satisfaction of the whole debt. The whole debt is discharged.
5. Waiver: When a party to a contract abandons his right under the contract, the other party is released from his obligations. Example: A pays Rs 1000 to B to paint a wall for him. Later on A forbids B to paint the picture. B is no longer bound to perform the promise.
6. Merger: When a superior right and an inferior right coincide and meet at one and the same person, the inferior right vanishes into the superior right. This is known as merger. Example: A has taken a house on lease from B for 10 years. After one year A buys the house from B. His rights of a lessee vanish into his rights of ownership and the contract of lease comes to an end.

VI. By Lapse of Time: The Limitation Act provides the time limit in which certain rights can be enforced. If that time limit expires, the promisee cannot enforce the promisor and promisor is discharged. Example: A owes Rs 10,000 to B. The last date for the repayment of the loan has expired and B does not file a suit against A for two years. B loses the right to recover the money back.

VII. By Operation of Law: This covers the following cases:

- Death: If a contract involves personal skill or ability, death of the promisor would terminate the contract.
- Insolvency: When a person is adjudged insolvent and hands over all his property to the official receiver/assignee, he is supposed to have the right to earn his livelihood in the ordinary way and therefore the courts, under certain circumstances and subject to certain conditions, discharge him from all debts which were payable in insolvency but remain unpaid. He does not remain liable to pay those debts.
- Merger: A contract is discharged when any firm merges with another firm.

- Material alteration: A change which affects or alters, in a specific manner, the rights and liabilities of the parties is called material alteration. A material alteration made in a written document or contract by one party without the consent of the other, will make the contract void, e.g. an indorsee of a promissory note/ altering the amount of note.

VIII. By Breach of Contract: Breach is the non-performance of the promise by the promisor. It entitles the promisee to rescind the contract. It, therefore, operates as a mode of discharging a contract.

Breach of Contract and its Remedies: As we discussed in the previous part breach of contract is a mode of discharge of the contract. Though the obligation created by the contract comes to an end but the aggrieved party is entitled to several remedies that are discussed in this part. The remedies depend upon whether the breach is (a) Actual or (b) Anticipatory or Constructive.

1. Actual Breach: Where a person fails to perform a contract when the performance is due, the other party can hold him liable for breach i.e. he can rescind the contract and sue for damages.

   A. At the time when performance is due: When a party to the contract fails to perform or refuses to perform his obligations at the time when the performance is due, he is committing a breach of contract. Example: A promised to supply B, 500 tables on 10th Jan. A does not supply the Tables on 10th Jan. A is guilty of breach of contract and B becomes the aggrieved party.

   B. During the performance of the contract: When a contract is being performed the promisor fails to perform the promisee to accept the remaining part, it is also a breach of contract. If the promisor is not allowed to perform the remaining part then the promisee has committed a breach of contract. Example: The defendant Co. agreed to buy 4000 tons of goods. After 2000 tons of goods had been delivered the company told the plaintiff that it did not require any more goods. The company committed a breach of contract.

2. Anticipatory Breach: When a party to the contract, before the date of performance arrives, repudiates his liability under the

contract or makes the performance of the contract impossible, there is an anticipatory (constructive) breach of contract. Anticipatory breach may be express or implied. Example: A promises to marry B in the month of April. But in the month of March A marries C. The marriage between A and B becomes impossible, this is a case of anticipatory breach.

Consequences of Anticipatory Breach: If a promisor is guilty of anticipatory breach, the promisee has got two options open to him:

He may treat the anticipatory breach as the actual breach of contract and can rescind the contract.

He may ignore the notice or the conduct of the promisor and may wait till the due date of performance and then if the promise is not performed he may treat it as breach of contract. If the promisee chooses the second course of action, he keeps the promise alive for the benefit of the promisor also and may lose his right to sue the promisor if:

i. The promisor performs the promise on the due date:
ii. They develop circumstances which discharge the contract legally.

Remedies of Breach of Contract: When a contract is broken the party who suffers from such breach is entitled to the following relieves:

1. Rescission of the contract: He would not be required to perform his promises. Example: A, an advocate promises to plead B's case in the court of law if B gets him (A) a table before the date of hearing. B does not deliver a table to A. A can rescind the contract and becomes free from the obligation of pleading B's case.
2. Suit for Damages: The injured party can also file a suit for compensation for the loss it has suffered because of the breach of the contract. Example: A contracts to buy B's car for Rs. 60,000 but B breaks his promise. B must pay to A, by way of compensation, the excess, if any, of the contract price which B can obtain for the car at the of the breach of promise.
3. Suit upon Quantum Meruit: The expression 'Quantum Meruit' means 'as much as earned', i.e. reasonable remuneration for the services performed. The rule is invoked where there is no agreement for remuneration for the work done. Thus where a party to the contract has performed part of his promise and is prevented by the act or conduct of the other party, from

completing it, he may sue on a Quantum Meruit. Example: A agreed to write a story for B, which B would publish in iinstalments in his weekly magazine. B agreed to pay a lump sum amount for the entire story. After a few instalments were published, B abandoned the magazine. Held A could recover on Quantum Meruit for the work done under the contract.

4. Suit for Specific performance of the contract: Specific performance means the actual carrying out of the contract. In certain cases the court may direct the party in default to fulfill his promise. This remedy may be granted to the injured party instead of or in addition to the awarding of damages. It is usually granted where monetary compensation is not an adequate remedy. But it would not be granted if the court cannot supervise the contract (e.g. mining operations)or if the contract is for personal services. Example: A, a renowned painter agrees to paint a picture for B. Later on he refuses to do so. B pleads with the court that he cannot get such a painting with any amount of money. Even if court is satisfied with the plea of B, it cannot grant specific performance because A cannot be compelled to paint a picture.

5. Suit for Injunction: Injunction is the specific performance of the negative terms of the contract. It is an order of the court prohibiting a party from doing something. Example: A agrees to do a musical programme at the theatre of B on the eve of the Christmas and also agrees not to perform in any other theatre on that day. Later on a agrees to perform in the theatre of P.B cannot enforce a specific performance of A's musical programme in his theatre (because court cannot effectively supervise it) but he can ask the court to restrain A from performing in P's theatre.

RULES REGARDING DAMAGES

Damages under Contract act are awarded by way of compensation for loss to the plaintiff only and not by way of punishment to the guilty party. Following are the rules for the damages:

- When a contract is broken, only those damages "which naturally arose in the usual course of things from such breach" can be recovered. These are known as general or ordinary damages.
- In certain cases even special damages can also be recovered. Special damages are those 'which the parties knew, when they

made the contract to be likely to result from the beach of it.' (Sec. 73)

- Compensation for the breach of quasi contract would be the same as the compensation for the breach of contract.
- "... In estimating the loss of damage, arising from a breach of contract, the means which existed of remedying the inconvenience caused by the nonperformance of the contract must be taken into account".
- Under a contract for the sale of goods the measure of damages is the difference between the contract price and the market price at the date of breach.
- Damages are not awarded with a view to punishing the defendant except
  — For a breach of promise to marry and
  — For a wrongful dishonour by the banker of cheque of the customer. These are known as Exemplary or Vindictive Damages.
- In case the court finds that though the defendant has been guilty of a breach of contract, the breach has not caused any appreciable loss to the plaintiff, it awards only nominal damages, like costs of the suit etc.
- Even if the parties agree about damages for breach of contract, only actual damages, not exceeding the agreed amount, can be recovered. These are known as liquidated damages (Sec.74)
- Plaintiff would not be denied damages for the loss suffered on the ground that the assessment of damages is difficult. (Sec.75).
- Mitigation of loss: it is the duty of the plaintiff to take steps to minimize the loss resulting from breach.
- Cost of suit: The plaintiff can recover not only damages for the loss sustained but also costs of getting the decree of damages.
- Interest as damages: As regards breach of contract of sale, the court is empowered to award interest, at such rate as it thinks fit, on the amount of the price.

Kinds of Damages

1. General or Normal Damages: The amount of general or ordinary damages is restricted to only that loss which arises:(a)

naturally and (b) in the usual course of things from such breach (Sec. 73)

2. Special Damages means loss which would result not in the ordinary course, but because of special circumstances and the parties know, at the time when they entered into the contract, that this is likely to result from the breach of it.

3. Liquidated Damages: (Sec. 74) "When a contract has been broken, if a sum is named in the contract as the amount to be paid in case of such breach, or if the contract contains any other stipulation by way of penalty, the party complaining of the breach is entitled whether or not actual damage or loss is proved to have been caused thereby, to receive from the party who has broken the contract reasonable compensation not exceeding the amount so named or, as the case may be, the penalty stipulated for".

   Example: A contracts with B to pay B Rs.10000, if he fails to pay B Rs. 9000 on a given day. A fails to pay B Rs.9000 on that day. B is entitled to recover from A such compensation, not exceeding Rs. 10000, as the court considers reasonable.

4. Vindictive or exemplary Damages: As explained earlier, damages for breach of contract are granted to compensate for the loss suffered by the plaintiff and not with a view to punish or penalize the wrong done by the defendant. Hence the damages granted are not vindictive, exemplary or 'punitive'.However there are following two exceptions to this general rule. (i) In case of a breach of promise to marry. (ii) In case a banker, wrongfully, dishonouring the cheque of a customer having sufficient funds to his credit. The rule of damages'. "A stipulation for increased interest from the date of default may be a stipulation by way of penalty" [Sec.74].

5. Nominal Damages: Where the aggrieved party does not suffer any monetary loss, sometimes the Courts grant a nominal amount like cost etc. just to establish that the plaintiff has won the case against the defendant.

CONTRACT OF AGENCY

DEFINITION OF AGENT AND PRINCIPAL

(Sec. 182) "An agent is a person employed to do any act for another or to represent another in dealing with a third persons. The person for whom such act is done or who is so represented, is called the principal."

Test of Agency: The true test of agency is the authority that one person possesses to create contractual relationship with the person he is representing and the person to whom he represents. Where a person is in the habit of advising another in business deals he does not become the agent of the other.

Agent and Servant: A servant is a person who acts under the direct control and supervision of his master while an agent does not. "A principal has the right to direct what the agent has to do; but a master has not only that right but also the right to say how it is to be done" An agent is, therefore, sometimes described as 'Superior Servant. An agent binds the principal with the third parties but a servant does not create relations between his master and third persons.

Who may employ agent? (Sec. 183), "Any person who is of the age of majority according to the law to which he is subject, and who is of sound mind, may employ an agent." "Whatever a person can do personally he can do through an agent." Thus a guardian of a minor can appoint an agent for the minor.

Who may be an agent? A minor or even a person of unsound mind can act as agents but they would not be responsible to the principal or to the third parties in cases where a person competent to contract would have been responsible.

Consideration for the contract of agency: (Sec. 185) "No consideration is necessary to create an agency." Principal's agreement to be represented by the agent is deemed to be sufficient detriment to support the promise by the agent to act as such and be liable to the principal for negligence.

CREATION OF AGENCY

The relationship of principal and agent may be created in any of the following ways:

1. By Express Agreement: "The authority of an agent may be express or implied." (Sec. 186) "An authority is said to be express when it is given by words spoken or written." (Sec. 187): Example: A asks B to sell his cow for a commission of 10% on sales. B agrees to do so Agency has been created. The agreement need not be in writing. But in certain cases,

law requires the agreement to be in writing, e.g. for sale or purchase of land, the law requires the agent to be appointed by executing a formal power of attorney.

2. By Implied Agreement: Sec. 187: "... An authority is said to be implied when it is to be inferred from the circumstances of the case, and things spoken or written, or the ordinary course of dealing..." Example: A owns a shop. The shop is managed by B, and he is in the habit of ordering goods from C in the name of A for the purposes of the shop, and of paying for them out of A's funds with A's knowledge. B has an implied authority from A to order goods from C in the name of A for the purposes of the shop.

   i. Agency by estoppel (Sec. 237): "When an agent has without authority done acts or incurred obligations to third persons on behalf of his principal, the principal is bound by such acts or obligations if he has, by his words or conduct, induced such third persons to believe that such acts and obligations were within the scope of the agent's authority." Example: A starts manufacturing plastic products. A, B and C are sitting together. B in the present of A tells C that A has appointed him (B) as selling agent of his product. A does not contradict this statement, though he had not appointed him as his agent. Later on C enters into a contract with B on the presumption that B is A's agent. A would be bound by this transaction. A would be precluded from denying that B is his agent.

   ii. Agency by holding out: The principle of holding out is a part of the law of estoppel. But agency by holding out requires some positive or affirmative conduct by the principal. Example: A sends his servant to buy goods from B on credit. B gives the goods to A's servant and A pays for them. Later on A's servant, without A's asking for it, buys goods from B on A's credit and runs away. A would be liable to pay for the goods, thought a servant is not an agent, but by paying for the credit purchases made by his servant, A held out that his servant was his agent also and as such he would be liable for the purchases made by his servant.

   iii. Agency of Necessity: If a person protects the property or interest of another where such property or interests are in imminent danger and the instructions of the owner cannot be obtained, the former would be deemed to be an agent of the latter so as to make the latter liable for whatever he has done provided the former has acted bonafide in the interests of the latter. The principle of necessity also extends to cases where an agent exceeds his authority if the following conditions are fulfilled:

- The agent was not in a position to communicate with the principal.
- The agent takes reasonable and necessary course in the circumstances.
- The agent acts bonafide.

Example: A sends some bananas to B with the instructions that B should send them to C. When B takes delivery of the bananas, he finds that the bananas are not in a condition to sustain the journey to C's place and would perish before reaching. B, therefore, sells them at the best possible price. A would be bound by this sale under agency by necessity. In cases of accident and emergency a master of a ship can sell or pledge the goods in order to save their value and such sale or pledge would be binding on the owners of the cargo.

Husband and Wife: A wife can bind the husband for the contracts in which she enters for the purchase of household necessities suiting to the couples joint style of living provided they are living together and the wife is the in-charge of domestic establishment and the husband has not made reasonable allowance to the wife for her needs.

Example: H and W are husband and wife respectively. W chooses to live separately and buys goods on credit from A. On her failure to pay for the purchases A cannot recover the money from H because they are not living together.

However, a husband can escape the liability if he can prove that:

i. He had warned the tradesman from supplying the goods on credit to his wife;

ii. He had already supplied sufficient articles in question to his wife

iii. He had supplied sufficient means to his wife for the purchase of articles in question. But if the wife is deserted by her husband and thus forced to live separately, she may of necessity become agent of her husband and can pledge her husband's credit for necessaries to the extent a reasonable maintenance makes it necessary.

Agency by Ratification: A person may become another's agent after having done some work for the latter, if the latter ratifies the act. When a person adopts an act done on his behalf but without his authority he is said to have ratified it.

Example: A, without authority, buys goods for B. Afterwards B sells them to C on his own account; B's conduct implies a ratification of the purchase made for him by A. Implications of Ratification:

i. Ratification relates back to the date of the act. It is tantamount to prior authority. This means that the agency comes into existence not from thè time when the act is ratified but from the time when the act was done. i.e. (Ratification is equivalent to an antecedent authority).

ii. No Authority for future: The ratification of an act done without authority does not confer authority to do similar acts in future.

CONDITIONS OF A VALID RATIFICATION

Ratification is enforceable only when the following conditions are fulfilled.

- Must contract as agent: The agent must contract as agent for a principal in contemplation; or the agent should not make the contract for himself.
- Only named Principal can ratify: Only that principal who was named or was identifiable at the time of the contract, can ratify the contract. He can do so even if the agent never intended that he should do so.
- Example: A make a contract with B on behalf of his uncle, D. Later on C, A's elder brother want to have the benefit of the contract and wants to ratify the same. C cannot do so. D, when comes to know of the contract, wants to ratify the same; he can do so and enjoy the benefit of the contract even if A does not want it.
- The principal should be in existence: Mere contemplation at the time of the contract is not sufficient. If the principal was not in existence at the time of the contract, he cannot ratify such contract.
- The Principal must be competent to contract at the date of the contract as well as at the date of ratification. Thus a minor

cannot ratify a contract made on his behalf after becoming a major.

- The principal must have full knowledge of the material facts (Sec. 198): "No valid ratification can be made by a person whose knowledge of the facts of the case is materially defective."
- The principal must ratify the whole transaction (Sec. 199).
- The principal must ratify the contract within a reasonable time after the contract is made.
- The act to be ratified should not be void or illegal though ratification can be made of voidable contracts or even of tortuous acts.
- Ratification of unauthorized act cannot injure third person.
- Ratification by Govt: Acts done by public servant in the name of the Government may be ratified by subsequent approval in the same manner as private transaction.

Extent of Agents Authority

It is necessary to know all dimensions of his (agent) authority. They are as follows:

A. Actual Authority: Actual authority is one which is conferred on the agent by the principal. It may be express or implied.

  1. Express Authority: An authority is said to be express when it is given by words spoken or written (Sec. 187).
  2. Implied Authority:
     i. An authority is said to be implied when it is inferred from the circumstances of the case.(Sec. 187)
     ii. An agent having authority to do an act has authority to do every lawful thing which is necessary in order to do such act. (Sec. 188)

B. Ostensible or Apparent Authority: Apparent or ostensible authority is that authority which an agent appears to be possessing though in fact he may not have.

C. Authority in Emergency: "An agent has authority, in an emergency, to do all such acts for the purpose of protecting his principal from loss as would be done by a person of ordinary prudence, in his own case, under similar circumstances." (Sec. 189).

DELEGATION OF AUTHORITY BY AGENT

"An agent cannot lawfully employ another to perform acts which he has expressly or impliedly undertaken to perform personally..." sub-agent may not enjoy the confidence of the principal ["A subagent is a person employed by, and acting under the control of, the original agent in the business of the agency" (Sec.191).

Exceptions: In the following circumstances delegation made by an agent to subagent would be proper:

Nature of agency:

Custom of Trade: Where it is a custom of trade that an agent appoints a sub-agent.

Ministerial Acts: Where the acts to be done are purely ministerial and do not involve the exercise of discretion, or personal or professional skill.

Express Delegation: Where the principal has expressly permitted delegation.

Implied Permission: Where the principal impliedly permits delegation i.e. from act or conduct it may be inferred that he has allowed delegation of authority.

In emergency: In case of emergencies an agent can always delegate the authority to a sub -agent.

DUTIES OF AN AGENT

1. To follow principal's directions or customs:
2. Skill and diligence to work:
3. To render proper account: (Sec. 213): "An agent is bound to render proper accounts to his principal on demand." He should always be ready to produce them to the principal.
4. To communicate with the principal (Sec. 214)
5. Not to deal on his own account: (Sec. 215)
6. To pay sums received for principal
7. Not to delegate authority (Sec. 190)
8. On Principal's death or insanity (Sec. 209)

RIGHTS OF AN AGENT

Right to Remuneration: Every agent is entitled to receive the remuneration agreed upon with the principal.

Right of retainer (Sec. 217)

Right of Lien (Sec. 221)

Right of indemnity

RIGHTS AND DUTIES OF PRINCIPAL TOWARDS AGENT

Rights of Principal

1. He can enforce the various duties of an agent.
2. He can recover compensation for any breach of duty by the agent.
3. He can forfeit agent's remuneration where the agent is guilty of misconduct in the business of agency.
4. Principal is entitled to any extra profit that the agent has made out of his agency. This includes illegal gratification, if any.
5. Principal is entitled to receive all sums that the transactions, entered into, by the agent, on behalf of the principal were void or illegal.

Duties of Principal

1. To Pay Remuneration:
2. Duty to Indemnify:
3. Compensation for injuries:
4. Should not prevent the agent from earning remuneration.

Principal's Liabilities to Third Parties for the Acts of the Agent

Liability for acts done by agent within authority

Ratification of acts beyond the scope of his authority

When an agent commits fraud or misrepresentation

Liability for tort: If an agent commits a tort in the course of and within the scope of his agency, the principal may in certain cases be liable for the same.

1. Notice given to agent as notice to principal (Sec. 229).
2. Liability under the principle of estoppel.

3. Liability when his name is not disclosed (Unnamed principal).
4. Liability when agent does not disclose his agency (undisclosed principal).

Agent and third Parties

"In the absence of any contract to that effect, an agent cannot personally enforce contract entered into by him on behalf of his principal nor is he personally bound by them...' If there is no contract providing for, or relieving the agent from, personal liability the agent would be liable in the following cases:

1. Foreign Principal.
2. Unnamed Principal.
3. Undisclosed Principal.
4. Incompetent Principal.
5. Where the agent exceeds his authority.
6. Where agent's authority is coupled with interest.
7. Custom of Trade.
8. Money received by mistake or fraud.

Termination of Agency

The contract of agency would come to an end in any of the following circumstances:

- By Agreement
- By Revocation by the principal
  - — If the authority has not been exercised
  - — Revocation may be expressed or implied (Sec. 207)
  - — Reasonable Notice of revocation
  - — Compensation. If the principal revokes the agency, without sufficient cause, he would have to compensate the agent for the premature termination. (Sec. 205)
  - — Agency is irrevocable in the following cases.
    a. Agency coupled with interest
    b. Where agent has partly exercised his authority
    c. Where an agent has incurred personal liability
- Renunciation by the Agent
- Completion of business

- Death or Insanity
- Insolvency of the principal
- Expiration of Time
- Destruction of the subject matter
- Dissolution of a company
- Principal or agent becoming alien enemy

Note: Avocent designs, manufactures, licenses, and sells software and hardware products, which provides connectivity and centralized management of information technology (IT) infrastructure. The company primarily operates in the US. It is headquartered in Alabama, United States and employs 1,099 people. For a case study visit company's site www.avocent.com

4

Company and Business Acts in India

PARTNERSHIP ACT, 1932

The law relating to partnership is contained in the Indian partnership Act, 1932. The Act came into force with effect from October 1, 1932. Prior to enactment of the aforesaid Act, partnership business used to be governed by the Indian Contract Act, 1872. Section 4 of the Indian Partnership Act, 1932 defines 'partnership' as follows: "a business carried on by all or any of them acting for all."

Essential elements of partnership:

- Association of two or more persons;
- Existence of a contract;
- Carrying on a business;
- Sharing of profits; and
- Prevalence of mutual agency.

But a partnership firm cannot create another partnership as it does not enjoy the status of the artificial legal person. There must exist a contract between persons who have agreed to form partnership. Such a contract may, however, be either express or implied, written or oral.

Partnership Deed: Partnership Deed is the document that defines the rights and obligations of partners. Besides names, address and occupation of partners it lays down the duration of partnership, nature of business, profit sharing ratio, right to interest, salary, commission etc.

REGISTRATION OF FIRMS

The registration of partnership firm is discretionary. The provisions relating to registration of partnership firm are contained in Chapter 7,

Sections 56 to 71 of the partnership Act.

Effect of Non-registration (Sec. 69)

An unregistered firm and its partners suffer from the following disabilities:

1. No Suit against other partners and firms
2. No suit against third parties
3. No claim of set off

DURATION OF PARTNERSHIP

Partnership may, from the point of view of its duration, be categorized into the following two classes:

1. Partnership for a fixed term or particular partnership
2. Partnership at will.

KINDS OF PARTNERS

There may be different kinds of partners in a partnership firm. The important classification of partners is being given below:

- Actual or active partners: Partners actively engaged in the conduct of the business are known as 'active' or 'actual' or ostensible partners.
- Dormant or sleeping partner: The nominal partner is one who lends his name to the partnership firm without any real interest in terms of investing money in the firm or sharing in profits.
- Nominal partner: the nominal partner is known to the outsiders and does not share the profits of the firm.
- Partner in profits only: A person who does not want to take risk of loss may agree to become a partner in profits only.
- Sub-partner: When a partner agrees to share his share of profit in a partnership firm with the outsiders, such an outsider is called a 'Subpartner'.
- Partner by estoppel or by holding out: If a partner, by his words or conduct holds out to another that he is a partner, he will be stopped from denying that he is not a partner. Such a partner neither contributes any capital nor participates in the management. He is only liable to third parties.

MINOR AS A PARTNER

According to Indian Contract Act an agreement of a minor is void, as void, as such he cannot enter into an agreement of partnership. Section 30 of the Partnership Act provides that a minor may be admitted to the benefits of partnership with the consent of all the partners.

Rights of Minor Partner

A minor admitted to the benefits of a Partnership has the following rights:

1. Right to share the profits. (2) Right to have the access to do the inspection
2. Right to file a suit for accounts or demand his share of property or profits.
3. Right to exercise option on attaining the age of majority, whether or not to continue in the firm.

Liabilities of Minor Partner

- The liability of a minor is limited to the extent of his share in the firm and therefore, unlike other partners, he is not personally liable.
- If the firm is declared insolvent his share in the firm vests in the official receiver or assignee but a minor cannot be declared insolvent.

RIGHTS, DUTIES AND LIABILITIES OF PARTNERS

Rights

- Right to take part in the conduct of business
- Right to be consulted
- Right of Access to the books
- Right to share profits
- Right to interest on capital
- Right to interest on advances
- Right to indemnity
- Right to act prudently in emergency
- Right to give consent for admission of a new partner
- Right to retire
- Right to carry on competing business after retirement.

Duties

A. Qualifying

- To attend his duties diligently
- To work without remuneration
- To contribute to losses
- To indemnify for willful neglect
- To use firm's a property exclusively for the firm
- To account for private profits [Sec.16(a)]

B. Others

- Duty to carry on business for the common advantage
- To indemnify for loss caused by fraud
- To give full information
- To render true accounts
- To be just and faithful

Liabilities

1. Liability of partner for acts of the firm: Every partner is liable, jointly with all the other partners and also severally, for all acts of the firm done while he is a partner
2. Liability of the firm for wrongful acts of the partner: Where, by the wrongful act or omission of a partner acting in the ordinary course of the business of a firm, or with the authority of his partners, loss or injury is caused to any third party, or any penalty is incurred, the firm is liable therefore to the same extent as the partner (Section 26).
3. Liability of the firm for misapplication by partners:
   i. When a partner acting within his apparent authority receives money or property from a third party and misapplies it, or
   ii. A firm in the course of its business receives money or property from a third party, and the money or property is misapplied by any of the partners while it is in the custody of the firm, the firm is liable to make good the loss (Sec. 27).
4. Liability for the loss caused by his own fraud.
5. Liability for the loss caused by his own willful neglect.

Authority of a Partner

a. Express Authority: A partner can express his views in the matters of the firm.

b. Implied Authority: "The act of partner which is done to carry on, in the usual way, business of the kind carried on by the firm, binds the firm". Thus the authority of a partner to bind the firm is called 'Implied authority".

c. Authority in an Emergency: A partner has authority in an emergency to do all such acts for the purpose of protecting the firm from loss as would be done by a person of ordinary prudence, in his own case, acting under similar circumstances, and such acts bind the firm.

RECONSTITUTION OF A FIRM

A change in the constitution of the firm occurs when a new partner is admitted or an old partner retires or dies. The partnership is reconstituted on:

- Admission
- Retirement
- Expulsion
- Insolvency
- Death of a partner
- Transfer of interests by a partner.

DISSOLUTION OF A FIRM

Dissolution of a firm means the decline of the firm. The Indian Partnership Act distinguishes between:

- Dissolution of firm, and
- Dissolution of partnership.

Section 39 provides that the dissolution of partnership between all the partners of a firm is called the "dissolution of the firm".

MODES OF DISSOLUTION

A firm may be dissolved in any of the following modes

i. By Agreement (Sec. 40)

ii. By Notice (Sec. 43)

iii. On the Happening of Certain Contingencies (Sec. 42)
   1. Expiry of fixed term
   2. Completion of adventure or undertaking
   3. Death of a partner
   4. Insolvency of a partner

iv. Compulsory (Sec 41): A firm is dissolved in the following circumstances:
   1. Insolvency of all partners or all except one
   2. Business becoming unlawful

v. Dissolution by the Court (Sec 44): Section 44 provides that the dissolution of a firm may take place on a suit filed by a partner on any of the following grounds, namely:
   1. Insanity of a partner [Section 44(a)]
   2. Permanent incapacity [Section 44(b)]
   3. Misconduct [Section 44(c)]
   4. Persistent breach of agreement [Section 44(d)]
   5. Transfer of interest [Sec.44 (e)]
   6. Continuous losses[Section 44(f)]
   7. Just and equitable causes [Sec.44(g)]

CONSEQUENCES OF DISSOLUTION

The consequences of dissolution are as follows:

- Continuous liability if fails to give a public notice [Sec. 45]
- Continuous authority of partners for purposes of winding up [Sec. 47]
- Right to have the business wound up [Sec. 46]
- Right to return of premium [Sec. 51]
- Rights where partnership contract is rescinded for fraud or misrepresentations [Sec. 52]
- Rights to impose restrictions [Sec. 53]
- Liability to share personal profits [Sec. 50]

Settlement of Accounts upon Dissolution

- Treatment of goodwill
- Meeting losses [Sec.48 (a)]
- Order of applications of assets [Sec.58(a)]

- Losses arising from insolvency of a partner
- Payment of firm's debts and separate debts [Sec. 49]

Public Notice

The Partnership Act requires that a public notice must be given in each of the following cases:

- On Minor Attaining Majority
- Retirement of a partner
- Expulsion of a partner
- Dissolution of the firm

SALE OF GOODS ACT 1930

The law defining their respective rights and obligations is contained in the Indian Sale of Goods Act, 1930. Before 1930, law relating to sale of goods was contained in the Indian Contract Act, 1872. The departures made by the Sale of Goods Act are in regard to the consideration, implied conditions and warranties etc.

ESSENTIALS OF A CONTRACT OF SALE OF GOODS

"A contract of sale of goods is a contract whereby the seller transfers or agrees to transfer the property in goods to the buyer for a price." [Sec. (4) 1]. Important features of a contract of sale:

Two Parties:

- Mutual Consent: Just the presence of two parties is not sufficient. The parties must agree on the transfer of property.
- Transfer of Property: What a contract of sale stipulates is the transfer of property i.e. the ownership of the goods and not the possession of the goods.
- Goods: Goods means every kind of movable property other than actionable claims and money. But it includes stock and shares, growing crops, grass and things attached to or forming part of the land which are agreed to be severed before sale or under the contract of sale. [Sec. 2(7)]. Since the price of the goods is expressed in terms of the money, money itself cannot be bought, and hence, money is not considered as goods.
- Price: Under a contract of sale, property in the goods is transferred to the buyer for a price. Price is the money consideration for the goods.

- Varied requirement as to delivery and payment: The contract may provide for the immediate delivery of goods or immediate payment of the price or both,

Requires no formalities:

Absolute or Conditional: An absolute contract of sale is technically called a 'sale'. Thus "where under a contract of sale the property in the goods is transferred from the seller to the buyer, the contract is called a sale.."[Sec. 4 (3)]. Thus a contract of sale is a generic term including:

- 'Sale' as well as 'an agreement to sell'
- Contract of Sale
- Sale Agreement to sell

DISTINCTION BETWEEN 'SALE' AND 'AGREEMENT TO SELL'

1. Transfer of Property: In a sale the buyer becomes the owner immediately (i.e. as soon as the contract of sale is made). But in an agreement to sell the seller continues to be the owner unless it becomes a sale by the expiry of certain time or by the fulfillment of the conditions agreed upon.
2. 'Jus in rem' and 'Jus in Personam: A sale creates 'Jus in rem' i.e. rights against the goods.
3. Risk of Loss: Risk prima facie passes with property (Sec. 26). The buyer would bear the risk of loss, even if goods are in the possession of the seller. But in case of an agreement to sell the ownership remains with the seller and as such the seller would be liable for the loss,
5. Consequences of default:
   a. When the buyer commits the default and does not pay the price of the contract is a 'sale. The seller can sue for the price, even if the goods are in the possession of the seller himself. But in 'an agreement to sell he cannot sue him (buyer) for the price of the goods even if the goods happen to be in the possession of the buyer.
   b. When the seller commits default and refuses to sell the goods or sells the goods to some other person, then if the contract is a sale the buyer can recover his goods, even from a second buyer (except under certain circumstances) and sue the seller for breach of contract

as well, but in case the contract is only an 'agreement to sell ' the buyer can only sue the seller for the breach of contract but cannot recover the goods.

6. Where the buyer becomes insolvent: Where the contract is a 'sale' the seller would have to part with the goods and can receive in buyer's insolvency, only ratable dividend for the price due. An agreement to sell, the seller may refuse to deliver the goods to the official receiver/assignee of the buyer's property unless he is paid the full price.
7. Insolvency of the seller: If it is a sale, the buyer can recover it from the official receiver/assignee. But in an agreement to sell buyer cannot recover the goods even if he has paid the price in advance.

SALE DISTINGUISHED FROM OTHER TRANSACTIONS

- Sale, barter and exchange: If the goods are exchanged for goods only it is called 'barter' and not sale. If money is exchanged for money (say $ 10 for Rs.450) it is called 'Exchange' only. But where goods are exchanged for a money consideration, it is called a sale. If the consideration consists partly of money and partly of goods, it would be a contract of sale.
- 'Hire purchase' and 'Agreement to sell': In a contract of sale there is an agreement to buy but in 'hire purchase', hirer has the option to buy the goods if he pays all the installments. Hence if he does not exercise his option, the owner cannot sue for breach of contract but can take his goods back. In an agreement to sell, if the buyer refuses to buy the goods the seller can sue him for breach of contract.
- Sale and contract for work and Labour: If the essence of the contract is the rendering of service and exercise of skill it is a contract of work and labour, though goods are also delivered under the contract. But if the delivery of goods is the essence of the contract although some labour on the part of the seller may be necessary, it would be a contract of sale.

Kinds of Goods

The goods are classified by sec 6, as follows:

Existing goods: Existing goods are those which are owned or possessed by the seller at the time of the contract of sale. Existing goods may be further classified into:

- Specific;
- Ascertained; and
- Unascertained.

"Specific goods means goods identified and agreed upon at the time a contract of sale is made" [sec.2(14)]. Ascertained goods are those which are identified and agreed upon after a contract of sale is made. The goods which are only defined by description and not specifically identified at the time a contract of sale is made are called unascertained goods.

Future Goods: Future goods means goods to be manufactured or produced or acquired by the seller after the making of the contract of sale." [Sec.2(6)], Example: A agrees to sell to B the entire crop of Onion, that his land would yield, at Rs.10,000 per ton. This is a contract for the sale of future goods because goods are still to be produced.

Contingent goods: Contingent goods are those the acquisition of which by the seller depends upon a contingency which may or may not happen [Sec. 6(2)]. Example: A agrees to sell the cow to B if A inherits C's property including the cow. C donates the entire property to a trust. The contract becomes void.

Perishing of Goods

After a contract of sale is made the subject matter of the contract may be destroyed or it may be found that the subject matter had already been destroyed before the date of making the contract, the effect of the two cases would be different.

A. Goods perishing before the contract of sale: (Sec.7) provides, "where there is a contract for the sale of specific goods the contract is void if the goods without the knowledge of the seller have, at the time when the contract was made, perished or become so damaged as no longer to answer to their description in the contract.'

B. Goods perishing after the contract of sale is made

   i. Perishing before sale but after an agreement to sell: "unless otherwise agreed, the goods remain at the seller's risk until the property therein is transferred to the buyer..."

ii. Goods perishing after sale: In sale, goods are destroyed after sale. The loss arising from the destruction or damage of the goods would be borne by the buyer.(Sec.26)

The Price

A. Meaning: "Price means the money consideration for a sale which of goods" [Sec.2(10)].

B. How to fix the price?

- By the contract: The price is a contract of sale may be fixed by the contract between the parties (Sec69).
- In an agreement: The price may be left to be fixed in manner of agreement (sec.9). Whatever manner of fixing the price has been agreed upon by the parties to the contract, that would be recognized by law. (3) Valuation by third party: The price may be left to be fixed by a third party.
- By the course of dealings: Where the price is neither expressed in the contract nor any manner of fixing the price is agreed, the price would be determined by the course of dealings between the parties.
- Reasonable price: What is a reasonable price is question of fact depending on the circumstances of each case. Generally the market price on the date of supply is taken to be a reasonable price.

C. Earnest or deposit: The money so paid is called earnest or deposit. If buyers commit a breach of the contract and seller files a suit for damages, the amount of damages shall be reduced by the amount of earnest money forfeited.

D. Taxes imposed after the contract of sale [sec.64 (A)]: Any tax, is imposed after making of the contract of sale of such goods, then the seller can recover the same from the buyer.

E. Payment of price a concurrent condition with that of delivery (sec.32): The seller shall be ready, and willing to give possession of the goods to the buyer in exchange for the price, and the buyer shall be ready and willing to pay the price in exchange for possession of the goods."

Time as Essence of Contract

A contract of sale of goods may stipulate the time for the payment of the price and also the time for delivery of goods.

- Regarding payment: "unless a different intention appears from the terms of the contract, stipulations as to time of payment are not deemed to be the essence of a contract of sale."
- Regarding delivery: as regards stipulation relating to the time of delivery of goods. (Sec.11).

LAW OF INSURANCE

The contract of insurance is called an aerator contract because it depends upon an uncertain event. Lord Mansfield described insurance as "a contract on speculation."

- Fundamental Principles of Insurance:
  - Good faith,
  - Insurable interest,
  - Indemnity,
  - Mitigation of loss,
  - Attachment of risk,
  - Causa proxima.
- Good Faith: A contract of insurance is a contract, uberrimae fidei, a contract based on utmost good faith and if the utmost good faith is not observed by either party the contract may be avoided by the other.
- Insurable Interest: The assured must have an actual interest called the insurable interest, in the subject-matter of the insurance; either he must own part or whole of it, or he must be in such a position that injury to it would affect him adversely.
- Indemnity: Excepting life assurance and personal accident and sickness insurance, a contract of insurance contained in a fire, marine, burglary or any other policy is a contract of indemnity.
- Mitigation of Loss: In the event of some mishap to insured property, the owner (the insured) must act as though he were uninsured, and make every effort to preserve his property.
- Risk Must Attach: A contract of insurance can be enforced only if the risk has attached.
- Causa Proxima: Make the insurer liable for loss, such loss must have been proximately caused by the peril insured against. Causa proxima non remota spectator.

- Contract of Insurance One from Year to Year: The general rule is the except in the case of life assurance a contract of insurance is a contract from year to year only,
- Premium: The premium is the price for the risk undertaken by the insurer. It is the consideration for the insurance.
- Days of Grace: The days of grace are the days allowed by the insurance company after the expiry of the stipulated period of insurance during which the assured can pay the premium in order to continue or to renew the policy of insurance.
- Policy: The policy is a formal and enforceable stamped document signed and issued by the insurance company embodying the terms of the contract between the parties.
- Interim Receipt, Certificate or Cover Note: A cover note or interim certificate is a document which the insurance company, on receiving the proposal, may issue pending the execution of a policy or the final decision of the directors as to acceptance or rejection of the proposal.
- Re-insurance: Re-insurance is a contract which insures the thing originally insured, and by which an insurer is to be indemnified against any loss which he may sustain by reason of being himself compelled to pay the assured under the original contract of insurance.
- Double Insurance: When the same subject-matter is insured with two or more insurers and the total sum insured exceeds the actual value of the subjectmatter, it is known as double insurance and it amounts to over-insurance.
- Subrogation: The right of subrogation is a necessary corollary of the principle of indemnity and is essential for its preservation.
- Contribution: Contribution is the right of the insurers to claim from others some payment towards the loss, and arises only where there is double insurance.

MARINE INSURANCE

The law telated to marine insurance is found in the Marine Insurance Act, 1963. A contract of marine insurance is an agreement whereby the insurer undertakes to indemnify the assured, in the manner and to the extent thereby agreed, against marine losses, that is to say, the losses incidental to marine adventure (Sec.3). There is a marine adventure when:

1. any insurable property is exposed to maritime perils;
2. the earnings or acquisition of any freight, passage money, commission, profit or other pecuniary benefit, or the security for any advances, loans, or disbursements is endangered by the exposure of insurable property to maritime perils;
3. any liability to third party may be insured by the owner of, or other person interested in or responsible for, insurable property by reason of maritime perils [Sec. 2(e)].

Maritime Perils: means the perils consequent on, or incidental to, the navigation of the sea, that it to say, perils of the seas, fire, war perils, pirates, rovers, thieves, captures, seizures, restraints and detainments of princes and peoples, jettisons, barratry and any other perils which are either of the like kind or may be designed by the policy [Sec. 2(e)].

Types of Policies

- Voyage Policy: Where the contract is to insure the subject-matter "at and from" or from one place to another or others, the policy is called a voyage policy.
- Time Policy: Where the contract is to insure the subject-matter for a definite period of time, the policy is called a time policy.
- Valued Policy: A valued policy is a policy which specifies the agreed value of the subject-matter insured.
- Unvalued Policy: An unvalued policy is a policy which does not specify the value of the matter insured, but subject to the limit of the sum insured, leaves the insurable value to be subsequently ascertained (Sec. 30).
- Floating Policy: A floating policy is a policy which describes the insurance in general terms, and leaves the name or names of the ship or ships and other particulars to be defined by subsequent declaration.
- Wager or Honour Policy: It is a policy in which the assured has no insurable interest or the insurer or underwriter is willing to dispense with the proof of interest.
- Insurable Interest: The person who effects an insurance, or issues instructions for effecting it, must have an insurable interest in the subject-matter. The assured must have insurable interest at the time of the loss thought he may not have been interested when the insurance was actually effected.

- Insurable Value: Insurable value is the amount of the valuation of the insurable interest for the purpose of insurance.
- Disclosure and Representation: The assured must disclose to the insurer every material circumstance which is known to him, and he is deemed to know everything which he ought to know in the ordinary course of business.
- Warranties: A warranty, according to sec. 35 of the Act, is an undertaking by the assured that some condition shall be fulfilled, or that a certain thing shall be or shall not be done, or whereby he confirms or negatives the existence of a particular state of facts. A warranty may be express or implied. An express warranty is a condition which is set forth in the policy or attached thereto; and an implied warranty is an essential condition implied by law, though not written in the policy.
- Sea-Worthiness: The ship must be sea-worthy at the commencement of the voyage, or if the voyage is divisible into distinct stages, at the commencement of each stage.
- Legality: So far as the assured can control the matter, the adventure shall be carried out in a lawful manner.
- The Voyage: The subject-matter may be insured by a voyage policy "from a port" or "at and from" a port.
- Perils- Perils are the risks which the underwriter agrees to take upon himself, and are inserted in the policy. Perils of the sea are all perils, losses, misfortunes of a marine character or a character incident to a ship as such. The purpose of the policy is to secure an indemnity against accidents which may happen, not against events which must happen.

Losses

Kinds of Losses: A loss may be either Total or Partial. Total loss may be subdivided into two classes:

1. Actual Total Loss, and
2. Constructive Total Loss.

The case of partial loss arises when the subject-matter of the insurance is partially lost. Partial loss is also of two sub classes:

i. Particular Average, and

ii. General Average.

FIRE INSURANCE

A fire insurance is a contract to indemnify the insured for destruction of or damage to property caused by fire.

- Average Clause: It is becoming very common in policies of fire insurance to insert a condition called the average clause, by which the insured is called upon to bear a portion of the loss himself. This condition is called the pro rata condition of average. Insurable interest, the insured must have insurable interest in the subject-matter both at the time of effecting the policy and at the time of the loss.
- The Risk: The risk in fire policy commences from the moment the cover note, or the deposit receipt, or the interim protection is issued and continues for the term covered by the contract of insurance.
- What is Fire: The word fire as used in the expression "loss by fire" is to be construed in its popular and literal sense, and means a fire which has broken bounds.
- Assignment: In English law policy of fire insurance can be assigned only with the consent of the insurer.

FIRE POLICIES

- Valued Policy: In the "valued policy" the insured can recover a fixed amount, agreed at the issue of the policy without the necessity for any further proof of value at the time of the fire.
- Re-instatement or Replacement Policy: A clause is inserted in the policy under which the insured can recover not the value of buildings or plant as depreciated, but the cost of replacement of the property destroyed by new property of the same kind, or the insurers may themselves reinstate the property instead of paying in cash.
- Consequential Loss Policy: The insured is indemnified for the loss of profits which he sustains through interruption or cessation of his business as a result of fire.

LIFE INSURANCE

Life assurance may be defined as a contract in which the insurer, in consideration of a certain premium, either in a lump sum or by other periodical payments, agrees to pay to the assured, or to the person for whose benefit the policy is taken, a stated sum of money on the happening of a particular event contingent on the duration of human life.

- Life Insurance is not a Contract of Indemnity: "The contract commonly called life assurance when properly considered is a mere contract to pay a certain sum of money on the death of a person, in consideration of the due payment of a certain annuity for his life.... This species of insurance in no way resembles a contract of indemnity."
- Insurable Interest: The assured must have at the time of the contract an insurable interest in the life upon which the insurance is effected.
- Person in his Own Life: A person is presumed to have an interest in his own life and every part of it, and can insure for any sum whatsoever, and as often as he pleases.
- Relatives: A wife has an insurable interest in the life of her husband, and vice versa.
- Persons not Related: A creditor has an insurable interest in the life of his debtor to the extent of the debt.

Policies

- Whole Life Policy: which matures only at the death whenever it may occur. Endowment Policy: in which the sum insured is payable after the expiration of certain term of years if the policy-holder is alive, or if he dies previously.
- Joint Life Policies: are issued under which the sum assured is payable at the death of the first of the two lives.
- Survivorship Policy: is also granted under which the sum assured is payable at the death of the last or survivor of two lives.
- Surrender Value: The amount which the insurers are prepared to pay in total discharge of the contract, in case the assured wishes to surrender his policy and extinguish his claim upon it.
- Loans on Policies: Where a policy has a surrender value, it also has a loan value, and assurance companies usually lend 95 per cent of the surrender value.
- Paid-up Policy Value: The amount to which the sum assured would be reduced at any time if the assured requested a

rearrangement of his contract so that no further premium should be payable.

- Principle of Good Faith and sec. 45 of Insurance Act: The general rule is that in all kinds of insurance the assured must disclose everything which is likely to affect the judgment of the insurer and what is stated must be truthful.
- Accident Insurance: An injury is accidental where it is the natural consequence of an unexpected cause, or the unexpected consequence of a natural cause. Accident insurance consists of three categories:
  a. Personal accident insurance, of three, including insurance against sickness;
  b. Property insurance, including burglary, fidelity, insolvency, etc
  c. Liability insurance, including motor insurance, workmen's compensation insurance, etc.

THE NEGOTIABLE INSTRUMENTS ACT, 1881

The law telated to negotiable instruments is primarily contained in the Negotiable Instruments Act, 1881. The word 'negotiable' means transferable from one person to another, and the term 'instrument' means 'any written document by which a right is created in favor of some person.' Thus, the negotiable instrument is a document by which rights vested in person can be transferred to another person in accordance with the provisions of the Negotiable Instruments Act, 1881. The Negotiable Instruments Act does not affect the provisions of Sections 31 and 32 of the Reserve Bank of India Act, 1934. But, the following are Not Promissory Notes. Ex. "I promise to pay B Rs. 500 and all other sums which shall be due to him."

Essentials or Characteristics of a Promissory Note:

- In writing.
- Promise to pay.
- Unconditional.
- Signed by the Maker.
- Certain Parties.
- Certain sum of money.
- Promise to pay money only.

- Number, place, date etc.
- It may be payable in installments
- It may be payable on demand or after a definite period
- It cannot be made payable to bearer on demand or even payable to bearer after a certain period (Sec. 31 of RBI Act).
- It must be duly stamped under the Indian Stamp Act

Bill of Exchange: A 'bill of exchange' is defined by Section 5 as "an instrument' in writing, containing an unconditional order, signed by the maker, directing a certain person to pay a certain sum of money only to or the order of, a certain person, or to the bearer of the instrument."

Characteristic features of a Bill of Exchange:

- It must be in writing.
- It must contain an order to pay and not a promise or request. Words, like 'Please pay Rs. 10,000 to A on demand and oblige, do not constitute the instrument a bill of exchange.
- The order must be unconditional.
- There must be three parties, viz., drawer, drawee and payee.
- The parties must be certain.
- It must be signed by the drawer.
- The sum payable must be certain or capable of being made certain.
- The order must be to pay money and money alone.
- It must be duly stamped as per the Indian Stamp Act.
- Number, date and place are not essential. Oral evidence may be obtained as to date and place of execution.

Cheque: A cheque is defined as 'a bill of exchange drawn on a specified banker and not expressed to be payable otherwise than on demand' (Section 6). Thus, a cheque is a bill of exchange with two added features, viz.:

i. It is always drawn on a specified banker;
ii. And it is always payable on demand and not otherwise.

Distinction between Promissory Note and Bill of Exchange

Promissory note differs from a bill of exchange in the following respects:

Promissory Note	Bill of Exchange
1. There are only two parties the maker (debtor) and the payee (creditor).	1. There are three parties the drawer, the drawee and the payee.
2. Contains an unconditional promise by the maker to pay the payee.	2. Contains an unconditional order to the drawee to pay according to the drawer's directions.
3. No prior acceptance is needed.	3. A bill payable 'after sight' must be accepted by the drawee or his agent before it is presented for payment.
4. The liability of the maker or drawer is primary and absolute.	4. The liability of the drawer is secondary and conditional upon nonpayment by the drawee.
5. No notice of dishonour need be given.	5. Notice of dishonour must be given by the holder to the drawer and the intermediate endorsers to hold them liable thereon.

Difference between Bill of Exchange and Cheque

Cheque	Bill of Exchange
1. Must be drawn only on a banker.	1. Can be drawn on any person including a banker.
2. The amount is always payable on demand.	2. The amount may be payable on demand or after a specified time.
3. The cheque is not entitled to days of grace.	3. A usance (time) bill is entitled to three days of grace.
4. Acceptance is not needed.	4. A bill payable after sight must be accepted.
5. A cheque can be crossed.	5. Crossing of a bill of exchange is not possible.
6. Notice of dishonour is not necessary. (The parties thereon remain liable, even if no notice of dishonour is given.)	6. Notice of dishonour is necessary to hold the parties liable thereon. (A party who does not receive a notice of dishonour can generally escape its liability thereon.)
7. Not to be noted or protested in case of dishonour.	7. Noted or protested to establish dishonour.
8. The protection given to the paying banker in respect of crossed cheques is peculiar to this instrument.	8. No such protection is available in the case of bills.

Holder and Holder-in -Due-Course: According to section 8, a holder of a negotiable instrument is "a person entitled in his own name to the possession thereof and to receive or recover the amount due thereon from the parties thereto." Thus, a person who has obtained the possession of an instrument by theft or under a forged endorsement is not a holder as is not entitled to recover the amount of the instrument.

A 'holder in-due-course': Is "a person who for consideration became the possessor of a promissory note, bill of exchange or cheque, if payable to bearer, or the payee or endorsee thereof, if payable to order, before the amount mentioned in it becomes payable and without having sufficient cause to believe that any defect existed in the title of the person from whom he derived his title (Section 9).

Privileges of a Holder in Due Course:

1. A person, who signed and delivered to another a stamped but otherwise inchoate (incomplete) instrument, is stopped form asserting, as against a holder in due course.
2. The maker or drawer, the acceptor, and all the intermediate endorsers continue to remain liable to the holder in due course until the instrument is duly satisfied.
3. Where a bill of exchange is drawn by a fictitious person and is payable to his order, the acceptor cannot be relieved from his liability to the holder in due course.
4. Where an instrument is negotiated to a holder in due course, the parties to the instrument cannot escape liability on the ground that the delivery of the instrument was conditional or for a special purpose only (Sections 46 & 47).
5. Not only that the title of the holder in due course is not subject to the defect in previous holder's title but once the instrument passes through the hands of a holder in due course, it is purged of all defects.
6. No maker of a promissory note and no drawer of a bill of exchange or cheque shall in a suit thereon by a holder in due course, be permitted to deny the validity of the instrument as originally made or drawn.
7. No maker of a note and no acceptor of a bill payable to order is, in a suit thereon by a holder in due course, permitted to deny the payee's capacity at the date of the note or bill to endorse it (Section 121).

    - Ambiguous Instrument (Sec.17): An ambiguous instrument is one which may be construed either as a promissory note or as a bill exchange. The holder may at his option treat it as either and the instrument shall be treated accordingly.

- Where Amount is stated differently in Figures and Words (Sec. 18): If the amount undertaken or ordered to be paid is stated differently in figures and in words, the amount stated in words shall be the amount undertaken or ordered to be paid.
- Inchoate Instruments (Sec.20): An inchoate instrument means an instrument that is incomplete in certain respects. The person so signing shall be liable upon the instrument, in the capacity in which he signed the same, to any holder-in-due- course for such amount. But, a person other than a holder-in-due course cannot recover from the person delivering the instrument anything in excess of the amount intended by him to be paid there under.
- Minor (Sec. 26): A minor may draw, indorse, deliver and negotiate negotiable instruments so as to bind all parties except himself.
- Agency (Sec. 27): Every person capable of binding himself or of being bound may so bind himself or be bound by a duly authorized agent acting in his name.
- Liability of Agent Signing (Sec. 28): An agent who signs his name to a P/N, B/E or cheque without indicating thereon that he does not intend thereby to incur personal responsibility, is liable personally on the instrument, except to those who induced him to sign upon the belief that the principal only would be held liable.
- Liability of Legal Representative (Sec.29): A legal representative of a deceased person who signs his name to a promissory note, bill of exchange or cheque is liable thereon, unless he expressly limits his liability to the extent of the assets received by him as such.
- Negotiable Instruments Made, etc.: Without Consideration (Sec.43): A negotiable instrument made, drawn, accepted, indorsed or transferred without consideration, or for a consideration which fails, creates no obligation of payment between the parties to the transaction.
- Partial Absence or Failure of Money Consideration (Sec.44): When the consideration for which a person signed a promissory note, bill of exchange or cheque consisted of money, and was originally absent in part or has subsequently failed in part, the sum which a holder

standing in immediate relation with such signer is entitled to receive from him is proportionately reduced.

- Partial Failure of Consideration not Consisting of Money (Sec. 45): When a part of the consideration for which a person signed a promissory note, bill of exchange or cheque, though not consisting of money, is ascertainable in money without collateral enquiry, and there has been a failure of that part, the sum which a holder standing in immediate relation with such signer is entitled to receive from him is proportionally reduced.
- Lost or Stolen Instruments [Sec. 58]: When a negotiable instrument has been lost, or has been obtained from any maker, acceptor or holder thereof by means of an offence or fraud, or for an unlawful consideration, no possessor or indorsee who claims through the person who found or so obtained the instrument is entitled to receive the amount due thereon from such maker, acceptor or holder, or from any party prior to such holder. However, if such possessor or indorsee is a holder in due course he shall be entitled to receive the payment thereof.
- Lost Instruments: When a bill or note is lost, the finder acquires no title to it as against the rightful owner. He is also not entitled to sue the acceptor or maker in order to enforce payment on it. If the finder obtains payment, the person who pays it in due course may be able to get a valid discharge for it. But the true owner can recover the money due on the instrument from the finder.

Stolen Instruments:

1. A person cannot enforce payment of it against any party thereto nor can he retain it against the party from whom he had stolen it.
2. If the thief negotiates the instrument to a purchaser for value who has notice of the theft, the transferee cannot acquire a better title than the thief and thus cannot enforce payment.
3. If a person who has stolen a bill or note payable to bearer transfers it to a holder in due course, he confers a good title on him or any person deriving title from such holder.

Instruments Obtained for Unlawful Consideration

1. The instrument is void.
2. A holder in due course, however, obtains a good title to an instrument which was originally made or drawn or subsequently negotiated for an unlawful consideration.

Forged Instruments: The most common species of forgery is fraudulently writing the name of an existing person. It is also a forgery to sign the name of a fictitious person or non-existing person. Even a man's signature of his own name may amount to forgery, if it is put with the intention that the signature should pass for the signature of another person of the same name.

Legal Position:

1. A forged signature is worthless and confers no title.
2. The holder of a forged instrument cannot enforce payment thereon nor can he give a valid discharge therefore.
3. The true owner can compel the debtor to pay it over again to him.
4. Even a holder in due course cannot claim payment on a forged instrument.
5. A person whose signatures have been forged may, by his conduct, be stopped from denying its genuineness to an innocent holder.

CHEQUE

A cheque is the usual method of withdrawing money from an account with a banker. A cheque, in essence, is an order by the customer of the bank directing his banker to pay on demand, the specified amount, to or to the order of the person named therein or to the bearer. Section 6 defines a cheque as "bill of exchange drawn on a specified banker and not expressed to be payable otherwise than on demand.

Requisites of a Cheque:

- Written Instrument. A cheque must be an instrument in writing.
- Unconditional Order. A cheque must contain an unconditional order.
- On a Specified Banker Only. A cheque must be drawn on a specified banker.

- A Certain Sum of Money. The order must be only for the payment of money and that too must be specified.
- Payee to be certain. A cheque to be valid must be payable to a certain person.
- Payable on Demand. A cheque to be valid must be payable on demand and not otherwise.
- Amount of the Cheque. A mount of the cheque must be clearly mentioned.
- Dating of Cheques. The drawer of a cheque is expected to date it before it leaves his hands.

A cheque hearing an earlier date is ante-dated and the one bearing the later date is called post-dated. In India, a cheque that bears a date earlier than six months is a stale cheque and cannot be claimed for. In England, cheque can remain in circulation for a period of twelve months.

Crossing of Cheques: Crossing of a cheque is a direction to the paying banker by the drawer that payment should not be made across the counter. The payment on a crossed cheque can be collected only through a banker. Section 123, defines crossing as, "Where a cheque bears across its face an addition of the words 'and company' or any abbreviation thereof, between two parallel transverse lines, or of two parallel transverse lines simply, either with or without the words 'not negotiable', that addition shall be deemed a crossing and the cheque shall be deemed to be crossed generally. A cheque having the cross mark such as 'X' is not generally regarded as a crossed cheque. A cheque that is not crossed is called an open cheque.

Significance of Crossing: Payment cannot be claimed across the counter on a crossed cheque, crossing of cheques serves as a measure of safety against theft or loss of cheques in transit. By crossing a cheque, a person, who is not entitled to receive its payment, is prevented from getting the cheque encashed at the counter of the paying banker.

Types of Crossing: Crossing may be of two types: (1) General or (2) Special.

- General Crossing: The term general crossing implies the addition of two parallel transverse lines.
- Special Crossing: 'Special Crossing' implies the specification of the name of the banker on the face of the cheque. Section 124 in this regard, reads: Where a cheque bears across its

face, an addition of the name of a bank, either with or without the words 'not negotiable', that addition shall be deemed a crossing, and the cheque shall be deemed to be crossed to that banker." The object of special crossing is to direct the drawee banker to pay the cheque only if it is presented through the particular bank mentioned therein. Thus, it makes the cheque system still safer.

- Not Negotiable Crossing: By including the words 'not negotiable', the cheque is deprived of its special feature of negotiability. Such a cheque is like any other goods where the title of the transferee is always subject to the title of the transferor. A bank, therefore, should be extra careful in paying such cheques.
- Account Payee Crossing (A/c Payee Crossing): An A/c payee crossing signifies that the drawer intends the payment to be credited only to the payee's account and in none else. The addition of 'A/c payee' to a crossing has no legal sanctity and the paying banker may ignore such a direction without being liable for any damages.
- Not Negotiable, A/c Payee Crossing: The instrument is rendered not negotiable plus A/c payee crossing directs the collecting banker to collect it for the payee only and warns that if the amount is collected for someone else, he may be held liable for damages.

Who can Cross a Cheque?:

- The drawer of a cheque.
- The holder of a cheque.
- The Banker. A cheque once crossed need not remain so being forever. The drawer has the right to cancel the crossing by writing the words 'pay cash' and putting his 'full signatures'.

Marking of Cheques

Marking or certification is a method adopted when the paying banker verifies the customer's account and indicates thereon that there are enough funds in his Account to meet that cheque. The marking of a cheque may be done at the instance of the drawer or at the instance of the payee or at the instance of the collecting banker. The effect of marking is different in the three cases.

- Marking at the Instance of the Drawer: The banker acquires a right to retain money to meet such a cheque. Marking only certifies the genuineness of the drawer's signature and the sufficiency of funds and not the endorsements.
- Marking at the Request of the Payee or Holder: It constitutes nothing more than an intimation that at the time of marking, the bank has a sufficient balance to the credit of the drawer.
- Marking Between Bankers: This marking is an appropriation of funds in the banker's hands for a specific purpose he is entitled to deduct the amount of such marked cheque when estimating the balance available for meeting other cheques.
- Marking of Post-dated Cheques: It has been held anomalous and invalid. Marking of such a cheque amounts to a promise, requiring consideration to support it.

Material Alterations: A material alteration may be defined as "an alteration which alters the business effect of the instrument if used for any business purpose. Any change made in the instrument that causes it to speak a different language from what is originally intended, or which changes the legal identity of the instrument in its terms or in relation or parties thereto is a material alteration."

Examples of material alteration are:

i. Date
ii. The time of payment
iii. The place of payment
iv. The sum payable
v. The number of parties
vi. The relationship between parties
vii. Legal character of the cheque
viii. Opening a crossed cheque
ix. Converting an order cheque into a bearer cheque.

Effect of Material Alteration (Section 87): It renders the same void as against any one who is party thereto at the time of making such alteration and does not consent thereto unless it was made in order to carry out the common interest of the original parties, and any such alteration, if made by an endorsee, discharges his endorsers from all liability to him in respect of the consideration thereof."

Examples of Alterations Which are not Material:

i. filling the blanks of the instrument (Section 20);

ii. conversion of blank endorsement into endorsement in full (Section 49);

iii. crossing of cheques (Section 125);

Forgery: No protection is granted to paying banker for making payment of cheques bearing forged signature of the customer. Payment of a cheque bearing forged signature of the customer is deemed to be a payment without the authority of customer and hence constituted breach of the implied contract between banker and the customer.

The Paying Banker: The 'paying banker' is a term used to denote the position and duties of the dawee banks in payment the cheques of their customers. Thus, 'paying banker' is a banker upon whom a cheque is drawn. The job of a paying banker in regard to the payment of cheques is highly risky. However, this obligation of the paying banker to honour his customer's cheque is subject to certain conditions:

Statutory Protection Available to a Paying-Banker: Section 31 holds the paying banker liable for payment to a wrong person. But, the banker, despite his efforts, may inadvertently happen to pay a cheque to a wrong person claiming payment under a clever forgery of endorsement.

Payment in Due Course

(Section 10) The following conditions must be satisfied before a payment of negotiable instrument can be called as a payment in due course:

1. Payment must be in accordance with the apparent tenor of the instrument.
2. Payment must be made in good faith and without negligence.
3. Payment must be made to the person in possession of the instrument.
4. Payment must be made under circumstances which do not afford a reasonable ground for believing that he is not entitled to receive payment of the amount mentioned therein.
5. Payment must be made in money only.

When Banker Must Refuse Payment?

1. Where the customer countermands the payment: A banker must refuse to honour cheque, payment for which has been stopped by the drawer.

2. On receipt of a notice of customer's death
3. On customer's becoming insolvent
4. On receipt of a notice of the customer's insanity
5. On receipt of Garnishee order: Where Garnishee Order is absolute, i.e., attaching the whole amount, payment on cheques received after the receipt of such an order must be refused.
6. On assignment of Credit balance: On receipt of a notice of assignment signed by the customer of credit balance of his account.
7. On suspicious misuse by trustee If the banker feels suspicious,that the trustee intends to use the amount of the cheque for his personal use.
8. On suspicious as to the title Where the banker believes that the person presenting the cheque is not entitled to receive the payment thereon.
9. In case of a joint account to be operated by all jointly where the cheque is not signed by all of the joint account holders.
10. Where the cheque is irregular, ambiguous or otherwise materially altered.
11. Where the cheque is presented after a period of six months from the date it bears, i.e., it has become stale.

When Banker May Refuse Payment

In the following cases the banker may dishonour a cheque without incurring any liability thereon:

- Where the cheque is post-dated. Refusal to pay a post-dated cheque before its due date does not make a banker liable for wrongful dishonour.
- Where the funds of the customer are insufficient.
- Where a cheque is not duly presented. (For instance, a cheque presented after business hours).

Negotiation: A negotiable instrument may be transferred by negotiation or assignment. When a negotiable instrument is transferred by negotiation, its transferee, if holder in due course, gets a better title than its transferor.

- Negotiation By Mere Delivery: (Section 47) A bill or cheque payable to bearer is negotiated by mere delivery of the instrument. Delivery may be actual or constructive. Actual delivery means change of actual possession. It is a constructive delivery when the possession is given to the transferee's agent, clerk or servant on his behalf.

- Payable to bearer: An instrument is payable to bearer (1) where it is made so payable, or (2) where it is originally made payable to order but the only or the last endorsement is in blank. A cheque which is originally drawn payable to bearer remains bearer even though it is subsequently endorsed in full. The rule is once a bearer cheque always a bearer cheque or (3) where the payee is a fictitious person.
- Negotiation By Endorsement and Delivery: Instruments payable to a specified person or to the order of a specified person can be negotiated only by endorsement and delivery.

Endorsement/Indorsement

1. It must be written on the instrument itself and be signed by the indorser.
2. The endorsement must be of the entire instrument.
3. Where in a negotiable instrument payable to order, the payee or endorsee is wrongly designated or his name is mis-spelt, he should sign the instrument in the same manner as given in the instrument.
4. Where there are two or more endorsements on an instrument, each endorsement is deemed to have been made in the order in which it appears on the instrument, until contrary is proved.
5. An endorsement may be blank or full. It may also be restrictive.

Kinds of Endorsements: According to the Negotiable Instruments Act, 1881, endorsement may take any of the following forms:

1. Conditional Endorsement: It is one which makes the transfer of the property in a negotiable instrument from the endorser to the endorsee dependent upon the fulfillment of a stated condition. For example, where the endorsement states "Pay 'X' if he reaches Delhi". In such a case, 'X' can claim payment on the instrument only if he reaches Delhi.
2. Endorsement in Blank: Where the endorser just puts his signature without specifying the endorsee, the endorsement is said to be in blank (Section 16). For example, a cheque is payable to 'X or order' and 'X' merely signs on the back of it, will constitute endorsement in blank.

3. Endorsement in Full: Where along endorser's signature, the name of the endorsee is specified, the endorsement is called 'endorsement in full' (Section 16). "Pay Y or order" and is signed by 'X', the payee, it constitute 'endorsement in full.'
4. Restrictive Endorsement: An endorsement is restrictive which prohibits from the further negotiation of a negotiable instrument.
5. Endorsement 'Sans Recourse': An endorsement of a negotiable instrument may be express words in the endorsement exclude his own liability thereon (Section 52). Such endorsement is called 'Endorsement Sans recourse' or 'without recourse to me'. For example, where X endorse a cheque as: 'Pay Y or order Sans Recourse' or 'Pay Y or order without Recourse to me'. 'X' will not be liable on the instrument if it is dishonoured.
6. Sans Frais: Indicates that no expenses should be incurred on account of the bill.
7. Facultative Endorsement: The endorser waives his right to receive notice of dishonour.
8. Partial Endorsement: Where the negotiable instrument is endorsed in part of the amount. Such an endorsement is not valid.

Effect of Endorsement: The effect of an endorsement in blank and delivery of an instrument originally made, drawn, payable to order is to convert it into one payable to bearer and transferable by mere delivery.

The effect of restrictive endorsement is (a) to prohibit or exclude further negotiation, or (b) to constitute the endorsee an agent of endorser to endorse the instrument, or (c) to constitute the endorsee as agent to receive its contents for some other specified persons.

The Collecting Banker: One of the principal functions of a banker is to receive instruments from his customer in order to collect the proceeds and credit them to his customer's account. When acting in this capacity he is called a "collecting banker".

Statutory protection to a collecting banker

1. For Crossed Cheques only.
2. Collection for customers.
3. Acted in Good Faith and Without Negligence.

BILL OF EXCHANGE AND PROMISSORY NOTE

Kinds of Bills

1. Inland Bill: "a promissory note, bill of exchange or cheque drawn or made in India and payable in or drawn upon any person resident in India". (Section 11).
2. Foreign Bills: According to Section 12, a foreign bill is negotiable instrument which is note an inland instrument.
3. Trade and Accommodation Bills: A trade bill is a bill of exchange issued in respect of a genuine trade transaction Such bills are drawn by the seller on the buyer in respect of payment of the price of the goods sold and purchased.
4. Time Bills (Usance Bills): Time bills, also called as usance bills, are bills payable at a fixed period after date or sight of the bills.
5. Demands Bills:A bill of exchange or a promissory note is payable on demand when -

1. It is made payable 'on demand'or 'at sight'or'on presentation' (Section 21)
2. No time for payment is mentioned therein (Section 19)

6. Clean and Documentary Bill: Where the banker is instructed to deliver to the drawee of the bill the documents of title against acceptance of the bill, the bill is called as Documents against Acceptance of Bill (D/A Bill) and where the documents are to be released only against payment, it is called as Documents against Payment of Bill (D/P Bill).

Parties to a Bill of Exchange

1. The Drawer
2. The Drawee
3. The Payee
4. The Holder
5. The Indorser
6. The Indorsee
7. Drawee in Case of Need: Such a person whose name is mentioned as an alternative drawee is called a drawee in case of need'.

8. Acceptor for Honour: An acceptor for honour is a person who, on the refuse by the original drawee to accept the bill or to furnish better security when demanded by the notary, accepts the bill in order to safeguard the honour of the drawer or any indorser.

Parties to a Promissory Note

1. The Maker
2. The Payee
3. The Holder
4. The Indorser
5. The Indorsee

Capacity of Parties: The capacity of a party to draw, accept, make or endorse a bill or note is co-extensive with his capacity to enter into contract.

Acceptance: The acceptance of a bill is the indication by the drawee of his assent to the order of the drawer. An acceptance of a bill may be general or qualified.

Presentment: Presentment of a negotiable instrument is made for two purposes.

1. For acceptance, and
2. For payment.

Dishonour: A bill of exchange may be dishonoured either by nonacceptance or by non-pay-ment.

Dishonour by Non-Acceptance: Section 91 enumerates the circumstances when a bill will be considered as dishonoured by non-acceptance.

Dishonour by Non-Payment: A negotiable instrument is said to be dishonoured by non-payment when the maker, acceptor or drawee, as the case may default in payment upon being duly required to pay the same (Section 92).

Compensation: Section 117 lays down rules for determining the amount of compensation to the holder or an endorser in the event of dishonour of a negotiable instrument, which includes:

- Compensation to holder.
- Compensation to Endorses.

- Compensation against banker.
- Discharge of One or More Parties

One or more parties to a negotiable instrument is/are discharged from liability in the following ways:

1. By cancellation [Sec. 82 (a)].
2. By release [Sec. 82 (b)].
3. By payment [Sec. 82 (c) and 8]
4. By allowing drawee more than 48 hours to accept (Sec.83)
5. By taking qualified acceptance (Sec. 86).
6. By not giving notice of dishonour.
7. By non-presentment for acceptance of a bill (Sec.61)
8. By delay in presenting cheque (Sec.84).
9. By material alteration.
10. By negotiation back.

FACTORIES ACT, 1948

In common parlance, generally factory and industry are understood interchangeable. That is incorrect. The term industry refers to a steady and systematic activity in which a trade is organised, whereas a factory is the place where such activities are being carried on.

The entire day-to-day administration of the factories is governed by the principal Act of 1948 amended Act, which is an improvement of 1934 Act. This Act extends to the whole of India, including Jammu and Kashmir. Unless otherwise provided, it also applies to factories belonging to the Central and State Governments. (Section 116) The Bhopal tragedy of 1984 has created an awareness among the public for preventing pollution and this has made the government to take steps in amending the present 1948 Act by incorporating Chapter IV A from Sections 41 A to 41 H, pertaining to provisions as regards hazardous processes.

OBJECT OF THE ACT

The object of the Factories Act of 1948 is:

- To improve health, welfare and safety of the workmen.
- To regulate by imposing restriction as to hours of work including rest and provisions for availing of leave.

- To make stringent provisions as regards employment of women and young persons and duration of their work.

MEANING OF THE TERM 'FACTORY'

Factory means any premises including the precincts therefore -

- Wherein ten or more workers are working or were working on any day of the preceding twelve months, and in any part of which a manufacturing process is being carried on with the aid of power, or is ordinarily so carried on, or
- Whereon twenty or more workers are working or were working on any day of the preceding twelve months, and in any part of which a manufacturing process is being carried on without the aid of power, or is ordinarily so carried on.

Factory does not include a mine as it is covered by Indian Mines Act, 1952 or a mobile unit belonging to the armed forces of the Union, a railway running shed or a hotel, restaurant or eating place. To put it in a nutshell, factory means

- Any premises including precincts
- Where ten or more persons are engaged in manufacturing process with the aid of power or
- Twenty or more persons are engaged in manufacturing process without the aid of power.

Manufacturing Process - Section 2 (k)

Manufacturing Process means any process for -

- Making, altering, repairing, ornamenting, finishing, packing, oiling, washing, cleaning, breaking up, demolishing or otherwise treating or adopting any article or substance with a view to its use, sale, transport, delivery or disposal, or
- Pumping oil, water, sewage or any other substance, or
- Generating, transforming or transmitting power, or
- Composing types for printing, printing by letter press, lithography taking photography and other similar process or book binding;
- Constructing, reconstructing, repairing, refitting, finishing or breaking up ships or vessels; or
- Preserving or storing any article in cold storage [Section 2 (k)].

Power [Section 2(g)]

It means mechanical or electrical energy transmitted as a step to carry out manufacturing and not energy generated by human or animal agency. Mere use of power not connected with activities of manufacturing will not make the premises a factory. [New Taj Mahal Hotel vs. Inspector of Factories, (1956) I.L.I.J.273].

Manufacturing process must be done with the aid of power, according to Section 2 (m). Use of power may be incidental or consequential to manufacturing process. According to Section 4, on application by the occupier of a factory, different departments or branches of the factory may be treated as separate factories. Likewise, two or more factories specified by the occupier can also be treated as a single factory by the State government by passing suitable orders.

Worker [Section 2 (l)]

Worker means a person employed directly or through any agency (including a contractor) with or without the knowledge of the principal employer, whether for remuneration or not, in any manufacturing process or in cleaning any part of the machinery or premises used for a manufacturing process or in any other kind of work incidental to, or connected within the manufacturing process, or the subject of the manufacturing process but does not include any member of the armed forces of the Union [Section 2 (1)].

In order to term a person as a worker, there must be employer - employee relationship. That is, the employer must not only be in a position to direct what work the employee should do but also how the work has to be done by him.

Rights of workers (Section 111A inserted by 1987 Amendment Act)

A worker shall have the right to (i) obtain from the occupier information related to workers' health and safety at work; (ii) get trained in the factory or at a training centre or institution when sponsored by the occupier and approved by the Chief Inspector; and (iii) represent to the Inspector, directly or otherwise, the matter of inadequacy of health or safety in the factory.

Occupier [Section 2(m)]

Any person who has an ultimate control and management over the affairs of the factory will be deemed to be an occupier.

- In a partnership firm, the individual partners and in the case of association of individuals, members thereof shall be regarded as occupier.
- In companies, the directors are regarded to be occupier because they are vicariously liable for the functions of the company.
- In government owned and controlled factories, the person or persons appointed to manage the affairs of the factory shall be deemed to be the occupier.
- In the case of partnership firm or association of individuals, and partner or member may be prosecuted. A manager cannot be regarded as an occupier, unless he is entrusted with the control and management of the factory.
- Owner, lessee or a licensee having control over the factory with regard to its management is deemed to be the occupier [Emperor vs. Ram Pratap, (1896) 20 Bom.423].

Licensing and Registration of Factories [Section 6]

Under Section 6, the State government may make rules regarding the submission of plans and approval, licensing and registration of factories. The site chosen to locate the factory must have the previous permission in writing of the State government of Chief Inspector of factories. Such permission will be granted to applicant unless he had duly complied with the directions of the government. Every application must be duly accompanied with a certified plan, showing all the details together with the challan representing the fees payable for such registration, licensing or renewal of licence. If permission is not granted either by the State government or the Chief inspector, within 3 months from the date of submission of such application, permission is presumed to have been granted.

On the refusal of the State government to grant permission, the aggrieved applicant can prefer an appeal within the 30 days from the date of refusal. Every order refusing to grant permission or licence must be a speaking order (a speaking order is an order passed after hearing both the sides and it is passed with reasons stated). Licence or permission cannot be denied merely on the direction by the government without hearing the applicant [Shihabudeen Kunju vs. State of Kerala, (1985) 2L.L.J.106].

Under Section 7, the occupier must give 15 days notice to the State government or chief inspector of factories before he begins to occupy or use any premises as a factory. Such notice should contain the following:

- The name and situation of the factory;
- The name and address of the occupier;
- The name and address of the owner of the premises or building (including the precincts thereof);
- The address to which communications relating to the factory may be sent;
- The nature of the manufacturing process to be carried on in the factory during the next 12 months;
- The total rated horse power installed or to be installed in the factory (not including the rated horse power of any separate stand-by plant);
- The name of the manager of the factory for the purpose of this Act;
- The number of workers likely to be employed in the factory; and
- Such other particulars as may be prescribed.

It is essential to intimate by notice the inspector with a copy addressed to the chief inspector of the factories if any new person is appointed as manager in a factory. Even an acting manager or a person without any designation as manager will be deemed to be an occupier if control and management of the factory is governed by them. In the absence of a designated person as manager who ever is an occupier is deemed to be an occupier. [Kama Kishore Jhunjhunwala vs. Prescribed Authority, (1976) 32 F.L.R.355].

Penalty for obstructing inspector (Section 9)

When a factory inspector is prevented or obstructed from exercising his powers, such person shall be punished with imprisonment for 6 months or fine upto Rs, 10,000 or with both.

Certifying Surgeons (Section 10)

Certifying surgeons are qualified medical practitioners, who are appointed by the State government for specified areas or factories. With the approval of the State government, a certifying surgeon may authorize and qualified medical practitioners to exercise any of the powers used by him. However, an occupier of a factory or any parson who becomes directly or indirectly interested in such factory cannot be appointed as a certifying surgeon. These restrictions could be exempted by the State Government in appropriate cases by passing orders in writing.

HEALTH, SAFETY AND WELFARE MEASURES

By way of implementing the recommendation of the Royal Commission on Labour in India, the present Factories Act, has underlined the importance of health, safety and welfare of the workers. It has made special provisions for health under Sections 11 to 20, for safety under Sections 21 to 40 including Chapter IV A (1987 Amendment Act) and welfare of the workers under Sections 42 to 50.

Health (Sections 11 to 20)

- Cleanliness (Section 11): House keeping is the modern term used for keeping the factory premises clean and tidy. Factories must not only be kept clean but must be maintained with cleanliness in such a way that accumulation of dirt and refuse must be avoided. Constant cleaning of effluvia (disagreeable vapours) arising from any drain is needed. Removal of dirt and refuse alone is not enough, but they have to be disposed of in a suitable manner without, causing detriment to the residents of the locality.
- Disposal of wastes and effluents (Section 2): Wastes and effluents are to be disposed of in order to maintain the hygiene inside the factory. However, such wastes cannot be let out without treatment. This is because wastes would pollute the surroundings. Norms laid down by the State Pollution Control Board have to be observed strictly in this regard.
- Ventilation and Temperature (Section 13): Ventilation and air circulation ensure normal health to the workmen. In order to maintain ventilation and fresh air circulation, temperature in the working place should be secured. For this purpose, the interior walls and roofs of the factory must be properly designed and provided with heat resisting or heatproof materials by way of insulation. Reasonable care should be taken for colour washing interior walls with psychologically pleasing colours such as light green, etc.
- Dust and Fumes (Section 14): Effective measures have to be adopted in order to prevent the workers inhaling dusts, fumes and other impurities that are present (which cannot be seen through naked eye) in the air. Control devices or tools have to be used for the purpose of preventing dust and fumes. Use of exhaust fans is highly recommended in such places. No stationary internal combustion engine is allowed to be operated

unless proper arrangements are made to prevent accumulation of injurious fume are caused thereon. [Gregeon vs. Hick Hargreavaes (1955) All E.R.860].

- Artificial Humidification (Section 15): In factories where artificial humidification is adopted from the point of view of manufacturing a product (e.g., in a textile mill), the norms prescribed by the Government must be strictly followed for increasing or decreasing or maintaining such artificial humidification, Humidifiers for keeping air moisture at even level shall be provided. Water used in these plants must constantly be changed and it must be pure. Otherwise it will give room for water borne diseases among workers.
- Overcrowding (Section16): Every worker requires at least 350 cubic feet (now after the commencement of the Act, 500 cubic feet) for the purpose of enabling him to work with ease and comfort ensuring mobility. However, while calculating the aggregate space, no account shall be taken of any space, which is more than 14 feet above the level of the floor. The Chief Inspector of Factories, by notice may specify the number of persons to be employed in a room.
- Lighting (Section17): Too much light throws glare on normal vision. Diffused light does not help to promote proper vision. Hence, the required light with minimum power must be provided. Glazed windows and sky lights through which rooms are ventilated have to be constantly cleaned from the inner and outer surfaces. Glares and shadows must be avoided from distorting the vision of eye. Otherwise, workmen would strain their eyes leading to risks.
- Drinking water (Section18): Potable, pure or wholesome drinking water shall be made available to workmen at convenient points, A notice board must be displayed indicating availability of such facility. The notice shall also contain the caption,' drinking water' in local language. If the strength of the workers increases beyond 250, cool water equipment must be provided to ensure supply of chilled water. The points at which drinking water is supplied shall legibly marked "Drinking water" in a language understood by a majority of employees. Such water points must be located beyond 6 meters or any washing place, urinals, latrine, spittoon and open drainage, carrying silage or

effluent. Shorter distance shall be permitted for locating water points only with the approval of Chief Inspector of Factories.

- Latrines and Urinals (Section 19): For a human being, two places are very important and both of them have to dept clean and tidy. They are - (i) Latrines and urinals; (ii) Places where people rest and relax. Factories where more than 250 workers are ordinarily employed, the latrine and urinal accommodation shall be of the prescribed sanitary type. The floors and internal walls upto a height of 3 feet and above from the floor level should be laid in glazed tiles. If tiles are not provided for, the latrines cannot be dept clean, as the bad water would pass through the pores of latrine walls. Sweepers shall be employed whose primary duty is to keep the latrines and urinals clean and washing places tidy.
- Spittoons (Section 20): Spittoons are nothing but pots that are specially provided for, into which, the workers have to spit. Workers cannot spit, as they like, as that would spoil the cleanliness and hygiene of the factory. Sufficient number of spittoons should be provided, taking into account the number of persons employed. A fine of Rs.5 would be imposed on any one who violated the rule.
- SAFETY (Sections 21 to 40): Safety must come prior to security. According to this concept, the present Factories Act ensures several safety measures as sound in Sections 21 to 40, which are enumerated below:
- Fencing of Machinery (Section 21): In every factory the following namely:
- Every moving part of a prime mover, and every fly-wheel connected to a prime mover, whether the prime mover or fly-wheel is in the engine house or not;
- The headrace and tailrace of every water wheel and water-turbine;
- Any part of a stock-bar, which projects beyond the headstock of a lathe;
- Every part of an electric generator, a motor or rotary converter;
- Every part of transmission machinery; and
- Every dangerous part of any other machinery must be fenced in a secured manner by substantial construction, which should

be constantly maintained. They have to be dept in proper position when the parts of machinery are in motion (Section 21).

The manager of the factory should take particular care to provide safeguard devices to deep the machine in tact, so that it cannot come into contact with workers and thereby cause injury.

- Work on or near Machinery in motion (Section 22): Such of those parts of machine that are in motion may have to be constantly examined in order to ensure that there is no friction, The examination, including lubrication on these moving parts of the machinery must be done only by the adult male workers with tight fitting clothes, It is better such tight fitting clothes are supplied by the occupier.
- Employment of Young persons on Dangerous machines (Section 23): Where complex machinery is functioning in a factory, it becomes very essential to stop any machinery either by striking a gear or for cutting off power. In old type of machines, driving belts were mounted on fast and loose pulleys. They were used forming part of transmission machinery. Hence, power must be cut off in order to prevent the driving belts riding upon moving shafts. Suitable, efficient mechanical device must be provided for instantaneously stopping the machines.
- Self-acting Machines (Section 25): In a factory, traversing part of a self acting machine together with a material carried on by it could be allowed to run over a space under which any person is liable to pass. However, such machinery shall be allowed to traverse both outward and inward directions only beyond a distance of 45 cms from any fixed structure. The fixed structure shall not be part of the machine. Workers must be capable of passing under the moving part of self-acting machine in connection with their employment.
- Casing of new machinery (Section 26): Power driven machinery, revolving shaft, spindle wheel and pinion should be properly encased, i.e., covered and guarded effectively. Spur wheel, helical wheel, fly wheel, friction gear not requiring adjustments which are in constant motion should be safely encased. Even hiring these machines without the safeguards is punishable with fine upto Rs.500 and imprisonment for 3 months or both.

- Prohibition of Employment of Women and Children near Cotton openers (Section27): Women and children are generally prohibited in being employed in pressing cotton in which a cotton opener is at work. If the feed end of a cotton opener is portioned by a separate wall or screen extending upto the ceiling or roof from the delivery end, then women and children could be employed on the side of the feeding end and definitely not at the delivery end.
- Hoists and lifts (Section28): In a factory where hoists and lifts are in use, their construction must have been done out of quality materials with adequate strength to withstand the strain of weight. Such lifts should be fitted with gates and enclosures. Lifts have to be thoroughly examined at least once in six months by competent persons, besides this, routine and other examinations have to be conducted. Entries have to be made recording the date of examination.
- Lifting machine, chains, and ropes and lifting tackles (Section29): Lifting machines and cranes that are used in a factory must be properly fastened and strongly coupled with chains and ropes. These chains and ropes tied up with the hoists sufficiently protect the lifts and cranes in contingencies like power failure or mechanical failure. The lifts should be fitted with ropes or chains connected with a cage so that the balance could be maintained with weights. The chief Inspector of factories has to ensure whether these lifts and cranes including the ropes are maintained properly.
- Revolving machinery (Section 30): In the case of use of revolving or grinding machines, it is necessary that the optimum speed should be indicated for the safe working of the machine. Although indications may be there signifying the maximum speed, the optimum speed must be written on the machine for the safe use of it. This would enable prevention of risk to the user and reduction of strain to the machine. Such a notice must be displayed on the peripheral space of the grinding stone, abrasive wheel, etc.

Hazardous Processes

Section 41-A-41-H: Hazardous process have become an important subject after the Bhopal gas tragedy. Precautionary measures and for handling situations involving hazardous processes have been highlighted under Chapter IV-A. What is hazardous process has become a major issue, so as to enforce the provisions under Chapter IV-A. It is for this reason; a new concept under hazardous processes has been introduced with effect from 1.10.1987. With view to avoid hazards, in storing, handling, transporting and using dangerous materials, these new provisions have been provided by way of addition to the existing ones under safety measures.

Welfare of Workers

The present Factories Act has provided several measures under Chapter V for welfare of the workers under Sections 42 to 48, dealing with washing facilities, facilities for storing and dressing, facilities for sitting, First-aid appliances, canteen, shelter, rest rooms, lunch rooms and crèches

- Washing facilities (Section 42): Suitable and adequate washing facilities, as prescribed by the State government have to be provided separately and exclusively for male and female workers. These places should be accessible. Facilities for storing and drying clothes (Section 43): Suitable places must be provided by the occupier to enable the workers to keep their clothes safe so that there is no risk of theft in that place.
- Sitting Facilities (Section 44): Arrangements shall be made for workers to sit and take rest where their work involves a standing posture.
- First Aid appliances (Section 45): The term first aid itself signifies immediate medical help required by the affected parties. First aid boxes containing essential medicines, including cotton must be provided for every department with not less than 150 workers. Where in a factory, 500 or more workers are employed, the occupier should provide an ambulance room, which is indispensable in the matter of giving medical attention to workers who have e sustained serious injuries.
- Canteen (Section 46): Factories employing 250 or more workers shall provide one or more canteens as per the rules of the State government. A managing committee consisting of representatives of employees and employers should manage such canteens.
- Shelters, rest rooms and lunch rooms (Section 47): Suitable shelters, rest rooms, lunch rooms with provision for drinking

water shall be provided for every factory employing 150 or more workers.

- Creches (Section 48): Creche is a room or place for accommodating children below the age of six. Such creche must be properly lighted and adequately ventilated. Trained women assistants shall be employed to attend to the children and maintain them clean and healthy.
- Welfare Officers (Section49): In factories, where 500 or more workers are employed, there shall be such number of qualified welfare officers employed by the management as per norms prescribed by the State government regarding their qualification, duties and conditions of service.

WORKING HOURS, HOLIDAYS & ANNUAL LEAVE

Adult [Section 2(a)], Adolescent [Section 2(b)] and Child [Section 2(c)]

An adult is a person who has completed the age of 18. An adolescent is a person who has completed the age of 15 but has not completed the age of 18. A child is a person who has not completed the age of 15.

It is very important to note that according to Section 67, a child who has not completed the age of 14 cannot be forced to work in a factory.

Working Hours

Weekly hours (Section 51): No adult worker shall be required or allowed to work in a factory for more than 48 hours in a week. At present it is reduced to 40 hours.

Work not done in the factory under direction of office will not be counted. [Superintendent & Remembrancer of Legal Affairs, Bengal Vs. J.J. Andrews, (1931) I.L.R. 50 Cal. 519].

Daily Hours (Section 54): No adult worker shall be required or allowed to work in a factory for more than 9 hours in any day and 40 hours in a week. However, to facilitate the change of shift, this limit may be exceeded, subject to the previous approval of the Chief Inspector of factories.

Where work of the same kind is carried out by two or more sets of workers working during different periods of the day, each of such sets is called a "group" or "relay" and each of such periods is called "shift" [Section 2(r)].

Classification of Workers: The manager of the factory shall classify the workers into such groups, as he may deem fit and proper. This would depend upon the nature of work, the number of workers in each group, wherein all the adult workers are not required for such work during the same period [Section 61 (4)]. For each group, which is not required to work on a system of shifts, the manager of the factory shall fix the periods during which the group may be required to work. [Section 61 (5)].

Group working on a system of shifts: The manager shall fix the period during which each relay of the group may be required to work on shifts. This is done in spite of the reason that there is already a pre-determined schedule that has been fixed as a system specifying the shift in which the respective relays have to work [Section 61 (6)].

Register of Adult Workers (Section 62): Registers disclosing the particulars of adult workers working in the factory shall be maintained by the manager incorporating the changes from time to time. Registers shall show (a) the name of each adult worker in the factory, (b) the nature of his work, (c) the group, if any, in which he is included, (d) the place or spot where his group works on shifts, the relay to which he is allotted; and (e) such other particulars as may be prescribed.

Work in accordance with Notice (Section 63): All adult workers who are required or allowed to work in the factory, shall be in accordance with the notice periods of work as displayed on the general notice board and in conformity with the entries made in the register of adult workers.

It shall be the duty of the occupier or manager in the factory, not to allow any adult worker beyond the stipulated period of hours of work. Furthermore, he shall not allow the total number of workers to exceed the number that has already been notified and allocated for work. The plea of payment of overtime wages would not justify employing a worker to do work beyond the usual hours of work.

Holidays (Sections 52 & 53)

No adult worker shall be required or allowed to work in a factory, on the first day of the week, which is a Sunday. This would mean that a worker, shall have a holiday for every six days of continuous work. However, the manager may call upon a worker to work on a Sunday. In such cases, one day holiday must be given either out of the 3 days preceding the Sunday or out of the 3 days succeeding the Sunday. Before making this arrangement, a manager shall deliver a notice to the office of the inspector expressing his intention to that effect.

Furthermore, notice must also be displayed in the factory, intimating such change. No substitution can however be made, in such a way that it makes a worker to work for more than 10 days consecutively. Sunday, shall for the purpose of calculating weekly hours of work be included in the preceding week, where any worker works on a Sunday.

Compensatory Holidays: It is mandatory that a worker shall be allowed compensatory holidays of equal number to the holidays so lost. This arises on account of the worker being deprived of the weekly holidays under Section 52 made by the State Government exempting the factory from such provisions. The compensatory holidays must be allowed to the workman within 2 months or within a month in which the substitution of such holidays becomes due. The manner in which compensatory holidays has to be allowed, is prescribed by the State Government.

Annual Leave with Wages (Section 79 to 82)

Section 78 to 84 of the Factories Act deal with annual leave with wages. If any award or agreement including settlement or contract of service provides for a longer annual leave with wages under provisions of Section 79 to 82, the worker shall be entitled to such leave. But there cannot be any award or settlement reducing the annual leave as provided under the Act.

Rules Relating to Annual Leave with Wages (Section 79)

There are two cumulative conditions that are said to be mandatory for the purpose of availing of annual leave with wages: (a) A worker should have put in continuous years of service which means that he should have actually worked for 240 days or more during the calendar year. (b) During that year, for every 20 days of actual work put in by him, a workman becomes eligible for one day rest leave in the succeeding year. In the case of a child, one day for every 15 days of work performed during the previous calendar year.

In spite of the fact that a worker might not have completed 240 days in a calendar year, the legal representative or nominee of such worker shall be entitled to claim such earned wages proportionately before the expiry of the second working day from the date of such discharge or dismissal or quitting.

(2) However, if a worker has been superannuated or has expired, then such earned wages must be settled before the expiry of two months from the date of such superannuation or death [Section 79 (2)].

(3) In calculating leave period, fraction of leave of half a day or more shall be treated as one full day's leave. The unavailed leave by a worker shall be carried forward to the succeeding year, provided no such accumulation of unavailed leave shall exceed 30 days in a year. In case of excess, unavailed earned leave would lapse. But the number of times the leave that may be taken during any year shall not exceed 3 times.

Other Provisions of Chapter VIII (Section 81 to 84): A worker who has been allowed earned leave for not less than 4 days in the case of an adult and 5 days in the case of a child, they shall be paid the wages due for the period before their leave begins respectively. If the employer does not make such payment, it shall be recoverable as delayed wages under the provisions of Payment of Wages Act, 1936.

Power to make rules (Section 83): The State Government may make rules directing managers of factories to keep registers containing prescribed particulars and requiring the register to be available for examination by Inspectors.

Power to exempt factories (Section 84): The State Government may exempt a factory from the operation of the leave rules, it is satisfied that its own leave rules provide benefits, which are not less favourable to the workers than that of the statutory leave rules.

Recent Amendments in the Act

Government has introduced the Social Security Scheme for the unorganized sector worker on a pilot basis in 50 districts of the Country, which was launched on 23/01/2004. This covers workers in the unorganized sector drawing not more than Rs. 6500 per month.

The scheme provides,

- A flat rate pension of Rs. 500 per month on retirement at the age of 60 and total disablement. Family pension in case of death of the workers.
- A personal accident insurance cover for rupees one lakh and
- Universal health insurance scheme for a worker and his family at the cost of Rs. 548 per annum for a family of 5 members or Rs. 365 per annum for a family of 3 members.

Further, the Ministry took several measures such as labour welfare funds, welfare fund for overseas Indian workers etc.

The Factories (Amendment) Bill, 2003 was introduced on the Lok Sabha on July 29, 2003. The bill proposes to amend Sec. 66 of the Factories Act, 1948 so as to provide flexibility in the matter of employment of women during night with adequate safeguard for their safety, dignity, honour and transportation from the factory premises to the nearest point of their residence.

The Parliamentary Standing Committee on labour and welfare examined the contents and submitted its report on August 27, 2003. The report of the II National Commission on labour was submitted to the Government on June 29, 2002.

The Factories Act, 1948 was passed with an intention of making the work life of persons employed in factories free from hazards and injuries. The protection is afforded to all workers - men, women, and children. Women and children are given special protection, as they are considered more vulnerable. As the employer prepares the environment, the law seeks to regulate the same in the interests of the workmen. The law provides for scrutiny of the place and approval of plans and specifications before they are registered under the Act for the purpose of ensuring health, safety and welfare of the workers. Appropriate standards are also prescribed. Working hours of adults are made subject to regulations. Employment of children below the age of 14 is prohibited. The law regulates the employment of minors who are permitted to work. Law provides for the entitlement of annual leave with wages. Special provisions are also envisaged to meet certain eventualities.

Labour reforms in India, is much desired, but also feared and misinterpreted. This issue has been a sensitive one ever since the liberalization era begins under the Narasima Rao Government in the early 1990. In the hurry to reform and to keep up with the globalization trend set in motion by the GATT (now replace by the WTO), the immediate forms was on the retrenchment of surplus workers' and the closure of 'SICK' Public and Private Sector units. The TATA's were the Pioneers in introducing a number of 'Firsts' in the field of labour welfare. Well ahead of any Indian legislation on this front, several benefits - the eight hour working day, free medical aid, provident fund, gratuity, leave with pay, maternity benefits were incorporated by the TATA's their work place climate.

INDUSTRIAL DISPUTES ACT, 1947

With the growing industrialization, the number of industrial workers in the country is also increasing rapidly. The ownership of the industries have changed hands from individuals to corporate houses. The expectations of workers have changed. The lifestyle has also undergone a change. The employer-employee relationship thus assumes a great importance in the changing scenario. Every one expects industrial harmony; it can be achieved only through satisfactory industrial relations.

INDUSTRIAL RELATIONS

Industrial relations' is a dynamic and developing concept. It refers to the general web of relationship normally obtaining between the employers and the employees and includes the complex relations between trade unions and management.

Industrial relations are an integral aspect of social relations arising out of employer-employee interaction in modern industries, which are regulated by the State in conjunction with organized social forces. The Encyclopedia Britannica (1961) states of industrial relations as "a concept extended to denote the relations of the State with employers. Workers and their organizations. The subject includes individual relations and joint consultations between employers and workers at their places of work; collective relations between employers and their organizations and trade unions; and the part played by the State in regulating these relations".

The State cannot remain a silent spectator in the hope that the relations will on their own reach the state of harmony. That is why under the industrial Disputes Act, the appropriate Government, where it feels that there may be an industrial dispute, refers the matter to adjudication suo moto. Thus, "industrial relations' is not merely a simple relationship; it is a functional, inter-related complexity and requires inter-disciplinary approach.

INTEREST GROUPS IN INDUSTRIAL RELATIONS

Interest groups in industrial relations are the parties involved in it. John Dunlop in the preface to his work "Industrial Relations System" (1958) says: "Industrial societies necessarily create industrial relations, defined as the complex of interrelations among workers, managers and government," The interest groups, therefore, are: as:

- Workers and their organizations
- Managers (employers) and their organizations
- The Government

Each group has different interests and priorities. The workers and their organizations want higher wages, good working conditions and other benefits like medical insurance, accident benefits etc. As against these, the employers and their organizations want maximum productivity at the lowest possible cost. They, therefore, offer lowest possible wages, although the unit may have capacity to pay higher wages, want long working hours and no other expenses. The interests of the first two groups are thus conflicting.

We have, however, seen that there are attitudinal changes in both the groups and they have realised that both of them need to be reasonable in their approach. The third interest group is the government. It is the responsibility of the government to ensure that there is an atmosphere of industrial peace and harmony. Thus, when the government apprehends that there may be an industrial dispute, it refers the matter for adjudication. The government endeavours to see that the industrial harmony is maintained even when there is an impending dispute.

INDUSTRIAL RELATIONS IN INDIA

In order to understand the issued and problems associated with industrial relations, it is desirable to study its various evolutionary phases. Practically speaking, the growth of industrial relations in India is in no way different from that of other parts of the globe. The various stages of industrial relations progressed from primitive stage to factory or industrial capitalism stage.

Ancient scriptures and laws of our country laid emphasis on the promotion and maintenance of peaceful relations between capital and labour. From the very early days, craftsmen and 3 workers felt the necessity of being united. The utility of unions has been stated in Sukla Yajurveda Samhita, "if men are united, nothing can deter them." Kautilyas's Arthashastra gives a comprehensive picture of the organization and functions of the social and political institutions of India and a good description of unions of employees, craftsmen or artisans. There were well-organised guilds, which worked according to their own byelaws for the management of the unions.

However, there were no organizations of workers during the Mughal rule. The labourers were entirely dependent on their masers and forced work was taken from them. Historical evidence further shows the existence of rules of conduct and prescribed procedure for the settlement of disputes for promoting cordial relations between the parties. The working relations, however, in those days were more or less of a personal character and are very much distinguishable from the present day industrial relations as have gradually developed with the growth of large scale industries.

A study of modern industrial relations in India can be made in three distinct phases which are as follows:

- The first phase can be considered to have commenced from the middle of the nineteenth century and ended by the end of the First World War.
- The second phase comprises the period thereafter till the attainment of independence in 1947, and
- The third phase represents the post-independence era.

OBJECTS AND SCOPE OF THE ACT

The object of the Industrial Disputes Act is to make provision for the investigation and settlement of industrial disputes. The Act is primarily meant for regulating the relations of employers and workmen, past, present and future. The principal aim of the Act is to encourage collective bargaining and to maintain industrial peace by preventing illegal strikes and lockouts and to provide lay off and retrenchment compensation.

The Act was passed with a view to removing certain shortcomings found in the working of the Trade Disputes Act, 1929. It came into force on the first day of April 1947 [sec. 1(3)].

It extends to the whole of India [Sec.1 (2)]. It extends to all industries whether they are carried on by private owners or by the Government. The Act has been amended from time to time. The latest amendment was made in 1984.

Thus, though the main object of the Act is to provide for investigation and settlement of industrial disputes, the amendment Act seeks to ensure speedier resolution of industrial disputes by removing procedural delays. Besides creating an efficient statutory machinery for the settlement of industrial disputes and thereby promoting industrial harmony, the Act also seeks to achieve certain other objects, referred to as 'certain other purposes' in the preamble.

These objects are:

- Promoting measures for securing and preserving amity and good relations between employer and workmen.
- Enquiring into any matter connected with or relevant to an industrial dispute.
- Promoting the settlement of industrial disputes.
- Adjudication of industrial disputes.

- Reference of individual disputes to grievance settlement authorities.
- Voluntary reference of disputes to arbitration.
- Prevention of illegal strikes and lock-outs.
- Compensation for lay-off and retrenchment of workmen.
- Provision for the payment of wages from the date of the award till the suit pending before courts of law is decided.
- Prevention of unfair labour practices.

These objects of the Act Center round the securing of industrial harmony and social justice.

DEFINTIONS

The following are some of the important definitions:

Appropriate Government: It means in relation to any industrial dispute concerning any industry carried on by or under the authority of the Central Government or by a railway company, or any controlled industry as may be specified, or n relation to an industrial dispute concerning banking or an insurance company, a mine, or an oil-field or a major port, the Central Government; and In relation to any industrial dispute other than those specified above, the appropriate Government would be the State Government. The general rule is that an industrial dispute arising between an employer and his employees would be referred for adjudication by the State Government except in the cases mentioned above. The definition is exhaustive.

Average pay [Sec.2 (aaa)]: This clause lays down the manner of calculating the average pay for the purpose of payment of compensation at the time of retrenchment of a workman. The determination of average pay is to be made in a different way in the case of

- Monthly paid workmen,
- Weekly paid workmen, and
- Daily paid workmen.

The average pay is calculated in the following manner for the different categories of workers:

- In the case of monthly paid workmen, the average of the wages paid for three complete calendar months;
- In the case of weekly paid workmen, the average of the wages paid for four complete weeks;

- In the case of daily paid workmen, the average of the wages paid for twelve full working days.

The period of three months, four weeks or twelve days as specified above, must precede the day on which the average pay becomes payable. In case a workman has not worked for the period specified above, the average pay shall be calculated as the average of wags paid to the workmen for the period he actually worked.

Award [Sec.2 (d)]: An award is an interim or final determination of an industrial dispute or any question relating thereto and by a labour court, industrial tribunal, national industrial tribunal or an arbitrator under Section 10-A. Interim award means a provisional or temporary relief. Determination implies decision one-way or the other. An order of labour Court, industrial Tribunal or National Industrial Tribunal granting or refusing to grant any of the relief's, which have been asked for would fall within the term 'award'.

Closure [Sec.2 (cc)]: It means the permanent closing down of a place of employment or part thereof. Public Utility Service: The phrase public utility service means.

- Any railway service or any transport service for the carriage of passengers or goods by road, water or air;
- Any section of an industrial establishment on the working of which the safety of the establishment or the workmen employed therein depends;
- Any postal, telegraph or telephone service;
- Any industry which supplies power, light or water to the public;
- Any system of public conservancy or sanitation;
- Any industry specified in the First Schedule which the appropriate government many, if satisfied that public emergency or public interest so requires, by notification in the Official Gazette, declare to be a public utility service for a specified period not exceeding six months in the first instance. The appropriate government, if necessary, may extend it from time to time.

Industry [Sec.2 (j)]: In the light of the judgment in Bangalore Water Supply Case, the term 'Industry' has been defined in Sec.2 (j) as amended in 1982 as follows: 'Industry' means any systematic activity carried on by co-operation between an employer and his workmen (whether such workmen are employed by such employer directly or by or through any agency including a contractor) for the production, supply or distribution of goods or services with a view to satisfy human wants or wished (not being wants or wishes which are merely spiritual or religious in nature). It makes no difference whether or not

a. Any capital has been invested for the purpose of carrying on such activity; or

b. Such activity is carried on with a motive to make any gain or profit.

'Industry' includes:

- Any activity of the Dock. Labour Board established under Section 5-A of the Dock Workers (Regulation of Employment) Act, 1948.
- Any activity relating to the promoting of sales or business or both carried on by an establishment.

Industrial Dispute [Sec.2 (k)]: It means any dispute or difference between:

- Employers and employees;
- Employers and workmen; or
- Workmen and workmen, which is connected with
  a. The employment or non-employment
  b. The terms of employment or,
  c. The conditions of labour of any reason

In the ordinary language an industrial dispute is implied to mean a dispute between the workmen and the management.

The definition of 'industrial dispute' contains the following two limitations:

- The adjective 'industrial' related the dispute to an industry as defined in the Act, and
- The definition expressly states that not disputes and differences of all sorts but only these, which bear upon the relationship of employers and workmen and the terms of employment and the conditions of labour, are contemplated.

Individual and Collective Disputes: The industrial disputes may be:

1. Individual disputes or
2. Collective disputes.

Now Section 2A of the Act provides that where any employer discharges, dismisses, retrenches or otherwise terminates the services of an individual workman, any dispute or difference between that workman and his employer connected with, or arising out of such discharge, dismissal, retrenchment or termination shall be deemed to be an industrial dispute even if no other workman nor any union of workman is a party to the dispute. A collective dispute may relate to any of the following matters:

- Wages, bonus, profit sharing, gratuity, compensatory and other allowances.
- Hours of work leave with wages, holidays.
- Rules of discipline, retrenchment of workmen, closure of establishment, rationalisation.

All collective disputes are industrial disputes and not vice versa.

Lay-off [Sec.2 (kkk0]: It means the failure, refusal or inability of an employer on account of the shortage of coal, power or raw material or the accumulation of stocks or the breakdown of machinery or natural calamity or for any other connected reason to give employment to a workman whose name is borne on the muster rolls of his industrial establishment and who has not been retrenched. Lay-off does not involve alteration in the conditions of service. A lay off is not the same this as the order of dismissal. It is more akin to an order of suspension.

Lock-out: It means temporary closing of a place of employment or the suspension of work or the refusal by an employer to continue to employ any number of persons employed by him. Under the present definition, two alternative acts of the employer constitute a lockout.

- Temporary closing of a place of employment or suspension of work; or
- Refusal to continue to employ any number of persons employed by him.

The First Schedule: The appropriate Government may, if satisfied that public emergency or interest so requires, by notification in the official Gazette, declare any industry specified in the First Schedule to be a public utility service for the purposes of the industrial Disputes Act for such period as may be specified in the notification.

Retrenchment [Sec.2 (oo)]: The term as used in the industrial Disputes Act means the termination by the employer of the service of a workman for any reason whatsoever otherwise than as a punishment inflicted by way of disciplinary action. Thus, the discharge of a workman on the ground that she did not pass the test, which would have enabled her to be confirmed, was 'Retrenchment' [Santosh Gupta Vs State Bank of Patiala, AIR (1980) SC 687.

'Retrenchment' does not, however, include-

- Voluntary retirement of a workman; or
- Retirement of the workman on reaching the age of superannuation if the contract of employment between the employer and workman contains a stipulation in the behalf; or
- Termination of the service of a workman on the ground of continued ill health.

Settlement [Sec.2 (p)]: It means-

- A settlement arrived at in the course of conciliation proceedings which may be held by a conciliation officer or Board of Conciliation, and includes
- A written agreement between the employer and workmen arrived at otherwise than in the course of conciliation proceeding where such agreement has been signed by the parties thereto in the prescribed manner and a copy thereof has been sent to an officer authorised in this behalf by the appropriate Government and the conciliation officer.

Strike [Sec.2 (q)]: It means-

- A cessation of work by a body of persons employed in any industry acting in combination; or
- A concerted refusal of any number of persons who are or have been so employed to continue to work or to accept employment; or
- A refusal under a common undertaking of any number of such persons to continue to work or to accept employment.

But mere absence of a workman from work does not amount to taking part in a strike within the meaning of the Industrial Disputes Act, 1947. There should be some evidence to show that his absence was the result of some concert between him and other persons and they would not continue to work.

Workman [Sec.2(s)]: 'Workman' means any person (including an apprentice0 employed in any industry to do any manual, unskilled, skilled, technical, operational, clerical or supervisory work for hire or reward. His terms of employment may be express or implied. For the purpose of any proceeding under this Act in relation to an industrial dispute, 'workman' includes any person who has been dismissed, discharged or retrenched in connection with, or as a consequence of that dispute, or whose dismissal, discharge or retrenchment has led to that dispute.

Authorities Under the Act

The Act provides for the constitution of various authorities for the purpose of prevention and settlement of industrial disputes. These are as under -

- Works committee
- Conciliation officers
- Board of conciliation
- Courts of inquiry
- Labour courts
- Industrial tribunals, and
- National tribunals

A brief description of the constitution, powers and duties of the various authorities is given below:

1. Work Committee (Sec.3): Constitution: Section 3 of the Act empowers the appropriate Government to constitute a works committee by a general or special order in a manner, which may be prescribed. There are two conditions, which must be satisfied before a works committee can be constituted:

   i. The establishment must be an industrial establishment.

   ii. One hundred or more workmen should either be presently employed or should have been employed on any day in the preceding twelve months.

   The works committee must be composed of the representatives of the employers and the workmen engaged in the industrial establishment and must be equal in number. It is further provided that the representatives of the workmen shall be chosen in the prescribed manner and in consultation with the registered trade union.

2. Conciliation Officers (Sec.4): As in the case of a Works Committee, the constitution of which is left to the discretion of the appropriate Government, so also in the case of conciliation

officers the appropriate government may as per Section 4 of the Act, appoint by notification in the official Gazette, such number of conciliation officers as it thinks fit.

3. Board of Conciliation: In similar manner, a board of conciliation may also be constituted to promote the settlement of industrial disputes. A board will consist of a chairman and two or four other members, as the appropriate government thinks fit. The chairman shall be an independent person and the other members shall be person's appointed in equal numbers to represent the parties to the dispute on the recommendation of the parties concerned. If any party fails to make a recommendation with in the prescribed time, the appropriate government shall appoint such persons as it thinks fit to represent that party.

   Conciliation proceedings before a board are similar in nature to those before a conciliation officer. But members of the boards of conciliation enjoy more powers than those enjoyed by conciliation officers. However, unlike a conciliation officer, the board cannot admit a dispute in conciliation on its own; the board has no jurisdiction until the government makes a reference to it.

4. Courts of Inquiry (Sec.6): The appropriate Government may, by notification in the official Gazette, constitute a Court of Inquiry 9hereinafter called the court) for inquiring into any matter appearing to be connected with or relevant to an industrial dispute [Sec.6 (1)].

5. Labour Courts (Sec.7): The appropriate Government may, constitute one or more Labour Courts for adjudication of industrial dispute relating to any matter specified in the Second Schedule. These courts shall also perform such other functions as may be assigned to them under the Act [Sec.7 (1)].

The Second Schedule: Matters within the jurisdiction of labour courts are as follows:

- The propriety or legality of an order passed by an employer under the standing orders;
- The application and interpretation of standing orders;
- Discharge or dismissal of workmen including reinstatement of, or grant of relief to, workmen wrongfully dismissed;

- Withdrawal of any customary concession or privilege;
- Illegality or otherwise of a strike or lock-out; and
- All matters other than those specified in the Third Schedule.
- A labour court shall consist of one person only to be appointed by the appropriate Government.

6. Industrial Tribunals (Sec.7-A): The appropriate Government may, by notification in the official Gazette, constitute one or more Industrial Tribunals (hereinafter called the tribunals) for the adjudication of industrial disputes relating to any matter, whether specified in the Second Schedule or the Third Schedule and for performing such other functions as may be assigned to them under this Act [Sec. 7-A (1)].

The Third Schedule: Matters within the jurisdiction of industrial Tribunals.

- Wages including the period and mode of payment.
- Compensatory and other allowances;
- Hours of work and rest intervals;
- Leave with wages and holidays;
- Bonus, profit sharing, provident fund and gratuity.
- Shift working otherwise, than in accordance with standing orders;
- Classification by grades;
- Rules of discipline;
- Rationalisation;
- Retrenchment of workmen and closure of establishment; and
- Any other matter that may be prescribed.

7. National Tribunals (Sec. 7-B): The Central Government may, by notification in the official Gazette, constitute one or more National Industrial Tribunals (hereinafter called National Tribunal) for the adjudication of industrial disputes which, in the opinion of the Central Government, involve questions of national importance or are of such a nature that industrial establishments situated in more than one State are likely to be interested in, or affected by, such disputes [Sec.7-B (1)].

   Notice of Change: The object of Section 9-A of the Act is to prohibit an employer from making any change in the conditions of service applicable to his workmen in respect of any matter specified in the Fourth Schedule unless he has complied with the following conditions.

- A notice in prescribed manner of the nature of the change proposed to be effected must be given to the workmen likely to be affected by such change; and
- A period of twenty-one days from the date of notice must have expired.

The appropriate Government has the power to include any other rules or regulations in this category by notification in its official Gazette. The matters in respect of which notice is required are enumerated in the Fourth Schedule to the Act and are as follows

- Wages including the period and mode of payment.
- Contribution paid or payable by the employer to any provident fund or pension fund.
- Compensatory and other allowances.
- Hours of work and other rest intervals.
- Leave with wages and holidays
- Starting, alteration or discontinuance of shift working otherwise than in accordance with standing orders.
- Classification by grades.
- Withdrawal of any customary concession or privilege or change in usage
- Introduction of new rules of discipline or alteration of existing rules except in so far as they are provided in standing orders
- Rationalisation, standardisation or improvement of plant or technique, which is likely to lead to retrenchment of workmen.
- Any increase or reduction (other than casual) in the number of persons employed or to be employed in any occupation or process or department or shift not occasioned by circumstances over which the employer has no control.

Award and Settlement

Award [Sec.2 (b)] It means an interim or a final determination of any industrial dispute or of any question relating thereto by any Labour Court, industrial Tribunal or National Tribunal. It also includes an arbitration award made under Sec. 10-A.

Settlement [Sec.2 (p)] It means (a) a settlement arrived at in the course of a conciliation proceeding which may be held by a conciliation officer or a Board or conciliation, and includes (b) A written agreement between the employer and workmen arrived at otherwise than in the course of conciliation proceedings.

i. Where such agreement has been signed by the [parties thereto in the prescribed manner and
ii. A copy thereof has been sent to an officer authorised in this behalf by the appropriate Government and the conciliation officer.

The 'Award' of a Labour Court or industrial Tribunal or National Tribunal shall be in writing and shall be signed by its presiding officer [Sec. 16(2)].

STRIKES AND LOCK-OUTS

Meaning of Strike: According to Section 2(q) of the Act " 'strike' means a cessation of work by persons employed in any industry acting in combination, or a concerted refusal, or a refusal under a common understanding of any number of persons who are or have been so employed to continue to work or to accept employment."

The ingredients of a strike as laid down in this section are:

- Cessation of work,
- Plurality of workmen who should cease to work or stop working,
- Refusal should be by a concerted action or under common understanding, and
- Refusal should be by persons who are or have been so employed in an industry.

Meaning of Lock-out: Section 2(1) defines lock-out thus: "Lock-out" means temporary closing of a place of employment, or the suspension of work, or the refusal by an employer to continue to employ any number of persons employed by him.

The requirements of lock-out, according to this definition are:

- Temporary closure of the place of employment;
- Suspension of work;
- Refusal to employ;
- By an employer; and

- To continue to employ any number of persons employed by him.

Illegal strikes and lock-outs (Sec.24): A strike or a lock-out shall be illegal if

- It is commenced or declared in contravention of Sec.22 or Sec.23; or

  It is continued in contravention of an order made under Sec.10 (3) or Sec. 10-A (4-A), [Sec.24 (1)].

Penalties Regarding Strikes and Lock-outs

1. Penalty for illegal strike [Sec.26 (1)]: Any workman, who commences, continues or otherwise acts in furtherance of a strike, which is illegal, shall be punishable with imprisonment for a term, which may extend to one month, or with fine, which may extend to Rs.0 or with both.
2. Penalty for illegal lock-out [Sec.26 (2)]: Any employer, who commences, continues or otherwise acts in furtherance of lock-out, which is illegal, shall be punishable with imprisonment for a term which may extend to one month, or with fine which may extend to Rs.1, 000 or with both.
3. Penalty for instigation etc. (Sec.27): Any person who instigates or incites others to take part in, or A otherwise acts in furtherance of, a strike or lockout, which is illegal, shall be punishable with imprisonment for term which may extend to six months or with a fine which may extend to Rs.1,000 or with both. In the case Raja Kulkarni Vs. State of Bombay AIR (1954) SC 73, it was held that Sec.27 did not impose any unreasonable restriction upon the fundamental rights guaranteed by Articles 19(1)(a) and (19(1)(c) of the constitution.
4. Penalty for giving financial aid for illegal strike and lock-out (Sec.28): Any person who knowingly expends or applies any money in direct furtherance or support of any illegal strike or lock-out shall be punishable with imprisonment for a term which may extend to six months, or with fine which may extend to Rs.1, 000 or with both.

Lay-off and Retrenchment

Meaning of lay-off: According to Section 2(kkk) lay-off (with us grammatical variations and cognate expressions) means the failure, refusal or inability of an employer to give employment to a workman, whose name is borne on the muster roll of his industrial establishment and who has not been retrenched. They lay-off may be due to shortage of coal, power or raw materials or the accumulation of stocks or breakdown of machinery. A workman shall be deemed to be laid off for the day if he presents himself for work at the appointed time during normal working hours on any day and the employer does not give employment to his within two hours of his so presenting.

Meaning of retrenchment [Sec 2 (oo)]: Retrenchment means the termination by the employer of the services of a workman for any reason whatsoever, otherwise than as a punishment inflicted by way of disciplinary action. It, thus, implies this discharge of surplus labours or staffs by the employer for any reason.

Retrenchment, however, does not include-

- Retrenchment of worker either (a) voluntarily, or (b) on reaching the age of superannuation if the contract of employment between the employer and the employee concerned contains a stipulation in that behalf;
- Termination of the service of workman on the ground of continued ill health;
- Termination of the service of the workmen as a result of the nonrenewal of the contract of employment provided a stipulation in that behalf is contained in the contract.

Some Distinctions

1. Lay-off and lock-out: Both lay-off and lock-out resemble each other in some respects. Both are of a temporary nature and arise out of an emergency, though the nature of emergencies in each case is different. Both in lay-off and lock-out the relationship of employer and workmen is only suspended and is not terminated. However, there are following points of distinction between lay-off and lock-out:
    - Lay-off generally occurs in a continues business, whereas lockout is closure of business for the time being.
    - In case of lay-off the employer is unable to give employment to one or more workmen on account of the reasons specified in Section 2(kkk), whereas in case of lock-out the employer deliberately closes the business for reasons, which have no connection with the causes specified in Section 2(kkk).

- In case of lay-off, the employer may be liable to pay compensation as provided in Section 25-C, but this liability cannot be invoked in case of lock-out. The liability of the employer in cases of lock-out will depend upon whether the lockout was justified and legal or not.
- Lock-out is resorted to by the employer as a weapon of collective bargaining while lay-off is due to trade reasons.
- The Act imposes certain penalties on lock-out but there are none in case of lay-off.

2. Lay off and closure: A lay-off is different from closure of business. Lay-off does not mean closing of the business. Lay off means temporary suspension and not discontinuance of the business. Closure, on the other hand, means closing of the business permanently or temporarily for an indefinite period by the management. In the case of closure there in no question of laying-off workers. The workers are discharged i.e. relationship of employer and workman comes to an end.
3. Lock-out and closure: The distinction between the closure and the lock-out is well settled. In case of a closure, the employer does not merely close down the place of business, but he closes business itself while lock-out indicates the closure of the place of business and not the closure of the business itself. Lock-out means suspension of the work and a discontinuance of the carrying on the business. If an employer shuts down his place of business as an instrument of coercion, or as mode of exerting pressure on the employees there would be lockout. If, on the other hand, he shuts down his work because he cannot, for instance, get the raw materials or because he is unable to sell the goods or because he is losing money, that would not be a lock-out.
4. Lock-out and retrenchment: The points of distinction between lock-out and retrenchment are as follows:
   - Lock-out is temporary while retrenchment is permanent
   - In case of retrenchment the relationship of employer and employee comes to an end at the instance of the employer, in case of lock-out the relationship is only suspended, it does not come to an end.
   - Lock-out is with a motive to coerce the workmen; while the intention behind retrenchment is to dispense with surplus labour.

- Lock-out is due to an industrial dispute, while in the case of retrenchment there is no such dispute.

It is gratifying to note that apart from the fundamental rights, our Constitution embodies within itself, in Part IV, Directive Principles of State policy. The functions and duties of the states as contained in the directive principles have given rise to the concept of social justice. The old idea of laissez faire has given place to a new idea of welfare state. The philosophy of social, economic and political justice have been given a place of pride in our Constitution, as well as in the aims and objectives of ILO. The development and growth of industrial law presents a close analogy to the development and growth of constitutional law. A series of labour enactments covering labour welfare and social security were enacted for protecting and promoting the overall welfare of different categories of working class. The central and some state governments have enacted laws on industrial relations. The three enactments by the central government in the field of industrial relations are (a) the Trade Unions Act, which provides for registration of trade unions;(b) the Industrial Employment (standing orders) Act which makes provision for certification of standing orders; and (c) the Industrial Disputes Act which lays down a machinery for the prevention and settlement of industrial disputes.

MINIMUM WAGES ACT, 1948

The Minimum Wages Act of 1948 is not only a measure of social security for the poverty stricken workers, but it is also a device for improving the standard of living of the downtrodden and thereby paving the way for their betterment and ultimate welfare.

The continuing tendency among the employer is only to exploit the labourers who happen to be illiterates and who never possessed the necessary prowess to fight against the ingenuity of the employers.

The Minimum Wages Act:

- Assures wages so as to help the workers to eke out their livelihood, at least to an extent of sustaining the adversities, namely, rise in the cost of living.
- Prevents the employers from exploiting the labourers by paying wages far below their needs; and
- Lays down principles for fixation of wages on a need based scale.

DEFINITION

Though Minimum Wages has not been defined anywhere in the Minimum Wages Act, however it can be defined generally. In common sense, minimum wages is the bare subsistence money required by the worker not only to meet the basic needs such as food, shelter and clothing but it is also includes monies required for medical expenses, education for children and traveling expenses to a worker in a family. Family must consists of husband, wife, and two children.

OBJECTS AND SCOPE OF THE ACT

The Minimum Wages Act contemplates

- The wages that are paid to the workers should meet their physical needs and at the same time.
- Keep them above starvation level.
- It should ensure sustenance for their family; and
- Also enable them to subsist by preserving their efficiency as workmen in day-to-day life.

Norms to be followed for fixation of minimum wages:

a. Irrespective of the financial adversities and other problems, an employer, has to pay compulsory minimum wages to his workmen.

b. Wages paid to workmen must be sufficient to provide, a standard family, with food, shelter, clothing, medical care and education for their children. This is known as fair wage.

c. (i)Fair wage is not a living wage. It is a mean between living wage and minimum wage. The minimum wage itself is slightly above the bare minimum. [Sandash Ltd., Vs. Union of India A.I.R. (1958) S.C. 578] (ii) Living wage meets the normal ne4ds of an average worker as a human being, living in a civilized society. Living wage not only ensures bare physical subsistence, but also maintenance of health and decency, conducive to the general interest of the public. [Bijoy Cotton Mills. Vs. State of Ajmer A.I.R. (1955) S.C.33.] (iii) Concept of minimum wage, fair wage and living wage is bound to change in accordance with the growth and development of industries and living standard of the employees. [Standard Vacuum Refining Co. of India vs. Its Workmen A.I.R. (19610 S.C. 895] (iv) Fair wage, although may be set at the level of minimum wage at the beginning, yet, it can be enhanced in gradual stages depending upon the capacity of the industry to pay. Hence, the lowest limit of fair wages is at the level of minimum wage and its upper limit may be enhanced to the level of living wage. [Express News paper Pvt. Ltd. Vs. Union of India A.I.R. (1959) S.C.R. 12]

d. (i) Wages required by the employees is more relevant than the financial capacity of the industries to meet the requirement of the labourers. [Arbuda Bhavan vs. State of Maharashtra 91991) Lab.I.C. 1671 Bom.] (ii) Satisfaction of the workers from the point of view of providing them a suitable pay packet serves as a good dev ice to motivate the workers to contribute to the growth of the industries. [Hindustan Antibiotics Ltd. Vs. Their Workmen A.I.R. (1967) S.C.948.]

e. Minimum wages are paid solely on the requirements of the worker of the family.

f. The directive principals of the State policy in Article 43 of the Indian Constitution imposes an obligation on then State to formulate suitable legislation in providing economic organizations in the form of industrial nits in such away so as to ensure a living wage to workmen.

Components in the Minimum Wage

- It must be understood that wages that are paid to a workman is not paid exclusively to him, but it is paid to his family as a unit. Therefore, such a wage should enable a worker to sustain his family by meeting certain necessary expenses which are inevitable; such as (a) Medical expenses
- Expenses to meet education for his children; and
- In some cases, transport charges

Concept of Minimum Wage

Minimum wages that are fixed for workmen has some significance:

- Minimum wages are not fixed on Equation principle, namely, money payable towards wags must be commensurate with the labour output.
- Equally, minimum wages are not based on the Economic principle, namely those who are able financially, must be capable of paying more to the workers.

- On the other hand, it is based on Ethical principle of pre-judging and assessing the needs of a workman and his family as a unit and making provision for his wages. To put it in a nutshell, minimum wages are considered to be need-based wages, which is according to the directive principle of our Constitution.

Cost of Living Index [Section 2 (d)]: The framework of minimum wags depends upon cost of living index, now known as Consumer Index. Cost of living forms an integral part in the fixation of wages for workers. But then, the cost of essential commodities increases now and then because of which a workman finds it hard to lead his life. The essential requirements for providing a staple food consisting of protein, carbohydrates, fat, vitamin, etc., are computed and calculated in terms of price from the available essential commodities. Calculation of Cost of Living Index: Upto 100 points they merge with the salary. Over and above 100 points, when there is an increase in the cost of these essential commodities, the workers find it difficult to procure these commodities to eke out their livelihood. This renders the position of a workers equivalent to a stage termed as 'between the cup and the lip."

Minimum Wages, Fair Wages and Living Wages

Fixation of wage is no doubt a subtle task, which requires a device for balancing the demand of social justice and the need for improving the sources of national income from the point of raising the standard of living. Payment of wages is mandatory. Irrespective of the fact whether an industry is big or small. Whether it makes profit or not, minimum wages must be paid to the workmen concerned. A human being must always be allowed to lead a docent life; hence it is not permitted to pay wages, which is hardly sufficient to make the workman to keep his body and soul together. Minimal requirements of the worker concerned should be provided under minimum wages. A living wage has been define4d as the wage received for normal needs of an average employee regarded as a human being living in a civilized community. A living wage enables a worker to enjoy comfort in life. The wages mentioned above are not static as they keep on changing according to the economic scenario of the nation. To neutralize or standardize the two extreme wage limits, namely, minimum wage and living wage, concept of fair wage is introduced as a via media, as given below:

- Ideal wage
- Living wage

- Fair wage
- Minimum wages

A fair wage is said to be a mean between minimum wage and living wage. Every attempt was made to introduce a fair wage, but then it could not be fixed at the upper limit. Hence, sometimes, fair wage also descends to the level of minimum wage.

Minimum wage is said to be the starting stage from the point of view of offering social security to workmen. Laborer's demand should always be viewed with sympathy and hence minimum wages must be paid compulsorily. If an employer is unable to pay even minimum wages or it becomes impossible on his part to carry on his business, then it would be better for his to close his business.

For the purpose of understanding the Minimum Wages Act, it essential to know the following definitions contained in the Act "Appropriate Government' [Section 2(b)] means-

a. In relation to any scheduled employment carried on by or under the authority of the central Government or a railway administration or in relation to a mine, oil-field or major port, or any corporation established by the Central Government, and

b. In relation to any other scheduled employment, the State Government.

c. Competent authority means the authority appointed by the appropriate Government by notification in its official Gazette to ascertain from time to time the cost of living index number applicable to the employees employed in the scheduled employment specified in such notification;

d. "Cost of living index number" in relation to employees in any scheduled employment in respect of which minimum rates of wages have been fixed, means the index number ascertained and declared by the competent authority by notification in the official Gazette to be the cost of living index number applicable to employees in such employment;

e. "Employer" means any person who employs, whether directly or through another person, or whether on behalf of himself or any other person, one or more employees in any scheduled employment in respect of which minimum rates of wages have been fixed under this Act, and includes, Except in sub-section (3) of Section 26;

f. "Prescribed" means prescribed by rules made under this Act;

g. "Scheduled employment" means an employment specified in then Schedule, or any process or branch of work forming part of such employment;

h. "Wages" means all remunerations, capable of being expressed in terms of money, which would if the terms of the contract of employment, express or implied, were fulfilled, be payable to a person employed in respect of his employment or of work done in such employment and includes house rent allowance.

i. "Employee" means any person who is employed for hire or reward to do any work skilled or unskilled, manual or clerical, in a scheduled employment in respect of which minimum rates of wages have been fixed; and includes an out-worker to whom any articles or materials are given out by another person to be made up, cleaned, washed, altered ornamented, finished, repaired, adapted or otherwise processed for sale for the purposes of the trade or business of that other person where the process is to be carried out either in the home of the outworker or in some other premises not being premises under the control and management of that other person; and also includes an employee declared to be an employee by the appropriate Government; bout does not include any member of the Armed Forces of Union.

Fixation and Revision of Minimum Wages: Fixation and revision of minimum wags could be studied under the following three heads.

- Fixation of minimum wages, how it is done and to whom it is applicable (Section 3).
- Contents of minimum wages (Section 4).
- Procedure for fixing and revising minimum wages (Section 5). Sections 3, 4 and 5 are said to be the operative sections under the Minimum Wages Act.

Fixation of Minimum Wages [Section 3]: The responsibility for fixing the minimum rates of wages is that of the appropriate Government. Section 3 provides that the appropriate Government-

- Shall fix the minimum rates of wages payable to employees employed in an employment specified in Part I or Part II of the Schedule to the Act and in an employment added to either part by notification in the official Gazette [Sec.3 (1)(a)].

- May, in respect of employees employed in an employment specified in Part II of the Schedule, instead of fixing minimum rates of wages for the whole State, fix such rates for a part of the State or for any specified class or classes of such employment in the whole State or part thereof [Provision to Sec. 3(1)(a)].
- Shall review at such intervals not exceeding five years, the minimum rates of wages so fixed and revise the minimum rates if necessary [Sec.3 (1)(b)].

Procedure for Fixing and Revising Minimum Wages (Sec.5): In fixing minimum rates of wages in respect of any scheduled employment for the first time the appropriate Government may follow either of the following methods:

- It shall appoint as many committees and sub-committees as it considers necessary to hold enquiries and advise it in respect of such fixation or revision, as the case may be: or
- It shall, by notification in the official Gazette, publish its proposals, for the information on persons likely to be affected theory and specify a date, not less than two months from the date of the notifications on which the proposals will be taken into consideration [Sec.5 (1)].

Safeguards in Payment of Minimum Wages:

- Wages in kind (Sec.11). Minimum wages payable under this Act will be paid in cash [Sec.11 (1)]. But where it has been the custom to pay wages wholly or partly in kind, the appropriate Government may by notification in the official Gazette, authorize the payment of minimum wages either wholly or partly in kind [Sec.11 (20]. The appropriate Government may by notification in the official Gazette authorize the provision of the supply of essential commodities at confessional rates [Sec.11 (3)].
- Payment of minimum rates of wages (Sec.12). Where in respect of any scheduled employment minimum wages have been fixed, the employer shall pay to every employee wages at a rate not less than the minimum rate of wages fixed for that class of employees in the employment. Such wages shall be paid without any deductions except as may be authorized. Where the contract rate of wages is higher, the statutory obligation does not come into play [Sec.12 (1)]. Section 12 of the Act does not affect

the provisions of the Payment of Wages Act, 1936 [Sec.12 (2)].

ENFORCEMENT OF THE ACT

Inspectors (Sec.19). The appropriate Government may, by notification in the official Gazette, appoint inspectors for the purposes of this Act, and define the local limits within which they shall exercise their functions [Sec. 19(1)]. The powers and functions of the inspectors so appointed are almost similar to those of the inspectors appointed under the Payment of Wages Act, 1936. The inspectors have e to see that the provisions of the Minimum Wages Act are complied with.

Claims (Sec.20). The appropriate Government may, by notification in the official Gazette, appoint an Authority to hear and decide for any specified area all claims

- Arising out of payment less than the minimum rates of wages; or
- In respect of the payment of remuneration for the day of rest under Sec.13 (1)(b) or for work done on days of rest under Sec.13 (1)(c);
- In respect of wages at the overtime rate under Sec. 14 to employees employed or paid in that area [Sec.20 (1)].

Offences and Penalties: Penalties for offences (Secs.22 and 22-A). Any employer who-

- Pays to any employee less than the minimum rates of wages fixed for that employee's class of work, or less than the amount due to his under the provision of this Act; or
- Contravenes any rule or order made under Sec.13, Shall be punishable with imprisonment for a term, which may extend to six months, or with fine, which may extend to Rs.500, or with both [Sec.22]. In imposing any fine for offence under Sec.22, the court shall take into consider on the amount of any compensation already awarded against the accused in any proceedings taken under Sec.20 (Proviso to Sec.22). Further, any employer who contravenes any provision of this Act or of any rule or order made there under shall, if no other penalty is provided for such contravention by the Act, be punishable with fine which may extend to Rs. 500 [Sec.22-A].

Contracting Out [Sec.25]: According to the Section 25 of the Act, any agreement or contract between the employer and the employee by which the employee gives upon his right to minimum, wages or any privilege or concession accruing to his under the Act is null and void, in so far it purports to reduce the minimum rate of wages fixed under the Act. I it immaterial whether the contract or agreement was entered into either before or after the commencement of the Act.

Exemptions and Exceptions (Sec. 26): The appropriate Government may-

- Direct that provisions of this Act shall not be applicable in relation to the wages payable to disabled persons [Sec 26(1)].
- Direct by notification in the official Gazette that the provisions of the Act or any of them shall not apply to all or any class of employees, employed in any scheduled employment [Sec.26 (2)].
- Exempt some specified employments from the application of some or all the provisions of this Act [Sec 26(3)].

Nothing in this Act shall apply to the wages payable by an employer to a member of his family who is living with him and his dependent on him. A member of the employer's family includes his or her spouse or child or parent or brother or sister (Explanation to Sec 26(3)].

Recent Amendments in the Act: On the basis of recommendations of Central Advisory Board in its meeting held on December 19, 2003, the National Minimum Wage has been raised from Rs. 55 to Rs. 66 per day with effect from February 1, 2004.

This act is of interest to women workers, as it sets minimum wages for employees, which include those working on a temporary basis, Piece rate workers and workers paid daily wages. In addition, no employee can be asked to work more than 9 hours a day without additional wages being paid and the normal working hours must be fixed.

This act aims at statutory fixation of minimum wages with a view to prevent the exploitation of workers. It seeks to achieve social justice to workers by securing the enjoyment of minimum wage fixed under the law. There are three levels of wage. They are the living wage, the fair wage and the minimum wage. The components of the minimum wage are set by the standards necessary to cover the basic needs of the workman and to preserve his efficiency. Receipt of the subsistence plus wage fixed under the Act is declared to be the fundamental right under Articles 23 and 21 of the Constitution. The responsibilities fundamental to the scheme envisaged under the Act are two fold. Firstly, the responsibility of fixing and revising the minimum wage is apportioned between the central and state governments. Secondly, the consequential responsibility of paying the same to the workmen is laid on the employer, both public and private, governed by the Act. Two methods are envisaged for fixation and revision of the minimum wage. They are substantially similar. Choice of the mode is left to the discretion of the government. Based upon the necessity, the government may either appoint a committee for enquiry and advice or formulate the proposal and publish the same inviting objections. A separate machinery is constituted for hearing and deciding the claims under Act. With a view to ensure quick and inexpensive justice, summary procedure is envisaged.

WORKMEN'S COMPENSATION ACT, 1923

The Workmen's Compensation Act, 1923, was the first social security measure introduced in Indian prior to independence. The statement of objects and reasons appended to the Bill at the time of its introduction clearly indicates the need to protect workmen from hardship arising from accidents due to the complexity of modern industry.

OBJECT AND SCOPE OF THE ACT

The Act considers compensation payable by an employer to his workmen in the case of an accident as a measure of relief and social security. It enables a workman to get compensation irrespective of his negligence. It also lays down the various amounts payable in case of an accident depending upon the type and extent of injury. The employer now knows the amount of compensation he has to pay and is saved of many uncertainties to which he was subject before the Act came into force.

Accordingly, payment of compensation is the main object of the Act. But yet, it seeks to reduce the number of accidents, mitigates the effect of accidents by providing suitable medical treatment, makes the industry more attractive to labour, increases labour efficiency and provides for a cheaper and quicker disposal of disputes relating to compensation, through special tribunals.

DEFINITIONS

Section 2 gives the definitions of the terms used in the Act. Some of the important definitions are as follows:

Partial Disablement [Section 2(1)(g)]: A disablement may be partial or total. A partial disablement only reduces the earning capacity of a workman, while a total disablement incapacitates a workman, from all work, which he was capable of performing at the time of the accident. Partial disablement may be of temporary or permanent nature. A temporary partial disablement means any disablement, which temporarily reduces the earning capacity of workman in any employment in which he was engaged at the time of the accident causing the disablement. A permanent partial disablement means such a disablement as permanently reduces the earning capacity of workman in every employment, which he was capable of undertaking at the time of the accident causing the disablement. But, every injury specified in part II of schedule I of this Act shall be deemed to result in permanent partial disablement.

The distinction between these two types of disablement depends on the fact as to whether an injury results in reduction of earning capacity in all the employments which the workman was capable of doing or only in that particular employment in which workman was engaged at the time of accident.

Total Disablement [Section 2 (1)(l)]: Total disablement means such disablement as incapacitates a workman for all work which he was capable of performing at the time of the accident resulting in such disablement. In order to constitute total disablement, disablement must be of such a character that the person concerned is unable to do any work and not merely the work, which he was performing at the time of the accident.

A total disablement may be temporary or permanent. A permanent total disablement shall be deemed to result from

- The permanent total loss of the sight of both eyes; or
- From an injury specified in Part I of Schedule I or from any combination of injuries specified in Part II thereof where the aggregate percentage of the loss of earning capacity as specified in the said Part II against those injuries, amounts to one hundred per cent or more.

A carpenter suffered from injury in the course of his employment, which resulted amputation of left hand above elbow. Since a carpenter cannot work with one hand, disablement was held to be total and not a partial [Pratap Narain Singh Deo Vs Srinivas Sabata and another [AIR (1976) SC 222].

Employer's Liability for Compensation: Section. 3 provides for employer's liability to pay compensation to a workman. It lays down that the following conditions must exist before an employer may be held liable to pay compensation to a workman

1. Some personal injury must have been caused to a workman;
2. Such an injury must have been caused by an accident;
3. The accident must have arisen out of and in the course of employment; and
4. The injury must have resulted either in the death of the workman or in his total or partial disablement for a period exceeding three days.

But the employer shall not be liable (except in the case of the injury resulting in the workman's death) to pay compensation in the following cases:

- If the injury did not result into the total or partial disablement of the workman for a period exceeding three days;
- If the workman was at the time of the accident under the influence of drink or drug, or
- If the workman willfully disobeyed an order expressly given or a rule expressly framed for the purpose of securing safety of workman; or
- If the workman willfully removed or disregarded any safety guard or other device which to his knowledge was provided for the purpose of securing his safety.

In the case of disease, no compensation shall be payable to a workman in respect thereof, unless the same is directly attributable to an injury caused by an accident arising out of and in the course of his employment. But in respect of the occupational diseases, specified in Schedule III of the Act, contracted by a workman it shall be presumed that the contracting of the disease amounts to an injury caused by an accident arising out of and in the course of his employment.

Accident Out of Employment: An accident arising out of employment implies a 'casual connection' between the injury and the accident and the work done in the course of employment. Employment should be the distinctive and the proximate cause of the personal injury whether physical or mental. In the case Dennis Vs White, (1917) A.C.479, it was laid down that "when a man runs a risk incidental to his employment and is thereby injured, the injury arises out of employment."

Accident in the Course of Employment: It suggests duration of employment or the period of time during which he employment continues. In the case Saurastra Salt Mfg. Co. Vs Bai Balu Raja (1958) SC 881, the

Supreme Court held "as a rule the employment of a workman does not commence until he has reached the place of employment and does not continue when he has left the place of employment".

Following points in this connection are important to note be noted:

- All movements of a worker from one place to another whether within the premises of the employer or to the premises of some other person in connection with the employment alone shall be taken to be the course of his employment.
- A person who is busy in performing his duty, under the terms of his employment, at any place, shall be taken to be working in the course of employment.
- Break for rest, refreshment, etc., within the premises of the employer is regarded as incidental to work and the worker is supposed to be in the course of his employment even for that period.
- When the workman uses transport provided by the employer for the purpose of going to and from the place of work, he is deemed to be in the course of employment during the time when he uses the transport. [Holmes Vs Great Northern Railway (1900) 2 Q.B.409].

Occupational Disease: Sub-section (2) declares that the contracting of an occupational disease by a workman shall be deemed to be an injury by accident within the meaning of Section 3, and unless the contrary is proved, the accidents shall be deemed to have arisen out of, and in the course of employment.

Employer Not Liable: Section 3(1) of the Act has mentioned the following circumstances in which the employer is not liable to pay compensation to a workman for personal injury caused by accident: They are

- In respect of any injury which does not result in the total or partial disablement of the workman for a period exceeding three days;
- In respect of any injury, not resulting in death, cause by an accident which is directly attributable to
- The workman having been at the time of the accident, under the influence or drink or drugs.
- The willful disobedience of the workman to an order expressly given, or to a rule expressly framed, for the purpose of securing the safety of workman; or

- The willful removal or disregard by the workman of any safety guard or other device, which he knew to have been provided for the purpose of securing the safety of workman.
- According to sub-section (4) of Section 3, if the occupational disease is not directly attributable to a specific injury by accident arising out of and in the course of his employment.
- According to sub-section (5), if the injured workman has instituted a suit in a civil court for damages in respect of the injury, against the employer or any other person, and
- If the accident causing injury or death did not arise out of and in the course of the workman's employment.

Amount of Compensation: The amount of compensation payable to a workman depends on

- The nature of the injury caused by accident;
- The monthly wages of the workman concerned; and
- The relevant factor for working out lump-sum equivalent of compensation amount as specified in Schedule IV (as substituted by the Amendment Act of 1984).

There is no distinction between an adult and a minor worker with respect to the amount of compensation.

Now Section 4 (as substituted by the Amendment Act of 1984) provides for compensation for

- Death;
- Permanent total disablement;
- Permanent partial disablement;
- Temporary disablement, whether total or partial.

Procedure for Claiming Compensation: An injured workman may either file a civil suit for damages against the employer or claim compensation under the Workmen's Compensation Act, 1923. He has to make a choice between these two reliefs. Section 3(5) of the Act provides that no claim for compensation can be made under the Act if the workman has filed a civil suit. It further provides that a workman cannot file a suit for damages in any court of law if

- He has filed a claim under the Workmen's Compensation Act, 1923; or

- There is an agreement between the workmen and his employer providing for the payment of compensation according to the provisions of the Workmen's Compensation Act, 1923.

In a civil suit for damages, the employer can put forward all the defences available to him under the law of torts. Moreover, a civil suit is a risky and costly affair. A claim under the Workmen's Compensation Act, 1923 is safe and less costly.

Appeal (Sec.30): Under Section 30 of the Act, an appeal lies to the High Court from following orders of the Commissioner:

- An order awarding as compensation, a lump sum whether by way of redemption of a half-monthly payment or otherwise or disallowing a claim in full or in part for a lump-sum.
- An order awarding interest or penalty;
- An order refusing to allow redemption of half-monthly payment;
- An order providing for the distribution of compensation among the dependants of a deceased workman, or disallowing any claim of a person alleging himself to be such dependent;
- An order allowing or disallowing any claim for the amount of an indemnity under the provisions of Section 12 (2);
- An order refusing to register a memorandum of agreement of registering the same or providing for the registration of the same subject to conditions.

According to the first proviso to this section, no appeal lies against any order unless a substantial question of law is involved, and in the case of an order other than an order refusing to allow redemption of a half-monthly payment, the amount in dispute is not less than three hundred rupees.

An appeal will not also lie, if the parties have agreed to abide by the decision of the Commissioner, or in which the order of the Commissioner gives effect to an agreement between the parties.

No appeal by an employer under clause (a) above shall lie, unless the memorandum of appeal is accompanied by a certificate by the Commissioner to the effect that the appellant has deposited with him the amount payable under the order appealed against.

The period of limitation for an appeal is 60 days, and the provisions of Section 5 of the Indian Limitation Act, 1908, will also apply to appeal under this section.

Amended Provisions in the Act: The minimum amount of compensation payable under the Workmen's Compensation Act yet has been enhanced from 50,000 to 80,000 in case of death and from 60,000 to 90,000 in case of permanent total disablement with effect from 08/12/2000. From the same date the ceiling of the Maximum amount of compensation has been doubled from Rs. 2.28 lakh to 4.56 lakh in case of death and from Rs. 2.74 lakh to 5.48 lakh in case of permanent total disablement.

The 39th session of Indian Labour conference was held on 16-18 October 2003 and deliberated various issues like child labour, bonded labour, women labour, etc.

India's first social security legislation was passed in 1923. The Workmen's Compensation Act was to provide injury compensation to industrial workers. The Act imposes obligation on the employer to pay compensation for accidents arising out of and in course of employment. The Act was amended in 1962 raising the wage limit to Rs.400 per month, and the 1976 amendment raised the wage limit to Rs.1, 000 per month, and a later amendment raised it to Rs.1, 600 per month.

The Compensation limits incase of death was raised from Rs.10,000 to 30,000 and for permanent and total disablement from Rs.14,000 to 40,000 by the same amendment. The term "workmen" in the Act refers to those employed in factories, mines, plantations, construction work and other hazards occupations, except those covered by Employee State Insurance Act, 1948, and clerical employees.

The Compensation is related to the extent of the injury or circumstances of death. However, the employee cannot claim any compensation if he sustains injuries under the influence of drugs, alcohol, etc. The Act provides for half monthly payment for temporary disablement. The compensation cannot exceed half the monthly wages. A Commissioner appointed by the Government administers the Act. The employer is required to file annual return giving details of the compensation paid, number of injuries and other particulars. If the workman contacts any occupational disease due to the employment in that particular job, it would be deemed to be an injury by accident arising out of and in the course of his employment for purposes of the Act. In this case, the compensation will be payable only if the workman has been in service of the employer for more than six months.

If the employer does not pay the compensation within one month from then date it fell due, the Commissioner may order recovery of not only the amount of arrears but also a simple interest at the rate of six per cent per annum on the amount due. If there is no justification for the delay in the opinion of the Commissioner, an additional sum not exceeding 50 per cent of such amount may be recovered from the employer by way of penalty.

Note: Avocent designs, manufactures, licenses, and sells software and hardware products, which provides connectivity and centralized management of information technology (IT) infrastructure. The company primarily operates in the US. It is headquartered in Alabama, United States and employs 1,099 people. For a very good case study regarding this topic, reader can visit company's website www.avocent.com

5

Nature of Company and Formation

INTRODUCTION

The Companies Act, 1956 defines the word 'company' as a company formed and registered under the Act or an existing company formed and registered under any of the previous company laws (Section 3). Section 12 permits the formation of different types of companies. These may be:

- Companies limited by shares,
- Companies limited by guarantee, and
- Unlimited companies.

The majority of companies in India are with limited liability by shares. The common stock so contributed is denoted in money and is "the capital" of the company. The persons who contribute to it, or to whom it belongs, to are the members. The proportion of capital to which each member is entitled is his "share". Shares in a company are transferable.

FEATURES OF THE COMPANY

The following are the characteristic features of company:

1. Incorporated Association: A company must be incorporated or registered under the Companies Act. Minimum number required for the purpose is 7 in case of a public company, and 2, in case of a private company (Sec. 12). As per Section 11, an association of more than 10 persons, in case of banking business, and 20 in case of any other business, if not registered as a company under the Companies Act, or under any other law for the time being in force, becomes an illegal association.
2. Artificial Person: A company is created with the sanction of law and is not itself a human being, it is, therefore, called

artificial; and since it is clothed with certain rights and obligations, it is called a person. A company is accordingly an artificial person.

3. Separate Legal Entity: Unlike partnership, company is distinct from the persons who constitute it. Section 34(2) says that on registration, the association of persons becomes a body corporate by the name contained in the memorandum.

4. Limited Liability: The company being a separate person, its members are not as such liable for its debts. Hence, in the case of a company limited by shares, the liability of members is limited to the nominal value of shares held by them. Thus, if the shares are fully paid up, their liability will be nil. However, companies may be formed with unlimited liability of members or members may guarantee a particular amount. In such cases, liability of the members shall not be limited to the nominal or face value of the shares held by them. In case of unlimited liability companies, members shall continue to be liable till each paise has been paid off. In case of companies limited by guarantee, the liability of each member shall be determined by the guarantee amount, i.e., he shall be liable to contribute upto the amount guaranteed by him.

5. Separate Property: Shareholders are not, in the eyes of the law, part owners of the undertaking. In India, this principle of separate property was best laid down by the Supreme Court in Bacha F.Guzdar V. the Commissioner of Income Tax, Bombay (Supara). The Supreme Court held that a shareholder is not the part owner of the company or its property, he is only given certain rights by law, e.g., to vote or attend meetings, to receive dividends.

6. Transferability of Shares: Since business is separate from its members in a company form of organization, it facilitates the transfer of members' interests. The shares of a company are transferable in the manner provided in the Articles of the company (Sec. 82). However, in a private company, certain restrictions are placed on such transfer of shares but the right to transfer is not taken away absolutely.

7. Perpetual Existence: A company being an artificial person cannot be incapacitated by illness and it does not have an allotted span of life. The death, insolvency or retirement of its members

leaves the company unaffected. Members may come and go but the company can go for ever.

8. Common Seal: A company being an artificial person is not bestowed with a body of natural being. Therefore, it has to work through its directors, officers and other employees. But, it can be held bound by only those documents which bear its signatures. Common seal is the official signature of a company.

9. Company may sue and be sued in its own name: Another fall-out of separate legal entity is that the company, if aggrieved by some wrong done to it may sue or be sued in its own name.

Lifting of The Corporate Veil: In case of a dishonest and fraudulent use of the facility of incorporation, the law lifts the corporate veil and identifies the persons (members) who are behind the scene and are responsible for the perpetration of fraud. The concept of lifting the corporate veil is a changing concept. The veil of corporate personality, even though not lifted sometimes, is becoming more and more transparent in modern jurisprudence. The following are some such cases:

- For the protection of revenue.
- Where the company is acting as agent of the shareholders,
- Where a company has been formed by certain persons to avoid their own valid contractual obligation,
- Where a company has been formed for some fraudulent purpose or is a "sham",
- Where a company formed is against public interest or public policy,
- Where the holding company holds 100 per cent shares in a subsidiary company and the latter is created only for purposes of holding company
- Where the number of members falls below statutory minimum (Section 45)
- Where prospectus includes a fraudulent misrepresentation.
- Where a negotiable instrument is signed by an officer of a company [Section 147 (4)(c)].
- Holding and Subsidiary Companies (Secs. 212-213).
- Investigation into related companies. Section 239
- For investigation of ownership of a company. Sec 247

- Where in the course of winding of a company. Section 542
- Where breach of economic offence is involved.
- Where company is used as medium to avoid welfare legislation.
- Where device of incorporation is used for some illegal or improper purpose.
- To Punish for contempt of Court
- For determination of technical competence of company.
- Where company is a mere sham or cloak.

Illegal Association: (Section 11) No company, association or partnership consisting of more than 10 persons for the purpose of carrying on the business of banking and more than 20 persons for the purpose of carrying on any other business can be formed unless it is registered under the Companies Act or is formed in pursuance of some other Indian Law. Thus, if such an association is formed and not registered under the Companies Act, it will be regarded as an 'Illegal association' although none of the objects for which it may have been formed is illegal. However, Section 11 does not apply in the following cases: Stock Exchange, Association 'Not for Profit-making', Joint Hindu Family.

Effects of an Illegal Association: Following are the effects of an illegal association:

- Every member is personally liable for all liabilities incurred in the business.
- Members are punishable with fine which may extend up to Rs.10,000.
- Such an association cannot enter into any contract.
- Such an association cannot sue any of its members or any outsider, not even if the association is subsequently registered as a company.
- It cannot be sued by a member or an outsider for any debts due to it because it cannot contract any debt.
- It cannot be wound up even under the provisions relating to winding up of un-registered companies.
- While an unregistered firm can be dissolved, an illegal association cannot be dissolved because law does not recognize its very existence.
- The illegality of an illegal association cannot be cured by subsequent reduction in the number of its members.

- The profits made by an illegal association are, however, liable to assessment to income-tax.

Classification of Companies: Companies can be classified into three categories according to the mode of incorporation. If a company is incorporated by a charter granted by the monarch, it is called as Chartered Company and is regulated by that charter. For example, the East India Company came into being by the grant of a Royal Charter. Such type of companies do not exist in India. A company which is created by a Special Act of the Legislature is called a Statutory Company and is governed by the provisions of that Act. (E.g. The State Bank of India). A company brought into existence by registration of certain documents under the Companies Act, 1956 is called Registered Company. The liability of members of a registered company may be limited or unlimited (Section 12). It may be limited by shares, or by guarantee or by both (i.e., shares and guarantee).

A company limited by shares is a registered company having the liability of its member limited by its memorandum of association to the amount, if any, unpaid on the shares respectively held by them. A shareholder cannot be called upon to pay more than the amount remaining unpaid on his shares. His personal assets cannot be called upon for the payment of the liabilities of the company, if nothing remains to be paid on the shares purchased by him. Such a company is also known as a "Share Company."

A company limited by guarantee is one having the liability of its members limited by the memorandum to such amount as the members may respectively undertake by the memorandum to contribute to the assets of the company in the event of its being wound up. Such a company is also known as a "Guarantee Company". A pure "guarantee company" does not have a share capital. A company limited by shares as well as by guarantee is a hybrid form of company which combines elements of the guarantee and the share company. Such a company raises its initial capital from its shareholders.

Private and Public Companies: Either of the above kinds of companies (i.e., a limited liability company and an unlimited liability company) may be private or public (Section 12).

Private Company: A private company can be formed by merely two persons by subscribing their names to the Memorandum of Association. Such a company must have a minimum paid-up capital of Rs. 1 lakh, and by its articles must:

i. Prohibit an invitation to the public to subscribe to its shares and debentures;

ii. Restrict the rights of its members to transfer shares; and

iii. limit the number of its members to fifty, excluding its employee-members or past employee-members; provided that where two or more persons hold one or more shares in a company jointly, they shall, for the purpose of this definition, be treated as a single member.

iv. Prohibits any invitation or acceptance of deposits from persons other than its member, directors or their relatives.

Public Company: [Section 3(1) (iv)] Companies (Amendment) Act, 2000 defines a public company to mean a company which -

a. Is not a private company.

b. Has a minimum paid-up capital of five lakh rupees or such higher paidup capital, as may be prescribed;

c. Is a private company, which is a subsidiary of a company, which is not a private company. Minimum number of members required to form a public company is 7. however there is no limit to the maximum number of members. (Sec. 12).

Private Company which is a subsidiary of public company: A private company which is a subsidiary of a public company will be treated as a public company from the date of commencement of the Companies (Amendment) Act, 2000.

Deemed Public Company: The Companies (Amendment) Act. 2000 has, by introducing sub-section (11) to Section 43A, made a private company will not automatically become a public company on account of shareholding or turnover.

Conversion of Private Company into a Public Company: Section 44 provides for conversion of a private company into a public company. The procedure is as follows:

1. Special Resolution:
2. Increase in Members/Directors
3. The Word "Private" is to be deleted before the word limited in the name.
4. Within thirty days of the passing of the special resolution altering the articles, the company shall file with the Registrar (i) a

printed or typewritten copy of the special resolution, and (ii) a prospectus or a statement in lieu of prospectus [Sec.44(a)]

Conversion of Public Company into a Private Company: A public company having a share capital, and membership within the limits imposed upon private companies by section 3(1) (iii), may become a private company by following the procedure as given below:

1. Pass special resolution for altering the articles so as to include there in the necessary restrictions, limitation and prohibitions and to delete any provision inconsistent with the restrictions.
2. The word Private should be added before Limited.
3. The approval of the Central Government to the alternation in the articles for converting a public company into a private company should be obtained.
4. Within one month of the date of the receipt of the order of approval, a printed copy of the altered articles must be filled with the Registrar.
5. Within thirty days of the passing of the special resolution, a printed or type-written copy there of should be filed with the Registrar.

Holding and Subsidiary Companies: Where a company has control over another company, it is known as the Holding Company and the company over which control is exercised is called the Subsidiary Company. A Company is deemed to be under the control of another if;

1. That other controls the composition of its Board of Directors; or
2. The other company holds more than half in nominal value of its equity share capital
3. It is subsidiary of a third company which itself is a subsidiary of the controlling company. For example, where company 'B' is a subsidiary of company 'A' and company 'C' is a subsidiary of company 'B' then company 'C' shall be a subsidiary of company 'A'. If Company 'D' is a subsidiary of company 'C', then company 'D' shall also be a subsidiary of company 'B' and consequently also of company 'A'.

- One Man Company: A member may hold virtually the entire share capital of a company. Such a company is known as a "one-man company". This can happen both in a private company and a public company. The other member/members of the company may be holding just one share each. Such other members may be just dummies for the purpose of fulfilling the requirements of law as regards minimum membership.

- Non -Trading Company/Non - Profit Association: Such a company must have the objects of promoting of commerce, arts, science, religion, charity or any other useful object and must apply its profit, if any, or other income in promoting its object and must prohibit payment of any dividend to its members. As soon as it obtains a license and is registered accordingly, it will have the same privileges and obligations that a limited company has under the Companies Act, 1956.
- Govt. Companies: Section 617 defines a Government company as a company in which not less than fifty-one per cent of the paid-up share capital is held by the Central Government, or by any State Government or Governments or partly by the Central Government and partly by one or more State Governments. A subsidiary of a Government company is also treated as a Government company.
- Foreign Companies (591 to 602): A foreign company is a company which is incorporated into a country outside India under the law of that other country and has a place of business in India. There are of two types: (1) Companies incorporated outside India, establish a place of business in India after April 1, 1956; and (2) Companies incorporated outside India, which established a place of business in India before that date and continue to have an established place of business in India.
- Investment Companies: An investment company is a company the principal business of which consists in acquiring, holding and dealing in shares and securities. It involves only the acquisition and holding of shares and securities and thereby earning income by way of interest, dividend, etc.
- FERA Companies: The FERA companies are those companies which are incorporated in India in which the non-resident interest (viz., foreign equity share capital) was more than 40%. After the Amendment of FERA 1973 in the year 1993, the erstwhile FERA companies would not in future be subjected to obtain the prior approval of the RBI in respect of certain matters. FERA (Foreign Exchange Regulation Act).

- Finance Companies: A finance company means a non-banking company which is a financial institution within the meaning of clause (c) of sec.45 of the RBI Act, 1934.
- Public Financial Institutions (Sec. 4-A): The following financial institutions shall be regarded, for the purposes of the Companies Act, as public financial institutions, namely:

1. The Industrial Credit and Investment Corporation of India Limited (ICICI)
2. The Industrial Finance Corporation of India (IFCI)
3. The Industrial Development Bank of India (IDBI)
4. The Life Insurance Corporation of India (LIC)
5. The Unit Trust of India (UTI)
6. The Infrastructure Development Finance Company Ltd."

Sub-section (2) of Sec. 4-A empowers the Central Government to specify any other institution, as it may think fit, to be a public financial institution by issuing a notification in the Official Gazette.

FORMATION OF A COMPANY

We shall discuss the formation in three heads:

- Promotion: Promotion is a term of wide import denoting the preliminary steps taken for the purpose of registration and floatation of the company.
- Duties and Liabilities of Promoters: Duties: The promoters to make a full disclosure of all material facts relating to the formation of the company. He should not make any secret profit at the expense of the company he promotes, without the knowledge and consent of the company and if he does so, the company can compel him to account for it.
- Liabilities: For Non-disclosure: In case a promoter fails to make full disclosure at the time the contract was made, the company may either:
  - Rescind the contract and recover the purchase price where he sold his own property to the company, or
  - Recover the profit made, even though rescission is not claimed or is impossible, or
  - Claim damages for breach of his fiduciary duty. The measure of damages will be the difference between the market value of the property and the contract price.

- Registration (Sec 12, 33): Availability of Name: Section 20 states that a company cannot be registered by a name, which in the opinion of the Central Government is undesirable. Therefore, it is advisable that promoters find out the availability of the proposed name of the company from the Registrar of companies.
- Procedure: The promoters will have to get together at least seven person in the case of public company, or two persons in the case of a private company to subscribe to the memorandum of association.
- Documents to be Delivered: Section 33 states that the following three documents are required to be presented for the purpose of registration of a company:
- The memorandum of the company;
- The articles, if any;
- The agreement, if any, which the company proposes to enter into with any individual for appointment as its managing or whole time director or manager.
- Statutory Declaration of Compliance: Section 33 also requires a declaration to be filed with the Registrar of Companies along with the Memorandum and the Articles. This is known as "Statutory Declaration of Compliance."
- Consent of Directors: In case of a public company, if the first directors are appointed by the articles,then the following must be complied with before the registration of articles with the Registrar of Companies:
  - — Written consent of those directors to act, signed by themselves, or by an agent duly authorized in writing, and
  - — An undertaking in writing signed by each such director to take from the company and pay for his qualification shares (if any).
- Other Documents are usually delivered along with the aforesaid documents:
- The address of the registered office of the company (Sec. 146).
- Particulars regarding directors, manager and secretary, if any (Sec 303).

- These two documents are required to be submitted within 30 days of registration of the company:
- Certificate of Incorporation/Consequences of Incorporation: This certificate serves the same purpose in the case of a company which a birth certificate does in the case of a natural person.
- Effect of Certificate of Incorporation: The certificate of incorporation is conclusive evidence that all the requirements of the Companies Act in respect of registration and of matters precedent and incidental thereto have been complied with.
- Floatation/Capital Subscription: When a company has been registered and has received its certificate of incorporation, it is ready for "floatation", i.e., it can go ahead with raising capital sufficient to commence business and to carry it on satisfactorily. Section 70 makes it obligatory for every public company to take either of the following two steps:
- Issue a prospectus in case public is to be invited to subscribe to its capital, or
- File a 'statement in lieu of prospectus' with the Registrar, in case capital has been arranged privately. It must be done at least 3 days before allotment.
- Certificate to Commence Business: Where the company has issued a prospectus - Section 149(1) it shall not commence business or exercise any borrowing powers unless:
- Minimum subscription
- Every director of the company has paid to the company.
- No money is, or may become, liable to be repaid to the applicants.
- Filed with the Registrar a duly verified declaration by one of the directors or the secretary.
- Where the company has not issued a prospectus Section 149(2) requires that it shall not commence business or exercise its borrowing powers unless:
  - — It has filed with the Registrar a statement in lieu of prospectus;
  - — Every director of the company has paid to the company on each of the shares taken or contracted to be taken by him.

— Filed with the Registrar duly verified declaration by one of the directors or the secretary.

Penalty: every person at fault is liable to a fine upto Rs.5,000 for every day of default.

MEMORANDUM AND ARTICLES OF ASSOCIATION

The Memorandum of Association of a company is its charter which contains the fundamental conditions upon which alone the company can be incorporated. It tells us the objects of the company's formation and the utmost possible scope of its operations beyond which its actions cannot go. If anything is done beyond the powers, that will be ultra vires (beyond powers of) of the company and so void. It enables shareholders, creditors and all those who deal with the company to know what its powers are and what is the range of its activities.

- Form and Contents: Shall be in such one of the Forms in Tables B, C, D and E in Schedule I to the Companies Act, 1956 as may be applicable in the case of the company, or in Forms as near thereto as circumstances admit. Section 13 requires the memorandum of a limited company to contain: (i) the name of the company, with "limited" and "private limited" the name of the State, the objects of the company, the declaration that the liability of the members is limited; and the amount of the authorized share capital, divided into shares of fixed amounts.
- The Name Clause (Sec. 13(1(a)]: The last word in the name of the company, if limited by shares or guarantee is 'limited' unless the company is registered under Sec.25 as an 'association not for profit' (Sec. 13(1)(a) and 25)].
- The Registered Office Clause (Sec. 13(1)(b)]:This clause states the name of the State in which the registered office of the company will be situated. Every company must have registered office which establishes its domicile, and it is also the address at which company's statutory books must normally be kept and to which notices, and all other communication can be sent.
- The Objects Clause (Sec. 13(1)(d)]: The objects clause defines the objects of the company and indicates the sphere of its activities. A company cannot do anything beyond or outside its objects and any act done beyond them will be ultra vires

and void, and cannot be ratified even by the assent of the whole body of shareholders. Section 13, read along with Tables "B', 'C', 'D' and E', requires the company to divide its objects clause into two parts:

- — Main objects of the company to be pursued by the company on its incorporation and object incidental or ancillary to the attainment of the main objects; and
- — Other objects of the company not included in (a) above.

- Liability Clause [Sec. 13(2)]: This clause states the nature of liability of the members. In case of a company with limited liability, it must state that liability of members is limited, whether it be by shares or by guarantee. In case of companies limited by guarantee, this clause will state the amount which every member undertakes to contribute to the assets of the company in the event of its winding-up. In fact, the absence of this clause in the memorandum means that the liability of its members is unlimited.
- The Capital Clause [Sec. 13(4)(c)]: This clause states the amount of share capital with which the company is registered and the mode of its division into shares of fixed value, i.e., the number of shares into which the capital is divided and the amount of each share.
- The Association Clause [Sec. 13(4)(c)]: The names, addresses, descriptions, occupations of the subscribers, and the number of shares each subscriber has taken and his signature attested by a witness.

DOCTRINE OF ULTRA VIRES (BEYOND POWERS)

The company's activities are confined strictly to the objects mentioned in its Memorandum, and if they go beyond these objects, then such acts will be ultra vires. The object of declaring such acts as ultra vires is to protect the interests of shareholders and all others who deal with that company.

1. Ultra vires the directors (Not Void).
2. Ultra vires the Articles of Association (Not Void)
3. Ultra vires the Memorandum of Association/Company (Void)

Effects of Ultra Vires:

1. Injunction against the company.
2. Personal liability of directors to the company.

3. Personal liability of directors to third party.
4. Ultra vires contracts are void.

Exceptions to Doctrine of Ultra Vires:

1. Acquires some property
2. Property can be recovered, existing and is traceable
3. Ultra vires loan to pay its own debts - can recover the money from the company
4. Any person borrows money from the company - the company has right to sue and recover the money from him
5. The company may compel the director to refund the money
6. The company is held liable for the ultra vires torts (civil wrongs) of its employees when it is proved.
   - A company exists only for the objects which are expressly stated in its objects clause
   - Any act done outside the express or implied objects is ultra vires.
   - The ultra vires acts are null and void ab initio.
   - The members of a company (even a single member) can get an order of injunction from the Court restraining the company from going ahead with the ultra vires act.
   - If the directors have exceeded their authority such matter can be ratified by the general body of the shareholders, provided the company has the capacity to do by its memorandum of association.
   - Any property acquired by a company under an ultra vires transaction may be protected by the company against damage by third persons.
   - Directors and other officers can be held liable to compensate the company for any loss occasioned to it by an ultra vires act.
   - Directors and other officers shall be personally accountable to the third parties.
   - Money or property gained through an ultra-vires transaction available in specie or capable of being identified shall be restituted (restored) to the other party.
   - In case, an ultra-vires loan, taken by a company is used for payment of its intra-vires debts, the lender of the

ultra loan is substituted in place of the creditor who has been paid off and as such can recover the money.

ALTERATION OF MEMORANDUM

Section 16 states that the company can not alter the conditions contained in memorandum except in the cases and in the mode and to the extent express provision has been made in the Act.

- Change of Name: The name of a company may be changed at any time by passing a special resolution at a general meeting of the company and with the written approval of the Central Government.
- Change of Registered Office: (a) Change of registered office from one premises to another premises in the same city, town or village. A resolution passed by the Board of directors shall be sufficient. (b)Change of registered office from one town or city or village to another town or city or village in the same State Procedure.
- Special Resolution
- Confirmation of Regional Director
- Copy of Special Resolution and Confirmation by Regional Directors to be filed with RoC.
- Notice of new Location. Within 30 days the notice of the new location has to be given to the Registrar who shall record the same.
- Change of Registered Office from one State to another State. Can be done by a special resolution which is required to be confirmed by the Company Law Board (CLB).
- Alteration of Objects Clause (Section 17): Empowers a company to change the place of its Registered Office from one State to another or to alter its objects by passing a special resolution, if alteration is sought on any of the following grounds:
  - — To carry on its business more economically and more efficiently
  - — To attain its main purpose by new or improved means
  - — To enlarge or change the local area of its operation
  - — To carry on some business which under existing circumstances may be conveniently or advantageously combined with the business of the company

- To restrict or abandon any of the objects specified in the memorandum.
- To sell or dispose of the whole or any part of the undertaking.
- To amalgamate with any other company or body of persons.

- Alteration of Liability Clause (Sec. 38): The liability of a member of a company cannot be increased unless the member agrees in writing. Increase in liability may be by way of subscribing for more shares than the number held by him at the date on which the alteration is made or in any other manner.
- Alteration of Capital Clause (Section 94): provides that, if the articles authorize, a company limited by share capital may, by an ordinary resolution passed in general meeting, alter the conditions of its memorandum in regard to capital so as-
  - To increase its authorized share capital;
  - To consolidate and divide all or any of its share capital into shares of larger amount than its existing shares.
  - To convert all or any of its fully paid-up shares into stock, and reconvert the stock into fully paid-up shares of any denomination;
  - To sub-divide its shares, or any of them, into shares of smaller amount.
  - To cancel shares which have not been taken or agreed to be taken by any person.

ARTICLES OF ASSOCIATION

The articles of association of a company and its bye laws are regulations which govern the management of its internal affairs and the conduct of its business. They define the duties, rights, powers and authority of the shareholders and the directors in their respective capacities and of the company, and the mode and form in which the business of the company is to be carried out.

- Registration of Articles: Section 26 states that a public company limited by shares may register articles of association signed by the subscribers to the memorandum. There are actually three possible alternatives in which such company may adopt articles:
  - It may adopt Table A in full or,
  - It may wholly exclude Table A and set out its own regulations in full, or

— It may set out its own articles and adopt part of Table A.

- No Article Company (Sec. 28): A company limited by shares may either frame its own set of articles or may adopt all or any of the regulations contained in Table 'A' [Section 28(1)]. But if it does not register any Articles, Table 'A' applies.

SUBJECT MATTER OF ARTICLES/CONTENTS

The articles of a company usually deal with the following matters:

- The business of the company;
- The amount of capital issued and the classes of shares the increase and reduction of share capital;
- The rights of each class of shareholders and the procedure for variation of their rights;
- The execution or adoption of a preliminary agreement, if any; the allotment of shares; calls and forfeiture of shares for non-payment of calls;
- The allotment of shares; calls and forfeiture of shares for non-payment of calls:
- Transfer and transmission of shares;
- Company's lien on shares;
- Exercise of borrowing powers including issue of debentures;
- General meetings, notices, quorum, proxy, poll, voting resolution, minutes;
- Number, appointment and powers of directors;
- Dividends - interim and final - and general reserves;
- Accounts and audit;
- Keeping of books-both statutory and others.

Form and Signature of Articles [Sections 29 & 30]: The articles of association of any company not being a company limited by shares, will be in one such form in Tables 'C', 'D', and 'E' in Schedule I as may be applicable. Section 30 requires that articles shall:

- Be printed;
- Be divided into paragraphs numbered consecutively;
- Be signed by each subscriber of the memorandum of association.

Inspection and Copies of the Articles: A company will, on being so required by a member, send to him within seven days of the requirement, on payment of one rupee, a copy of the articles.

ALTERATION OF ARTICLES

A company may, by special resolution alter or add to its articles. A printed or type written copy of every special resolution altering the articles must be filed with the Registrar within 30 days of the passing of the special resolution.

Effect of Memorandum and Articles/Binding Force of Memorandum and Articles

- Members bound to company: Each member must observe the provisions of the articles and memorandum.
- Company bound to members: A company is bound to members by whatever is contained in its memorandum and articles of association.
- Member bound to member: The articles bind the member inter se, i.e., one to another so far as rights and duties arising from the articles are concerned.
- Whether company or members bound to outsiders?: No, the memorandum or articles do not confer any contractual rights to outsiders against the company or its members, even though the name of the outsiders is mentioned in the articles.
- Whether directors are bound by whatever is contained in the Articles? Yes, the directors of the company derive their powers from the articles and are subjected to limitations, if any, placed on their powers by the articles.

Constructive Notice of Articles and Memorandum: The memorandum and articles when registered become public documents and then they can be inspected by anyone on payment of a nominal fee. Every person dealing with the company is presumed to have read these documents and understood them in their true perspective. This is known as 'Doctrine of Constructive Notice'.

Doctrine of Indoor Management: The doctrine of indoor management allows all those who deal with the company to assume that the provisions of the articles have been observed by the officers of the company. In other words, they are not bound to enquire into the regularity of internal proceedings. An outsider is not expected to see that the company carries out its internal regulations.

Exceptions: The doctrine of indoor management is subject to the following exceptions:

1. Knowledge of Irregularity.
2. No knowledge of Articles: The rule cannot be invoked in favour of a person who did not consult the memorandum and articles and, thus did not rely on them.
3. Void or Illegal Transaction. The rule does not apply to transactions which are void or illegal ab initio, e.g., forgery.
4. Negligence: If an officer of a company does something which would not ordinarily be within his powers, the person dealing with him must make proper enquiries and satisfy himself as to the officer's authority. If he fails to make inquiry he cannot rely on the rule.
5. Doctrine does not apply where question is in regard to very existence of agency.
6. Doctrine is not applicable where a precondition is to be fulfilled before company itself can exercise a particular power.

STATEMENT IN LIEU OF PROSPECTUS

A prospectus, means any document described or issued as prospectus and includes any notice, circular, advertisement or other document inviting deposits from the public or inviting offers from the public for the subscription or purchase of any shares in or debentures of a body corporate. Thus, a prospectus is not merely an advertisement; it may be a circular or even a notice. A document shall be called a prospectus it satisfies two things:

- It invites subscriptions to shares or debentures or invites deposits.
- The aforesaid invitation is made to the public.

The Board attends to the following matters:

- Appointment of various expert agencies such as bankers, auditors, secretary, etc.
- Entering into underwriting contract, brokerage contracts.
- Making arrangements for the listing of shares on stock exchanges.
- Drafting a prospectus for the purpose of issue to the public.

Underwriting: Underwriting, in its simplest form, consists of an undertaking by some person or persons that if the public fails to take up the issue, he or they will do so. In return for this undertaking, the company agrees to pay the underwriter a commission on all shares or debentures, whether taken up by the public or by he underwriters.

Sub-Underwriting: The underwriters usually choose to spread their risk by using sub-underwriters who agree to take a certain number of shares for which they accept responsibility and for which they receive a commission out of the commission received by the underwriters. The difference between the commission paid by the company to the principal underwriters and the commission paid by them to the sub-underwriters is known as overriding commission.

Brokerage Contracts: There must be authority in the articles to pay brokerage, and the brokerage must be disclosed in the prospectus, or statement in lieu of prospectus, as the case may be, and it should pay a reasonable brokerage. (Sec. 76)

Listing of Shares on a Stock Exchange: The eligibility criteria for listing of securities of a company are:

i. Minimum issued equity capital of a company should be Rs. 5 crores [Rs. 3 crores where trading is screen-based], and
ii. The minimum public offer of equity capital shall be not less than 25 per cent.

Time of Floatation: The Board of Directors will decide about the time of issue of prospectus. It is advisable to consider the condition of the capital market, the investors' mood, fiscal and monetary policies of the Government and the state of business conditions before issuing a prospectus.

Dating of Prospectus: Sec. 55 states that every prospectus must be dated and the date is deemed to be the date of publication of the prospectus. Section 56 of the Companies Act lays down that the matters and reports stated in Schedule II to the Companies Act must be included in a prospectus.

Abridged Form of Prospectus: In stead of appending full prospectus, now 'abridged prospectus' need only be appended to the application form. Form 2-A has been prescribed as a format of abridged prospectus.

When 'Abridged Prospectus' Not Necessary?: In the following circumstances, an 'abridged prospectus' need not accompany the application forms:

i. A bonafide invitation to a person [Sec. 56(3)(a)]

ii. When shares or debentures are not offered to the public [Sec.56(3)(b)].

iii. Where offer is made only to existing members/debenture holders of the company by way of rights, whether with or without the right of renunciation [Sec.56(5) (a)].

iv. In the case of issue of shares or debentures which are in all respects similar to those previously issued and dealt in and quoted on a recognized stock exchange [Sec.56(5) (b)].

Registration of the Prospectus (Section 60): A copy of the prospectus duly signed by every director or proposed directors must be delivered to the Registrar before its publication.

Is the issue of prospectus compulsory?: when prospectus is not required to be issued?

The following are the circumstances:

i. A private company

ii. If the promoters or directors feel that they can mobilize resources through personal relationship and contacts.

iii. A memorandum containing the prescribed salient features of a prospectus.

iv. A bonafide invitation to a person to enter into an underwriting agreement Sec.56(3)

v. Application form is issued in relation to shares or debentures not offered to the public [Sec. 56(3)]

vi. Offered to existing holders of shares or debentures[Sec. 56(5)]

vii. The issue relates to shares or debentures previously issued [Sec. 56(5)]

viii. Where invitation is made in the form of an advertisement, ordinarily called as "prospectus announcement' [Sec. 66].

Shelf Prospectus and Information Memorandum [Section 60A and 60 b]: The Companies (Amendment) Act, 2000 has introduced two new sections, viz., Sections 60A and 60B relating to 'Shelf Prospectus' and 'Information Memorandum' respectively. 'Shelf prospectus' means a prospectus issued by any financial institution or bank for one or more issues of the securities or class of securities specified in that prospectus.

Information Memorandum (Section 60B): 'Information memorandum' means a process undertaken prior to the filing of a prospectus by which a demand for the securities proposed to be issued by a company is elicited, and the price and the terms of issue for such securities is assessed, by means of a notice, circular, advertisement or document [Section 2(19B)].

Statement in Lieu of Prospectus (Section 70): If a public company makes a private arrangement for raising its capital then it must file a statement in lieu of prospectus with the Registrar at least three days before any allotment of shares or debentures can be made.

If allotment of shares or debentures is made without filing the Statement in lieu of prospectus, the allottee may avoid it within two months after the statutory meeting, or where no such meeting is to be held, within two months of the allotment. Contravention also renders the company and every director liable to a fine up to Rs. 10,000.

Liability for Untrue Statements in the Prospectus: (Sections 62-63): The prospective shareholders are entitled to all true disclosures in the prospectus. The persons issuing the prospectus are bound to state everything accurately and not to omit material facts.

What is an untrue statement?: According to Section 65(1) if the statement is misleading in its form and context in which it is included; and where the omission form a prospectus of any matter going to mislead, being a prospectus in which an untrue statement is included.

Civil Liability (Section 62): The following persons shall be liable to pay compensation to every subscriber for loss or damage:

1. Director of the company at the time of the issue of the prospectus;
2. Person who has authorized himself to be named and is named in the prospectus as a director,
3. Every promoter of the company; and
4. Who has authorized the issue of the prospectus.

Remedies against the Company: Any person who, takes shares from the company may: 1. Rescind the contract to take the shares 2. Claim damages.

He must, however, take action to rescind the contract:

b. Within a reasonable time,

c. Before proceedings to wind up the company have commenced, and

d. Before he does anything. which is inconsistent with the right to repudiate, e.g., to accept dividends.

Remedies against Directors or Promoters: A shareholder who had been induced to take shares may claim:

i. Damages for fraudulent misrepresentation'

ii. Compensation under Section 62;

iii. Damages for noncompliance with the requirements of Section 56 regarding contents of the prospectus.

Damages for Fraudulent Misrepresentation: An allottee of shares may bring an action for deceit, i.e., fraudulent misrepresentation.

Compensation for untrue Statement [Sec. 62]: File a suit for compensation under Section 62. A claim can be made, whether the statements are fraudulent or innocent.

Remedies against Experts: The allottee of the shares is entitled to claim from the expert: (i) damages, (ii) compensation under Section 62.

Liability under Section 56: An omission from a prospectus of a matter required to be stated under Section 56(i.e., as per Sch.II) may give rise to an action for damages at the instance of a subscriber for shares, who has suffered loss.

Criminal Liability for Misstatement in Prospectus (Section 63): Every person authorizing its issue is punishable:

i. With imprisonment for a term up to two years, or

ii. With fine up to Rs. 50.000, or

iii. With both imprisonment and fine.

Liability under Section 68: Every person authorizing its issue. shall be punishable with imprisonment for a term which may extend to 5 years or with fine which may extend to Rs. 1,00,000 or with both.

Golden Rule for framing of Prospectus: The 'Golden Rule' for framing of a prospectus was laid down by Justice Kindersely in New Brunswick & Canada Rly. & Land Co. V. Muggeridge (1860). Briefly, the rule is: Those who issue a prospectus hold out to the public great advantages which will accrue to the persons who will take shares in the proposed undertaking.

Thus, the persons issuing the prospectus must not include in the prospectus all the relevant particulars specified in Parts I & II of Schedule II of the Act, which are required to be stated compulsorily but should also voluntarily disclose any other information within their knowledge which might in any way affect the decision of the prospective investor to invest in the company

SHARE & SHARE CAPITAL

Meaning of a Share. Section 2(46) defines a share "as a share in the share capital of a company and includes stock except where a distinction between stock and share is expressed or implied. A share signifies the following:

- The interest of a shareholder in the company; the right to receive dividend, attend meetings, vote at the meeting and share in the surplus assets of the company, if any, in the event of the company, being wound up;
- The liability of the shareholder in the company to pay calls on shares until fully paid up;
- The right of the shareholder to transfer the shares subject to the articles of association.
- Binding covenants on the part of the company as well as the shareholder, as given in the Articles of the company.
- Thus, a share of a company in the hands of a shareholder signifies a bundle of rights and obligations. A share is not a negotiable instrument.

Share Vs. Share Certificate: Sec. 82 of the Companies Act. 1956, describes a share as a moveable property transferable in the manner provided by the articles

of the company and Sec. 84, on the other hand, describes a 'share certificate' to mean a certificate, under the common seal of the company, specifying any shares held by any member.

SHARE VS. STOCK

Share: The share capital of a company is divided into a number of indivisible units of specified amount. Each of such unit is called a 'share'. Stock The term 'stock' may be defined as the aggregate of fully paid-up shares of a member merged into one fund of equal value. It is a set of shares put together in a bundle. The 'stock' is expressed in terms of money and not as so many shares. Stock can be divided into fractions of any amount and such fractions may be transferred like shares.

Distinction: Following are the main points of difference

Share	Stock
1. A share has a nominal value.	1. A stock has no nominal value.
2. A share has a distinctive number which distinguishes it from other shares.	2. A stock bears no such number.
3. Share can be issued originally to the public	3. A company cannot make an original issue of stock. Stock can be issued by existing company by converting its fully paid up shares.
4. A share may either be fully paid up or partly paid up.	4. A stock can never be partly paid up, it is always fully paid up.
5. A share cannot be transferred in fractions. It is transferred as a whole.	5. A stock may be transferred in any fractions.
6. All the shares are of equal denomination.	6. Stock may be of different denominations.

Classes of Shares: The most common classes of shares are: (1) Preference, (2) Equity or Ordinary, and (3) Deferred or Founders'.

A public company and a private company which is a subsidiary of public company may not issue shares other than equity, preference and cumulative convertible preference shares (CCPS).

Preference Share: A preference share is one which carries the following two rights over holders of equity shares:

- A preferential right in respect of dividends at a fixed amount or at a fixed rate, and
- A preferential right in regard to repayment of capital on winding up.

The preference or priority of the preference shareholders is in relation to the rights of equity shareholders [Section 85].

Participating and Non-participating: If a preference share carries either one or both of the following rights then it is known as participating share:

- To participate further in the profits either along with or after payment of a certain rate of dividend on equity shares,
- To participate in the surplus assets at the time of winding up [Section 85].

Thus, if a preference share does not carry either of these rights, then it will be known as non-participating share .If a preference share carries the right for payment of arrears in dividend from future profits, then such a share is known as cumulative preference share. If a preference share does not carry the right to dividend in arrears, then such a preference share is known as noncumulative or simple. The preference shares are always presumed to be cumulative unless expressly described as non-cumulative.

Redeemable and Irredeemable: Redeemable preference shares are those shares which are to be redeemed by the company either at a fixed date, or after a certain period of time or at the option of the company as per Section 80.

Conditions:

Shares issued earlier cannot be converted into redeemable preference shares:

There must be authority in the articles. The shares can be redeemed only when they are fully paid up; it will only be redeemed:

a. Out of profits of the company which would otherwise be available for dividend, or

b. Out of the proceeds of a new issue of shares.

If there is a premium payable on redemption, it must have been provided out of profits or out of the securities premium account before the shares are redeemed. Where the shares are redeemed out of profits, a sum equal to the nominal amount of the shares redeemed is to be transferred out of profits to the "Capital Redemption Reserve Account."

Voting rights of preference shareholders: The preference shareholders will vote only on matters directly relating to preference shares.

i. Any resolution for winding up of the company,

ii. Any resolution for the reduction or repayment of share capital,

iii. Any resolution at any meeting, if dividend on cumulative preference shares remains unpaid for at least two years

Equity Share: 'Equity share' means a share which is not preference share [Section 85]. The rate of dividend is not fixed. The Board of Directors recommend the rate of dividend which is then declared by the members at the Annual General Meeting. New issues of share capital of a company limited by shares shall be of two kinds only, namely:

a. Equity share capital with voting rights; or With differential rights as to dividend, voting or otherwise in accordance with such rules and subject to such conditions as may be prescribed;

b. Preference share capital.

Prior to the Amendment to the companies Act in 2000, public companies were not allowed to issue equity shares with differential rights. Thus, companies are now allowed to issue non-voting equity shares. The holders of equity shares carrying voting rights shall have voting rights in proportion to the paid-up equity capital of the company [Section 87(1)].

Cumulative Convertible Preference Shares (CCPs): Such shares are issued as preference shares but are convertible into equity shares within a period of 3 years to 5 years, as may be decided by the company.

Deferred or Founders' Shares: A pure private company can issue shares of a type other than those discussed above [Section 90]. Thus, it may issue what are known as deferred shares. As deferred shares are normally held by promoters and directors of the company, they are usually called founders' shares. They are usually of a smaller denomination, say one rupee each.

ISSUE OF SHARES AT PAR, AT PREMIUM, AND AT DISCOUNT

A company may issue shares at par, or at a premium, or at a discount.

- Issue at Par: Shares are deemed to have been issued at par when subscribers are required to pay only the amount equivalent to the nominal or face value of the shares issued.
- Par Value of Shares: 'Par value' is the notional face value of the shares which a company issues to its investors.
- Issue at a Premium: If the buyer is required to pay more than the face value of the share, then the share is said to be issued or sold at a premium. The premium cannot be treated as profit and, therefore, cannot be distributed as dividend. The amount of premium received in cash and the equivalent of it received in kind must be kept in a separate bank account known as the 'Securities Premium Account'. As per SEBI guidelines, 2000 every company entitled to make a public issue can offer its shares at par or premium.
- Issue at a Discount: If the buyer of shares is required to pay less than the face value of the share, then the share is said to be issued or sold at a discount. Certain conditions subject to which shares can be issued at a discount are as follows:

- Is authorized by a resolution:
- The issue must be of a class of shares already issued
- The maximum rate of discount must not exceed 10 per cent
- Not less than one year has, at the date of issue, elapsed since the date on which the company was entitled to commence business.
- Issued within two months of the sanction by the Company Law Board.
- Every prospectus must mention particulars of the discount allowed on the issue of shares.
- Issue of Sweat Equity Shares [Sec. 79A]: 'Sweat-equity shares' means equity shares issued by the company to employees or directors at a discount or for consideration other than each. 'Sweat equity shares' may be issued for providing know-how or making available intellectual property rights (say, patents) or value additions, by whatever name called.

Conditions:

a. Must be of a class of shares already issued.
b. Authorised by a special resolution.
c. The resolution specifies the number of shares, current market price, consideration, if any, and the class or classes of directors or employees to whom such equity shares are to be issued.
d. Not less than one year has, at the date of the issue, elapsed since the date on which the company was entitled to commence business.
e. Are issued in accordance with the regulations made by the Securities and Exchange Board of India.

    - Bonus Shares: A company may, capitalize profits by issuing fully paid-up shares to the members, thereby, transferring the sums capitalized from the profit and loss account or Reserve Account to the Share Capital [Section 205(3)]. Such shares are known as bonus shares and are issued to the existing members of the company free of charge. The issue of bonus shares is regulated not only by the Companies Act, 1956 but also by the guidelines issued by SEBI in this regard.

- Right Shares: The existing members of the company have a right to be offered shares, when the company wants to increase its subscribed capital. Such shares are known as "right shares" but they are not issued free of charge.

SHARE CAPITAL

- Meaning of share capital: It means the capital of a company, or the figure in terms of so many rupees divided into shares of a fixed amount, or the money raised by the issue of shares by a company.
- Nominal, Authorised or Registered capital: This is the sum stated in the memorandum as the share capital of a company with which it is proposed to be registered. This is the maximum amount of capital which it is authorised to raise by issuing shares, and upon which it pays stamp duty.
- Issued capital: It is the part of the authorized capital which the company has issued for subscription. The amount of issued capital is either equal to or less than the authorized capital.
- Subscribed capital: It is that portion of the issued capital which has been subscribed for the purchasers of the company's shares. The amount of subscribed capital is either equal to or less than the issued capital.
- Called-up capital: The company may not call up full amount of the face value of the shares. Thus the called-up capital represents the total amount called-up on the shares subscribed. The total amount of called-up capital can be either equal to or less than the subscribed capital.
- Uncalled capital: represents the total amount not called up on shares subscribed, and the shareholders continue to be liable to pay the amounts as and when called. The company may reserve all or part of the uncalled capital, which can then be called in the event of the company being wound up. It is known as Reserve Capital or Reserve Liability [Section 99].
- Paid-up capital: Paid -up capital is the amount of money paid-up on the shares subscribed.
- Alteration of share capital: Section 94 provides that, if the articles authorise, a company limited by share capital may, by an ordinary resolution passed in general meeting, alter the conditions of its memorandum in regard to capital to.

- Increase of authorised share capital: A company limited by shares, if the articles authorise can increase its authroised share capital by passing an ordinary resolution.
- Consolidate and sub-divide shares: Consolidation is the process of combining shares of smaller denomination, Sub-division of shares is just the opposite of consolidation.
- Convert shares into stock and vice versa: Stock cannot be issued in the first instance. It is necessary to first issue shares and have then fully paid-up and them convert them into stock. Also stock can be reconverted into fully paid-up shares by passing a resolution in general meeting.
- Diminish share capital: Section 94 provides that a company may cancel shares and diminish the amount of the share capital by the amount of the shares so cancelled. This constitutes diminution of capital and should be distinguished from reduction of capital.
- Reduce capital: (i) by reducing or extinguishing the liability of members for uncalled capital. (ii) By paying off returning capital which is in excess to the wants of the company, (iii) Pay off paid-up capital on the understanding that it may be called up again. (iv) A Combination of the preceding methods. (v) Write off or cancel capital which has been lost or is not represented by available assets.

Reduction of share capital without the sanction of the court: There are some cases in which there is reduction of share capital and no confirmation by the court is necessary. These are:

- Forfeiture of shares.
- Surrender of shares
- Diminution of capital
- Redemption of redeemable preference shares.
- Purchase of shares of a member by the company under section 402.
- Purchase of its own shares as per section 77A

Raising of Capital/Issue of Shares: Issue of shares may be made in 3 ways:

- By private placement of shares;

- By allotting entire shares to an issue-house, which in turn, offers the shares for sale to the public; and
- By inviting the public to subscribe for shares in the company through a prospectus.

Private Placement of Shares: Shares are issued privately to a small number of persons known to the promoters or related to them by family connections.

By an Offer for sale: The Issue-house publishes a document called an offer for sale, with an application form attached, offering to the public shares or debentures for sale at a price higher than what is paid by it or at par. This document is deemed to be a prospectus [Section 64(1)].

By inviting public through prospectus: The company invites offers from members of the public to subscribe from the shares or debentures through prospectus.

Issue of shares to existing shareholders: The capital is also raised by issue of rights shares' to the existing shareholders (Sec.81). In the case, the shares are allotted to the existing equity shareholders in proportion to their original shareholding.

Public Issue of Shares: Public issue of shares means the selling or marketing of shares for subscription by the public by issue of prospectus.

Allotment of Shares: It means and implies a division of the share capital into defined shares of a particular value or of different classes and assignment of such shares to different persons.

Share Certificate (Section 113): The share certificate states the name, address, occupation of the holder together with the number of shares and their distinctive number and amount paid-up. It must bear the common seal of the company, must be stamped and bear the signature of one or more directors.

Share Warrants (Section 114): A share warrant is a negotiable instrument. It entitles the bearer to the shares specified in it and he can transfer the ownership of shares by merely delivering the share warrant to the transferee.

Membership: Membership can be in the following ways:

1. The subscribers of the Memorandum
2. Every other person who agrees in writing to become a member
3. Every person holding equity share capital of a company

Member and Shareholder: In the case of an unlimited company or a company limited by guarantee, a member may not be a shareholder.

Modes of Acquiring Membership: By subscribing to the memorandum of association..

1. By agreement and registration.
2. By agreeing to purchase qualification shares.

Calls on shares: The company may ask for some payment at the time of application for shares (but money not less than 5 per cent of the nominal value) and another sum at allotment. The balance may be payable when called for.

Forfeiture of Shares: Forfeiture of shares means taking theme away from the member. This is absolutely a serious step for not only does it deprive the shareholder of his property but also, unless the shares are re-issued, it involves a reduction of capital.

DEBENTURES

According to Sec. 2(12), 'debenture' includes debenture stock, bonds and any other securities of a company, either constituting a charge on the assets of the company or not.

Characteristic features of a debenture:

1. Debentures is issued by a company and is usually in the form of a certificate which is an acknowledgement of indebtedness.
2. It is issued under the company's seal.
3. It is one of a series issued to a number of lenders.
4. It usually specifies a particular period or date as the date of repayment.
5. It generally creates a charge on the undertaking of the company or some parts of its property.
6. A debenture holder does not have any right to vote in the company meetings.

CLASSES OF DEBENTURES

Debentures may be classified according to the following characteristics, viz.,

1. Negotiability,
2. Security,

3. Permanence,
4. Convertibility, and
5. Priority.

1. Classification according to negotiability:
   - Bearer debentures.
   - Registered debentures.
2. Classification according to security:
   - Secured debentures.
   - Unsecured or naked debentures.
3. Classification according to permanence:
   - Redeemable debentures.
   - Irredeemable or perpetual debentures.
4. Classification according to convertibility:
   - Convertible debentures.
   - Non-convertible debentures.
5. Classification according to priority:
   - First debentures.
   - Second debentures.

Debentures with voting rights not to be issued (Sec. 117): A company cannot issue any debentures carrying voting rights.

Issue of debentures at a discount: Debentures can be issued at a discount, unless the Articles provide otherwise.

Debentures and debenture stock: The difference between debentures and debenture stock is the same as the difference between shares and stock.

Debenture trust deed: [New Sec. 117-A as inserted by the Companies (Amendment) Act, 2000]. A trust deed for securing any issue of debentures shall be in specified form and shall be executed within the prescribed period.

Appointment of debenture trustees and duties of debenture trustees [Sec. 117-B]: A person shall not be appointed as a debenture trustee, if he - (a) beneficially holds shares in the company (b) is beneficially entitled to moneys which are to be paid by the company to the debenture trustee (c) has entered into any guarantee in respect of principal debts secured by the debentures or interest thereon.

Liability of company to create security and debenture redemption reserve [New Sec. 117-C as inserted by the Companies (Amendment) Act, 2000]: Creation of debenture redemption reserve: Where a company issues debentures after the commencement of this Act, it shall create a debenture redemption reserve for the redemption of such debentures, to which adequate amounts shall be credited, from out of its profits every year until such debentures are redeemed.

Liability of trustees for debenture-holders (Sec.119): A trustee is liable for any breach of trust where he fails to show the degree of care and diligence required of him as trustee, having regard to the provisions of the trust deed conferring on him any powers, authorities or discretions.

REMEDIES OF DEBENTURE HOLDERS

1. He may sue for his principal and interest.
2. He may, petition under Sec. 439 for the winding up of the company by the Court. But in addition he has also the following courses open to him:
   - Debenture-holders' action.
   - Appointment of receiver.
   - Foreclosure.
   - Sale.
   - Proof for the balance

Creation of Charges: A company like any other person can, when it borrows money, give its-creditors security. Often it mortgages or charges its property to its debenture-holders.

Fixed and Floating Charges:

- Fixed charge: A fixed or specific charge is one which is created on some specific and definite assets of the company, e.g., a charge on land and building.
- Floating charge: A floating charge is an equitable charge which is created on some class of property which is constantly changing, e.g., a charge on stock-in-trade, trade debtors, etc.
- New financial instruments: Issuer of capital shall make instruments such as Deep Discount Bonds, Debentures wit Warrants, Secured Premium Notes etc., so that an investor can make reasonable determination of the risks, returns, safety and liquidity of the instruments.

COMPANY MANAGEMENT & REMUNERATION

- Directors: A company in the eyes of the law is considered to be an artificial person. The persons who are in charge of the management of the affairs of a company are termed as directors. They are collectively known as Board of directors or the Board.
- Only individuals can be directors (Sec. 253): No body corporate, association or firm can be appointed as director of a company.
- Number of directors: Minimum number (Sec.252): Every public company (other than a deemed public company) shall have at least 3 directors and every other company (e.g., a private company, a deemed public company) at least 2 directors.

APPOINTMENT OF DIRECTORS

1. First Directors (Sec. 254 and Clause 64 of Table A)
    - The Articles of a company usually name the first directors by their respective names or prescribe the method of appointing them.
    - If the first directors are not named in the Articles, the number of directors and the name of the directors shall be determined in writing by the subscribers of the Memorandum or a majority of them (Clause 64 of Table A).
    - If the first directors are not appointed in the above manner, the subscribers of the Memorandum who are individuals become directors of the company.
2. Appointment of directors by the company (Secs. 255 to 257, 263 and 264) Directors must be appointed by shareholders in general meeting. At least 2/3rds of the total number of directors shall be liable to retire by rotation. Such directors are called rotation directors. Appointment of a new director (Sec. 257):
    - Fourteen days' notice and deposit of Rs.500.
    - Consent in writing to act as director (Sec. 264).
    - Separate ordinary resolution for each appointment (Sec. 263).

    Retirement of directors where annual general meeting is not held: A director who is to retire by rotation at the annual general meeting shall not continue in office after the last day on which the annual general meeting in each year should have been held.

2. Appointment of director by directors (Secs. 260, 262 and 313)

   The directors of a company may appoint directors:

   - As additional directors (Sec. 260).
   - In a casual vacancy (Sec. 262).
   - As alternate director (Sec. 313).

3. Appointment of directors by third parties: The number of directors so appointed shall not exceed 1/3rd of the total number of directors, and they are not liable to retire by rotation.

4. Appointment by proportional representation (Sec. 265): The system of proportional representation ensures representation of the minority shareholders on the Board of directors.

5. Appointment of directors by the Central Government (Sec. 408):

Any director appointed by the Central Government shall not be required to hold any qualification shares.

- Directors as agents: A company, as an artificial person, acts through directors who are elected representatives of the shareholders.
- Directors as employees: Although the directors of a company are its agents, they are not employees or servants of the company for being entitled to privileges and benefits which are granted under the Companies Act to the employees.
- Directors as officers: For certain matters under the Companies Act, the directors are treated as officers of the company [sec.2 (30)].
- Directors as trustees: Directors are treated as trustees -
  — Of the Company's money and property; and
  — Of the powers entrusted to them.

QUALIFICATIONS AND DISQUALIFICATIONS OF DIRECTORS

A director must -

- Be an individual,
- Be competent to contract, and
- Hold a share qualification, if so required by the Articles.

Disqualification of directors (Sec. 274)

The following persons are disqualified for appointment as directors of a company:

- A person of unsound mind.
- An undischarged insolvent.
- A person who has applied to be adjudicated as an insolvent and his application is pending.
- A person who has been convicted by a Court of any offence involving moral turpitude and a period of 5 years has not elapsed from the date of expiry of the sentence.
- A person whose calls in respect of shares of the company held for more than 6 months have been in arrear.
- A person who is disqualified for appointment as director by an order of the Court under Sec. 203.
- Such person is already a director of a public company which
  - — Has not filed the annual accounts and annual returns for any continuous three financial years commencing on and after the first day of April, 1999; or
  - — Has filed to repay its deposit or interest thereon on due or redeem its debentures on due date or pay dividend and such failure continues for one year or more.

VACATION OF OFFICE, REMOVAL AND RESIGNATION OF DIRECTORS

Vacation of office by directors (Sec. 283):

- Statutory Vacation.
- Additional grounds in case of private companies.
- Acceptance of officer of profit.

Removal of directors: Directors may be removed by:

- — The shareholders,
- — The Central Government,
- — The Company Law Board.

- Removal by Share holders: In certain circumstances, the shareholders may remove the directors.
- Removal by Central Government: (Secs. 388-B to 388-E): The Central Government may, in certain circumstances, remove managerial personnel from office on the recommendation of the Company Law Board.

- Removal by Company Law Board (Sec. 402): Where, on an application to the Company Law Board for prevention of oppression (under Sec. 397) or mismanagement (under Sec. 398).

Resignation of directors: There is no provision in the Companies Act, 1956 relating to the resignation of office of a director.

Managerial Remuneration: Managerial personnel: The expression 'managerial personnel' refers to the:

- Managing director.
- Whole-time/part-time directors, or
- Manager.

Overall maximum managerial remuneration (Sec. 198): Remuneration must not to exceed 11 per cent: The total managerial remuneration of the directors and the manager in respect of any financial year shall not exceed 11 per cent of the net profit of the company for that financial year computed in the manner laid down in Sec. 349 and 350.

Meetings of Directors (Sec. 285 to 288)

1. Number of meetings - once in every 3 months (Sec. 285).
2. Notice of meetings (Sec. 286): Every officer of the company whose duty is to give notice and who fails to do so shall be punishable with fine which may extend to Rs.1,000.
3. Quorum for meetings (Sec.287): The quorum shall be 1/3rd of its strength or 2 directors, whichever is higher.

Powers of Directors

General powers of the Board (Sec. 291): The Board of directors of company is entitled to exercise all such powers and to do all such acts and things as the company is authorized to exercise and do.

Powers to be exercised at Board meetings (Sec. 292): The following powers, on behalf of the company,

- Make calls on shareholders in respect of money unpaid on their shares;
- The Power to authorise the buy-back of shares
- Issue debentures;
- Borrow money otherwise than on debentures
- Invest the funds of the company; and make loans.

Other powers: These powers are:

- To fill vacancies in the Board (Sec. 262);
- To sanction or give consent for certain contracts in which particular directors, their relatives and firms are interested (Sec. 297);
- To receive notice of disclosure of directors' interest in any contract or arrangement with the company (Sec. 299);
- To receive notice of disclosure of shareholdings of directors (Sec. 308);
- To appoint as managing director or manager a person who is already managing director or manager of another company (Secs. 316 and 386);
- To make investments in companies in the same group (Sec. 372).

Exceptions:

1. Directors acting mala fide.
2. Directors themselves wrong-doers.
3. Incompetency of Board.
4. Deadlock in management.
5. Residuary powers. i.e., powers not expressly conferred on the directors or shareholders, in a general meeting.

Powers to be exercised with the approval of company in general meeting (Sec. 293):

- To sell, lease or otherwise dispose of.
- To remit or give time for repayment of any debt.
- To invest (excluding trust securities) the amount of compensation received.
- To borrow moneys where the moneys to be borrowed (together with the moneys already borrowed by the company) are more than the paid-up capital.
- To contribute to charitable and other funds not directly relating to the business.

Audit Committee [Sec. 292-A as introduced by the Companies (Amendment) Act, 2000]: The Audit Committee shall act in accordance with terms of reference to be specified in writing by the Board.

Duties of Directors

1. Fiduciary duties, and
2. Duties of care, skill and diligence.

1. Fiduciary Duties: As fiduciaries, the directors must
   — Exercise their powers honestly and bona fide for the benefit of the company as a whole; and
   — Not place themselves in a position in which there is a conflict between their duties to the company and their personal interests.
2. Duties of care, skill and diligence: Directors should carry out their duties with reasonable care and exercise such degree of skill and diligence as is reasonably expected of persons of their knowledge and status.

Other duties of directors: The other duties of a director are -

- to attend Board meetings,
- not to delegate his functions except to the extent authorized by the Act or the constitution of the company, and
- to disclose his interest.

Liabilities of Directors

1. Liability to third parties:
   - Material misrepresentations.
   - Independently of the Act: Directors, as agents of a company, are not personally liable on contracts entered into an agent on behalf of the company.
   - Liability for acts ultra vires the company: Where a director enters into a contract, which is ultra vires the company, the director is personally liable for breach of implied warranty of authority.
   - Liability for frauds and torts.
2. Liability to the company: The liability of directors towards the company may arise from-
   - Ultra vires acts,
   - Negligence,
   - Breach of trust, and
   - Misfeasance.

Other Managerial Personnel:

- Managing Director: The term 'managing director' includes a director occupying the position of a managing director, by whatever name called.
- Manager: 'Manager', according to Sec. 2 (24), means an individual who has the management of the whole or substantially the whole of the affairs of a company.

- Managing Director and Manager Compared

Managing director	Manager
1. A managing director is entrusted with the substantial powers of the management.	1. A manager has the management of the whole, or substantially the whole of the affairs of a company.
2. A company may have two managing directors.	2. A company can have only one manager as he is vested with the management of the whole or substantially of the whole or substantially the whole of the affairs of the company.
3. A managing director must be a director.	3. A manager may or may not be a director.
4. A managing director is appointed by the directors from among themselves and appointed either resolution of the Board or general meeting.	4. A manager is usually appointed by the Board of directors.

Sole Selling Agents: The term 'sole selling agent' is not defined in the Act, it means an individual, firm or company who or which is given exclusive rights to sell in a particular area the goods of the company concerned.

Secretary: A company secretary means "a person who is a member of the Institute of Company Secretaries of India". According to Sec. 2 (45) of the Companies Act as amended in 1988 'secretary' means a company secretary within the meaning of Sec. 2 (1) (c) of the Company secretaries Act, 1980, and includes any individual possessing the prescribed qualifications appointed to perform the duties which may be performed by a secretary under this Act and any other ministerial or administrative duties.

MEETINGS AND RESOLUTIONS

GENERAL MEETINGS OF SHAREHOLDERS

1. Statutory Meeting (Sec. 165): Every company limited by shares and every company limited by guarantee and having a share

capital will, within a period of not less than one month and not more than six months from the date at which the company is entitled to commence business, hold a general meeting of the members of the company. This meeting is called the 'statutory meeting'. This is the first meeting of the shareholders of a public company and is held only once in the lifetime of a company.

Statutory report: The Board of directors shall, at least 21 days before the day on which the meeting is to be held, forward a report, called the 'statutory report', to every member of the company.

Procedure at the meeting: (a) List of members. (b) Discussion of matters relating to formational aspect. (c) Adjournment.

Objects of the meeting and report:

i. To put the members of the company in possession of all the important facts relating to the company.
ii. To provide the members an opportunity of meeting and discussing the management, methods and prospects of the company.
iii. To approve the modification of the terms of any contract named in the prospectus.

2. Annual General Meeting (Secs. 166 and 167):

Company to hold annual general meeting every year (Sec. 166)

Every company will in each year hold, a general meeting as its annual general meeting and shall specify the meeting as such in the notice calling it. There shall not be an interval of more than 15 months between one annual general meeting and the another. But the first annual general meeting should be held within a period of 18 months from the date of its incorporation.

The Registrar may, for any special reason, extend the time for holding any annual general meeting by a period not exceeding 3 months. But no extension of time is granted for holding the first annual general meeting. Every annual general meeting shall be called during business hours on a day that is not a public holiday. It shall be held either at the registered office of the company or at some other place within the city, town or village in which the registered office of the company is situated. As regards holding of the annual general meeting, no distinction is made between a public company and a private company. 21 days' notice (Sec.171): A general meeting of a company may be called by giving not less than 21 days' notice in writing. Annual general meeting a statutory requirement: The annual general meeting of a company is a statutory requirement. It has to be called even where the company did not function during the year. Canceling or postponing of convened meeting: Where an annual general meeting is convened for a particular date and notice is issued to the members, the Board of directors can cancel or postpone the holding of the meeting on that date provided power is exercised for bona fide and proper reasons.

Canceling of failure to hold annual general meeting: If a company fails to hold an annual general meeting:

- Any member can apply, under Sec. 167, to the Company Law Board for calling the meeting.
- The company and every officer who is in default shall be punishable with fine.

Powers of Company Law Board to call annual general meeting (Sec. 167): If default is made by a company in holding an annual general meeting in accordance with Sec. 166, any member of the company may apply to the Company Law Board for calling such a meeting.

Penalty for default (Sec. 168): If default is made by a company in holding a meeting in accordance with Sec. 166 or in complying with any direction of the Company Law Board in calling a meeting under Sec. 167, the company, and every officer of the company who is in default, shall be punishable with fine which may extend to Rs. 2,500 for every day after the first during which such default continues.

3. Extraordinary General Meeting (Sec. 169): A statutory meeting and an annual general meeting of a company are called ordinary meetings. Any meeting other than these meetings is called an extraordinary general meeting. It is called for transacting some urgent or special business which cannot be postponed till the next annual general meeting. It may be convened. (1) by the Board of directors on its own or on the requisition of the members; or (2) by the requisitionists themselves on the failure of the Board of directors to call the meeting.

1. Extraordinary meting convened by the Board of directors.

The Board of directors may call an extraordinary general meeting:

a. On its own.
b. On requisition of the members.

2. Extraordinary meeting convened by the requisitionists

Power of Company Law Board to order meeting (Sec. 186): If for any reason it is impracticable for a company to call; hold or conduct an extraordinary general meeting, the Company Law Board may call an extraordinary meeting.

II. Class Meetings: Under the Companies Act, class meetings of various kinds of shareholders and creditors are required to be held under different circumstances. Under Sec. 106, class meetings of the holders of different classes of shares are to be held if the rights attaching to these shares are to be varied.

Requisites of a Valid Meeting: A meeting can validly transact any business if the following requirements are satisfied:

1. The meeting must be duly convened by a proper authority.
2. A proper notice must be served in a prescribed manner.
3. A quorum must be present.
4. A chairman must preside the meeting aside.
5. Minutes of the proceedings must be kept

RESOLUTIONS

Kinds of Resolutions: There are three kinds of resolutions under the Companies Act, 1956. They are:

1. Ordinary resolutions;
2. Special resolutions; and
3. Resolutions requiring special notice

1. Ordinary resolution (Sec. 189 (1)]

   An ordinary resolution is a resolution passed at a general meeting of a company by a simple majority of votes (i.e., votes cast in favour of the resolution exceed votes cast against it) including the casting vote of the chairman, if any).

   When is an ordinary resolution required? Ordinary resolution is necessary for the following among other purposes:

   - Rectification of name or adoption of new name by a company where it resembles the name of an existing company with the previous approval of the Central Government [Sec. 22 (1) (a)].
   - Issue of shares at a discount [Sec. 79 (2)]
   - Alteration of share capital [Sec. 94 (2)].
   - Re-issue of redeemed debentures (Sec.121).

- Adoption of statutory report (Sec. 165).
- Passing of annual accounts and balance sheet, along with reports of Board of directors and auditors (Sec. 210).
- Appointment of auditors and fixation of their remuneration [Sec. 224 (1)].
- Appointment of first directors who are liable to retire by rotation [Sec. 255 (1)].
- Increase or reduction in the number of directors within the limit fixed by the Articles (Sec. 258).
- Appointment of managing/whole-time director (Sec. 269).
- Removal of a director and appointment of a director in his place [Sec. 284(1)].
- Approval of appointment of sole-selling agents (Sec. 294).
- Winding up a company voluntarily in certain events [Sec. 484 (1) (a)].
- Appointment and fixation of remuneration of liquidators in a members voluntary winding up [Sec. 490 (1)].
- Nomination of a liquidator in a creditors' voluntary winding up [Sec. 502 (1)].

2. Special resolution [Sec. 189 (2)]: A special resolution is one which satisfies the following conditions:
   - The intention to propose the resolution as a special resolution has been duly specified in the notice calling the general meeting.
   - The notice has been duly given of the general meeting.
   - The votes cast in favour of the resolution by members entitled to vote are not less than 3 times the number of votes cast against the resolution by members so entitled and voting.
   - An explanatory statement setting out all material facts concerning the subject-matter of the special resolution including, in particular, the nature of the concern or interest of every director and the manager, if any, shall be annexed to the notice of the meeting.

When is a special resolution required? Special resolution is necessary for the following among other purposes:

- Alteration of Memorandum for changing the place of registered office from one state to another with the leave of the Company

Law Board [Sec. 17(1) and (2)]. Special resolution is also required for changing the 'objects clause' of the Memorandum.

- Changes of name of a company with the consent of the Central Government (Sec. 21).
- Omission or addition of the word 'Private' from or to the name of a company (Sec. 21).
- Change of name of a charitable or other non-profit company by omitting the word or words 'Limited' or 'Private Limited' [Sec. 25 (3)].
- Alteration of the Articles of a company [Sec. 31(1)].
- Conversion of any portion of the uncalled capital into reserve capital (Sec. 99).
- Reduction of share capital [Sec. 100 (1)].
- Variation of shareholder's rights (Sec. 106).
- Removal of a company's registered office outside the local limits of any city, town or village [Sec. 146 (2)].
- Keeping registers and returns at a place other than the registered office [Sec. 163(1)].
- Payment of interest out of capital [Sec. 208 (2) and (3)].
- Applying to the Central Government for appointing an Inspector for investigating a company's affairs in some cases [Sec. 237 (a)].
- Appointment of sole selling or buying agent in the case of companies having paid-up share capital of Rs. 50 lakhs or more [Sec. 294-AA(3)].
- Fixing the remuneration of directors where the Articles require such resolution [Sec. 309 (1)].
- Allowing a director to hold an office of profit under a company [Sec. 314(1) and (1-B)].
- Alteration of Memorandum to render the liability of directors unlimited [Sec.323(1)].
- Applying to the Court to wind up a company [Sec. 433 (a)].
- Winding up a company voluntarily [Sec. 484 (1) (b)].
- Authorizing the liquidator of a company to accept shares as consideration for the transfer of its assets [Secs. 494 (1)].

- Disposal of books and papers of a company in voluntary winding up when its affairs' have been completely wound up [Sec. 550 (1) (b)].

3. Resolutions requiring a special notice (Sec. 190)

   A resolution requiring a special notice is not an independent class of resolutions. It is only a different kind of an ordinary resolution of which notice of the intention to move a resolution has to be given to the company . The notice will be given not less than 14 days before the meeting at which the resolution is to be served and at the day of the meeting.

ACCOUNTS, AUDIT AND PREVENTION OF OPPRESSION AND MISMANAGEMENT

Accounts: Books of account to be kept by company (Sec. 209): The Act requires every company to maintain at its registered office proper books of account with respect to

- All receipts and disbursements of money and the matters in respect of which the receipts and disbursements take place;
- All sales and purchases of goods of the company;
- The assets and liabilities of the company, and
- In the case of a company engaged in production, processing, manufacturing or mining activities, such particulars relating to utilisation of material or labour or to other items of cost as may be prescribed by the Central Government in the case of such class of companies. The object of this clause is to make efficiency audit possible.

Inspection of books of account (Sec. 209-A): The books of account and other books and papers shall be open to inspection during business hours (i) by the Registrar; (ii) by such other officer of the Government as may be authorized by the Central Government in this behalf. (iii) by such officers of the Securities and Exchange Board of India as may be authorized by it.

Statutory Books: In addition to the books of account required to be maintained by a company under Sec. 209, the company is also required to maintain some other books with a view to safeguarding the interest of shareholder. Such books are called statutory books and are as follows:

- Register of investments not held in company's name (open to inspection of members and debenture-holders) [Sec. 49 (7)].

- Register of charges (open to inspection of all) [Sec.143 (1)].
- Register of members (open to inspection of all) (Sec. 150 (1)).
- Index of members where their number is more than 50 (open to inspection of all) [Sec. 151 (1)].
- Register of debenture-holders (open to inspection of all) [Sec. 152 (1)].
- Index of debenture-holders where their number is more than 50 (open to
- inspection of all) [Sec. 152 (2)].
- Foreign register (and a duplicate) of members and debenture-holders, if any (open to inspection of all) (Sec. 158).
- Minute books containing minutes of proceedings of general meetings (open to inspection of members) [Sec. 193] (1)].
- Books of account and annual accounts [Secs. 209 (1) 210].
- Register of contracts, and companies and firms in which directors are interested (open to inspection of members) [Sec. 301 (1)].
- Register of directors, managing director, manager and secretary (open to inspection of all) [Sec. 303 (1)].
- Register of directors' shareholding (open to inspection of members and debenture-holders during 14 days before and 3 days after the annual general meeting and to the Registrar and the Central Government) [Sec. 307 (1)].
- Register of loans made, guarantees given or securities provided to companies under the same management (open to inspection of all) [Sec. 370 (1.C)]

Statistical Books: In addition to statutory books, there are many other books which are required to be maintained for the proper and efficient running of a company. These books are not only found to be desirable but often indispensable in practice. Some of the important statistical or non-statutory books are as follow:

- Share application and allotment book.
- Share call book.
- Register of share warrants.
- Register of share certificates.
- Register of share transfers.

- Register of lost share certificates.
- Register of balance tickets issued.
- Register of transfers certified.
- Agenda book.
- Register of lists of dividends.
- Dividend Mandate register.
- Register of debenture interest.
- Register of documents sealed.
- Register of powers of attorney.
- Register of probates.
- Register of directors' attendance

Auditors: To safeguard the interest of the shareholders, the Companies Act provides the employment of an auditor. The auditor is the servant of the shareholders and his duty is to examine the affairs of the company on their behalf at the end of a year and report to them what he has found about that company.

QUALIFICATIONS AND DISQUALIFICATIONS OF AUDITORS (SEC. 226)

Qualifications [Sec. 226 (1)]: A person shall not be qualified for appointment as auditor of a company unless he is a Chartered Accountant within the meaning of the Chartered Accountants Act, 1949.

Disqualifications (Sec. 226 (3)]: The following persons, even if they are otherwise qualified, shall he disqualified from being appointed as auditors of a company:

a. A body corporate.
b. An officer or employee of the company.
c. A person who is a partner, or who is in the employment of an officer or employee of the company.
d. A person who is indebted to the company for an amount exceeding Rs. 1,000 or who has given any guarantee of any third person to the company for an amount exceeding Rs. 1,000.
e. A person holding any security of that company after a period of one year from the date of commencement of the Companies (Amendment) Act, 2000.

Appointment of Auditors (Secs. 224 and 225): Appointment in annual general meeting: Every company shall, at each annual general meeting, appoint an auditor or auditors to hold office from the conclusion.

Restriction on the appointment of auditors: A company shall not appoint or re-appoint any person who is in full-time employment elsewhere or firm as its auditor if such person or firm is, at the date of such appointment or reappointment, holding appointment as auditor of more than the specified number of companies.

Compulsory re-appointment: At any general meeting a retiring auditor, by whatsoever authority appointed (Board of directors, general meeting, annual general meeting or Central Government), shall be re-appointed except in the following cases:

b. If he is not qualified for re-appointment;

c. If he has given notice to the company in writing or his unwillingness to be re-appointed;

d. If a resolution has been passed to the effect appointing somebody instead of him or providing expressly that he shall not be re-appointed; or

e. Where notice has been given of an intended resolution to appoint some person or persons in the place of a retiring auditor, and by reason of death, incapacity or disqualification of that person or of all those persons, the resolution cannot be proceeded with [Sec. 224 (2)]

Appointment by the Central Government: Where at an annual general meeting no auditors are appointed or re-appointed, the Central Government may appoint a person to fill the vacancy.

Appointment of auditors by a special resolution: Sec. 224-A puts another restriction that in the case of a company in which not less than 25 per cent of the subscribed share capital is held, whether singly or in any combination, the appointment or re-appointment at each annual general meeting of an auditor or auditors shall be made by a special resolution.

First auditors: The first auditors of a company shall be appointed by its Board of directors within 1 month of its incorporation. Subsequent appointment (Sec. 225): At the expiry of the term of an auditor, the members may, in the annual general meeting, appoint another person in his place.

Penalty (Sec. 232): If default is made by a company in complying with any of the provisions of Sec. 225, the company, and every officer of the company who is in default, shall be punishable with fine which may extend to Rs. 5,000.

Casual vacancy: The Board of directors may fill any casual vacancy in the office of an auditor.

- Removal of auditors: The first auditors of company appointed by the directors prior to the first annual general meeting of the company may be removed by the members in a general meeting even if their tenure of office has not expired.
- Remuneration of auditors: The remuneration of the auditors of a company shall be fixed by the company in general meeting or in such manner as the company in general meeting may determine.

Position of Auditors:

- As an agent of the members.
- As an officer of the company and
- As an employee of the company

Rights and powers of auditors:

- Right of access to books, accounts and vouchers (Sec. 227).
- Right to obtain information and explanations (Sec. 227)
- Right to visit branch offices and right of access to books, etc. (Sec. 228)
- Where the accounts of any branch office are audited by a person other than the company's auditor, the company auditor shall -
- Be entitled to visit the branch office, if he deems it necessary to do so, for the performance of his duties as auditor; and
- Have a right of access at all times to the books and accounts and vouchers of the company maintained at the branch office.
- Right to receive notice of general meeting and to attend them (Sec. 231)
- Right to receive remuneration.

Duties of auditors:

2. Acquaintance with the Articles and the Companies Act.
3. Report to members (Sec. 227).
4. Duty of care and caution.

Further duties:

1. Statutory report (Sec. 165)
2. Prospectus (Sec. 56).
3. Assistance in investigation (Sec. 240).

PREVENTION OF OPPRESSION AND MISMANAGEMENT

Special powers have been vested in the Company Law Board for the protection of members against oppression by the majority of shareholders and for intervention in case of mismanagement of a company's affairs. This has been done because the cardinal rule laid down in Foss v. Harbottle, that the minority is bound by the decision of the majority, is abused in many cases. Secs. 397 and 409 provide for remedial measures.

If the oppressed minority consider to wind up the company it would not relieve but on the contrary, they would be unfairly prejudiced by winding up, they may petition the Court under Sec. 397, and the Court may impose a solution on the disputants. A certain number of members (stated below) may apply to the Company Law Board for relief on the grounds that the affairs of the company are being conducted:

- In a manner oppressive to any member or members, or
- In a manner prejudicial to the interests of the company, or
- In a manner prejudicial to the public interest, or
- That material change has taken place in the management or control of the company and that by reason of, it may pass any orders with a view to bringing to an end the matters complained of, or apprehended.

If the Company Law Board is satisfied that the affairs of the company are being conducted as complained of, it may pass any order with a view to bringing to an end the matter complained of, or apprehended. The number of members necessary to make application is (i) in the case of a company having share capital, 100 members or 10 per cent of the total number of member, whichever is less, or members holding 10 per cent of the issued capital; (ii) in the case of a company not having share capital, 20 per cent of its total number of members. The Central Government is also entitled to apply to the Company Law Board for an order as above.

The Company Law Board may in its discretion make any order that it thinks fit, and in particular, it may provide for:

- The regulation of the company's affairs in future;

- The acquisition of the shares or interests of any members by other members or by the company;
- The consequent reduction of the share capital in case of (ii) above;
- Termination, setting aside or modification of any agreement, howsoever arrived at, between the company and the managing agent, secretaries and treasurers, managing director, any other director, or manager;
- Termination, setting aside or modification of any agreement between the company and any other person with the latter's consent;
- Setting aside any transfer, delivery of goods, payment, execution or other act relating to property made or done by or against the company within 3 months of the application which would amount to a fraudulent preference in the case of an individual's insolvency;
- Any other matter for which in the opinion of the Company Law Board it is just and equitable that provision should be made (Sec. 402). No compensation is payable for loss of office resulting from the termination of agreement by the Company Law Board. Any person whose agreement of office has been terminated cannot act for the company for 5 years thereafter without the leave of the Company Law Board. In addition to the above order, heavy penalties are provided.

WINDING UP

WINDING UP BY COURT

A winding up by the Court, or compulsory winding up, as it is often called, is initiated by an application by way of petition presented to the appropriate Court for winding up order.

GROUNDS FOR COMPULSORY WINDING UP

- Resolved to be wound up by the Court.
- If default is made in delivering the statutory report to the Registrar or in holding the statutory meeting.
- If the company does not commence its business within a year from its incorporation, or suspends its business for a whole year.

- If the number of members falls below seven (or in case of a private company, below two).
- If the company is unable to pay its debts.
- If the court is of opinion that it is just and equitable that the company should be wound up.
- Just & Equitable: (a) Main object-failed (b) Deadlock in management (c) Cannot carry on business except losses. (d) Mere bubble - and does not carry any business or does not have any property. (e) Majority of shareholder have adapted an aggressive policy towards the minority.

Who May Petition: The following persons may file petition:

- The company;
- Creditor;
- Contributory;
- All or any of the above parties;
- The Registrar;
- Any person authorized by the Central Government
- By virtue of Sec. 440, when a company is already being wound up voluntarily, the court may order winding up by it.

Voluntary Winding Up: A company may be wound up voluntarily:

- when the period (if any) fixed for its duration has expired or an event on the happening of which the company is to be wound up has happened and the company in general meeting has passed an ordinary resolution to wind up; or
- if the company passes a special resolution to wind up voluntarily (Sec. 484). There are two kinds of voluntary winding up, namely: Member's or Creditors'.

Winding up Under Supervision: Where a company is being wound up voluntarily the Court may order the continuation of voluntary winding up subject to its supervision with any terms or conditions. The liquidator will continue to exercise all powers subject to any restrictions laid down by the Court.

Consequences of Winding Up:

- As to Shareholders: A shareholder is liable to pay full amount of shares held by him.

- As to Creditors: A secured creditor may either (i) rely on the security and ignore the liquidation, or (ii) value his security and prove for the balance of his debt, or (iii) give up his security and prove for the whole amount. Unsecured creditors of an insolvent company are paid in this order: (i) preferential payment under Sec.530, (ii) other debts pari passu.
- As to Servants and Officers: A winding up order operates as a notice of discharge to the employees and officers of the company except when the business of the company is being continued (Sec. 444). A voluntary winding up also operates as a notice of discharge.
- As to Proceedings: After a winding up petition is presented the Court may stay all proceedings against the company.
- As to Costs: If the company, while in liquidation, brings or defends any action and is ordered to pay costs, they are paid first out of the assets of the company.

Offences Antecedent to or in Course of Winding Up:

- Offences of Officers: Every past and present officer of a company which is being wound up must assist the liquidator and if he fails to do so he is liable to be punished. He is liable to be imprisoned up to 5 years, or fined or given both punishments.
- Misfeasance Proceedings: In the course of winding up a company it appears that any person who has been found to be guilty of any misfeasance or breach of trust in relation to the company, the Court may, examine into the conduct of the person, director, managing agent, secretaries and treasurers, manager, liquidator or officer aforesaid, and compel him to repay or restore the money or property or any part thereof respectively with interest at such rate as the Court thinks just, or to contribute such sum to the assets of the company by way of compensation, notwithstanding that offence is one for which the offender may be criminally liable.

Liquidators:

- Compulsory Winding Up: The official Liquidator attached to High Court will become the liquidator on a winding up order being passed.
- Powers of Liquidator: (i) institute or defend any suit, prosecution, or the legal proceeding in the name of the

company, (ii) carry on the business of the company for its beneficial winding up, (iii) sell company's property, (iv) raise money on the security of the company's assets, and (v) do all other things necessary for the winding up.

- Duties of Liquidator: Summon meetings of creditors or contributories get in the property and pay the debts and distribute the balance among contributories. Keep the proper books of account, minutes books, and allow inspection thereof. Keep all the funds of the company in "the public account of India" in the Reserve Bank of India.
- Voluntary Liquidator: The voluntary liquidator is appointed by resolution in general meeting of the company and or of the creditors and his remuneration fixed. A voluntary liquidator is a paid agent of the company and is liable in damages if he neglects his duties as such.
- Disclaimer by a Liquidator: Section 535(1) empower the liquidator, with the leave of the Court to disclaim any onerous property of the company.

Note: VF Corporation (VFC) offers branded lifestyle apparel and related products in various product categories including jeanswear, outerwear, packs, footwear, sportswear and occupational apparel. The company operates in the US, Europe, Asia, Canada and Latin America. It is headquartered in Greensboro, North Carolina, and employs 46,600 people. For further knowledge regarding this chapter reader can visit www.vfc.com

6

International Business Environment

One of the most dramatic and significant world trends in the past two decades has been the rapid, sustained growth of international business. Markets have become truly global for most goods, many services, and especially for financial instruments of all types. World product trade has expanded by more than 6 percent a year since 1950, which is more than 50 percent faster than growth of output the most dramatic increase in globalization, has occurred in financial markets. In the global forex markets, billions of dollars are transacted each day, of which more than 90 percent represent financial transactions unrelated to trade or investment. Much of this activity takes place in the so-called Euromarkets, markets outside the country whose currency is used.

INTRODUCTION

This pervasive growth in market interpenetration makes it increasingly difficult for any country to avoid substantial external impacts on its economy. In particular massive capital flows can push exchange rates away from levels that accurately reflect competitive relationships among nations if national economic policies or performances diverse in short run. The rapid dissemination rate of new technologies speeds the pace at which countries must adjust to external events. Smaller, more open countries, long ago gave up illusion of domestic policy autonomy. But even the largest and most apparently self-contained economies, including the US, are now significantly affected by the global economy. Global integration in trade, investment, and factor flows, technology, and communication has been tying economies together. Why then are these changes coming about, and what exactly are they? It is in practice, easier to identify the former than interpret the latter.

The reason is that during the past few decades, the emergence of corporate empires in the world economy, based on the contemporary scientific and technological developments, has led to globalization of production. As a result of international production, co-operation among global productive units, the large-scale capital exports, "the export of production" or "production abroad" has come into prominence as against commodity export in world economy in recent years. Global corporations consider the whole of the world their production place, as well as their market and move factors of production to wherever they can optimally be combined. They avail fully of the revolution that has brought about instant worldwide communication, and near instant-transformation. Their ownership is transnational; their management is transnational. Their freely mobile management, technology and capital, the modern agent for stepped-up economic growth, transcend individual national boundaries. They are domestic in every place, foreign in none-a true corporate citizen of the world. The greater interdependence among nations has already reduced economic insularity of the peoples of the world, as well as their social and political insularity.

DEFINITION OF INTERNATIONAL BUSINESS

International business includes any type of business activity that can cross national borders. Though a number of definitions in the business literature can be found but no simple or universally accepted definition exists for the term international business. At one end of the definitional spectrum, international business is defined as organization that buys and/ or sells goods and services across two or more national boundaries, even if management is located in a single country. At the other end of the spectrum, international business is equated only with those big enterprises, which have operating units outside their own country. In the middle are institutional arrangements that provide for some managerial direction of economic activity taking place abroad but stop short of controlling ownership of the business carrying on the activity, for example joint ventures with locally owned business or with foreign governments.

In its traditional form of international trade and finance as well as its newest form of multinational business operations, international business has become massive in scale and has come to exercise a major influence over political, economic and social from many types of comparative business studies and from a knowledge of many aspects of foreign business operations. In fact, sometimes the foreign operations and the comparative business are used as synonymous for international business. Foreign business refers to domestic operations within a foreign country. Comparative business focuses on similarities and differences among countries and business systems for focuses on similarities and differences among countries and business operations and comparative business as fields of enquiry do not have as their major point of interest the special problems that arise when business activities cross national boundaries. For example, the vital question of potential conflicts between the nation-state and the multinational firm, which receives major attention is international business, is not like to be centered or even peripheral in foreign operations and comparative business.

SCOPE OF INTERNATIONAL BUSINESS ACTIVITIES

The study of international business focus on the particular problems and opportunities that emerge because a firm is operating in more than one country. In a real sense, international business involves the broadest and most generalized study of the field of business, adapted to a fairly unique across the border environment. Many of the parameters and environmental variables that are very important in international business (such as foreign legal systems, foreign exchange markets, cultural differences, and different rates of inflation) are either largely irrelevant to domestic business or are so reduced in range and complexity as to be of greatly diminished significance.

Thus, it might be said that domestic business is a special limited case of international business. The distinguishing feature of international business is that international firms operate in environments that are highly uncertain and where the rules of the game are often ambiguous, contradictory, and subject to rapid change, as compared to the domestic environment. In fact, conducting international business is really not like playing a whole new ball game, however, it is like playing in a different ballpark, where international managers have to learn the factors unique to the playing field. Managers who are astute in identifying new ways of doing business that satisfy the changing priorities of foreign governments have an obvious and major competitive advantage over their competitors who cannot or will not adapt to these changing priorities.

The guiding principles of a firm engaged in international business activities should incorporate a global perspective. A firm's guiding principles can be defined in terms of three board categories of products offered/ market served, capabilities, and results. However, their perspective of the international business is critical to understand the full meaning of international business. That is, the firm's senior management should explicitly define the firm's guiding principles in terms of an international mandate rather than allow the firm's guiding principles in terms as an incidental adjunct to its domestic activities. Incorporating an international outlook into the firm's basic statement of purpose will help focus the attention of managers (at all levels of the organization) on the opportunities (and hazards) outside the domestic economy.

It must be stressed that the impacts of the dynamic factors unique to the playing field for international business are felt in all relevant stages of evolving and implementing business plans. The first broad stage of the process is to formulate corporate guiding principles. As outlined below the first step in formulating and implementing a set of business plans is to define the firm's guiding principles in the market place. The guiding principles should, among other things, provide a long-term view of what the firm is striving to become and provide direction to divisional and subsidiary managers vehicle, some firms use "the decision circle" which is simply an interrelated set of strategic choices forced upon any firm faced with the internationalization of its markets. These choices have to do with marketing, sourcing, labor, management, ownership, finance, law, control, and public affairs.

Here the first two marketing and sourcing-constitute the basic strategies that encompass a firm's initial considerations. Essentially, management is answering two questions: to whom are we going to sell what, and from where and how will we supply that market? We then have a series of input strategies-labor, management, ownership, and financial. They are in their efforts to develop their own business plans. As an obligation addressed essentially to the query, with what resources are we going to implement the basic strategies? That is, where will we find the right people, willingness to carry the risk, and the necessary funds? A third set of strategies legal and control-respond to the problem of how the firm is to structure itself of implement the basic strategies, given the resources it can muster. A final strategic area, public affairs, is shown as a basic strategy simply because it places a restraint on all other strategy choices.

Each strategy area contains a number of subsidiary strategy options. The decision process that normally starts in the marketing strategy area is an iterative one. As the decision maker proceeds around the decision circle, previous selected strategies must be readjusted. Only a portion of the possible feedback adjustment loops is shown here.

Although these strategy areas are shown separately but they obviously do not stand-alone. There must be constant reiteration as one moves around the decision circle. The sourcing obviously influences marketing strategy, as well as the reverse. The target market may enjoy certain preferential relationships with other markets. That is, everything influences everything else. Inasmuch as the number of options a firm faces is multiplied as it moves into international market, decision-making becomes increasingly complex the deeper the firm becomes involved internationally. One is dealing with multiple currency, legal, marketing, economic, political, and cultural systems. Geographic and demographic factors differ widely.

In fact, as one moves geographically, virtually everything becomes a variable: there are few fixed factors. For our purposes here, a strategy is defined as an element in a consciously devised overall plan of corporate development that, once made and implemented, is difficult (i.e. costly) to change in the short run. By way of contrast, an operational or tactical decision is one that sets up little or no institutionalized resistance to making a different decision in the near future. Some theorists have differentiated among strategic, tactical, and operational, with the first being defined as those decisions, that imply multi-year commitments; a tactical decision, one that can be shifted in roughly a year's time; an operational decision, one subject to change in less that a year. In the international context, we suggest that the tactical decision, as the phrase is used here, is elevated to the strategic level because of the rigidities in the international environment not present in the purely domestic-for example, work force planning and overall distribution decisions. Changes may be implemented domestically in a few months, but if one is operating internationally, law, contract, and custom may intervene to render change difficult unless implemented over several years.

SPECIAL DIFFICULTIES IN INTERNATIONAL BUSINESS

What makes international business strategy different from the domestic are the differences in the marketing environment. The important special problems in international marketing are given below:

- Political and Legal Differences: The political and legal environment of foreign markets is different from that of the domestic. The complexity generally increases as the number of countries in which a company does business increases. It should also be noted that the political and legal environment is not the same in all provinces of many home markets. For example, the political and legal environment is not exactly the same in all the states of India.
- Cultural Differences: The cultural differences, is one of the most difficult problems in international marketing. Many

domestic markets, however, are also not free from cultural diversity.

- Economic Differences: The economic environment may vary from country to country.
- Differences in the Currency Unit: The currency unit varies from one nation to other nation. This may sometimes cause problems of currency convertibility, besides the problems of exchange rate fluctuations. The monetary system and regulations may also vary.
- Differences in the Language: An international marketer often encounters problems arising out of the differences in the language. Even when the same language is used in different countries, the same words of terms may have different meanings. The language problem, however, is not peculiar to the international marketing. For example: the multiplicity of languages in India.
- Differences in the Marketing Infrastructure: The availability and nature of the marketing facilities available in different countries may vary widely. For example, an advertising medium very effective in one market may not be available or may be underdeveloped in another market.
- Trade Restrictions: A trade restriction, particularly import controls, is a very important problem, which an international marketer faces.
- High Costs of Distance: When the markets are far removed by distance, the transport cost becomes high and the time required for affecting the delivery tends to become longer. Distance tends to increase certain other costs also.
- Differences in Trade Practices: Trade practices and customs may differ between two countries.

BENEFITS OF INTERNATIONAL BUSINESS SURVIVAL

Because most of the countries are not as fortunate as the United States in terms of market size, resources, and opportunities, they must trade with others to survive; Hong Kong, has historically underscored this point well, for without food and water from china, the British colony would not have survived along. The countries of Europe have had similar experience, since most European nations are relatively small in size. Without foreign markets, European firms would not have sufficient economies of scale to allow them to be competitive with US firms. Nestle mentions in one of its advertisements that its own country, Switzerland, lacks natural resources, forcing it to depend on trade and adopt the geocentric perspective. International competition may not be matter of choice when survival is at stake. However, only firms with previously substantial market share and international experience could expand successfully.

GROWTH OF OVERSEAS MARKETS

Developing countries, in spite of economic and marketing problems, are excellent markets. According to a report prepared for the U.S. CONGRESS by the U.S. trade representative, Latin America and Asia/ Pacific are experiencing the strongest economic growth. American markets cannot ignore the vast potential of international markets. The world is more than four times larger than the U.S. market. In the case of Amway corps., a privately held U.S. manufacturer of cosmetics, soaps and vitamins, Japan represents a larger market than the United States.

Sales and Profit

Foreign markets constitute a larger share of the total business of many firms that have wisely cultivated markets aboard. Many large U.S. companies have done well because of their overseas customers. IBM and Compaq, foe ex, sell more computers aboard than at home. According to the US dept of commerce, foreign profits of American firms rose at a compound annual rate of 10% between 1982 and 1991, almost twice as fast as domestic profits of the same companies.

Diversification

Demand for the most products is affected by such cyclical factors as recession and such seasonal factors as climate. The unfortunate consequence of these variables is sales fluctuation, which can frequently be substantial enough to cause lay offs of personnel. One way to diversify a companies' risk is to consider foreign markets as a solution for variable demand. Such markets, even out fluctuations by providing outlets for excess production capacity. Cold weather, for instance may depress soft drink consumption. Yet not all countries enter the winter season at the same time, and some countries are relatively warm year round. Bird, USA, inc., a Nebraska manufacturer of go carts, and mini cars, for promotional purposes has found that global selling has enabled the company to have year round production. It may be winter in Nebraska but its summer in the southern hemisphere-somewhere there is a demand and that stabilizes the business.

Inflation and Price Moderation

The benefits of export are readily self-evident. Imports can also be highly beneficial to a country because they constitute reserve capacity for the local economy. Without imports, there is no incentive for domestic firms to moderate their prices. The lack of imported product alternatives forces consumers to pay more, resulting into inflation and excessive profits for local firms. This development usually acts as prelude to workers demand for higher wages, further exacerbating the problem of inflation.

Import quotas imposed on Japanese automobiles in the 1980's saved 46200 US production jobs but at a cost of $160,000 per job per year. This cost was a result of the addition of $400 to the prices of US cars, and $1000 to the prices of Japanese imports. This windfall for Detroit resulted in record high profits for US automakers. Not only do trade restrictions depress price competition in the short run, but they also can adversely affect demand for year to come.

Employment

Trade restrictions, such as high tariffs caused by the 1930's smoot-hawley bill, which forced the average tariff rates across the board to climb above 60%, contributed significantly to the great depression and have the potential to cause wide spread unemployment again. Unrestricted trade on the other hand improves the world's GNP and enhances employment generally for all nations. Importing products and foreign ownership can provide benefits to a nation. According to the institute for international Economics-a private, non- profit research institute - the growth of foreign ownership has not resulted in a loss of jobs for Americans; and foreign firms have paid their American workers the same, as have domestic firms.

Standards of Living

Trade affords countries and their citizen's higher standards of living than otherwise possible. Without trade, product shortages force people to pay more for less, products taken for granted, such as coffee and bananas may become unavailable overnight. Life in most countries would be much more difficult were it not for the many strategic metals that must be imported. Trade also makes it easier for industries to specialize and gain access to raw materials, while at the same time fostering competition and efficiency. A diffusion of innovations across national boundaries is useful by-products of international trade. A lack of such trade would inhibit the flow innovative ideas.

FRAMEWORK FOR ANALYSING INTERNATIONAL BUSINESS ENVIRONMENT

Environmental analysis is defined as "the process by which strategists monitor the economic, governmental/legal, market/competitive, supplier/ technological, geographic, and social settings to determine opportunities and threats to their firms".

"Environmental diagnosis consists of managerial decisions made by analyzing the significance of the data (opportunities and threats) of the environmental analysis".

The definition of environmental analysis given above has been made in the context of the strategic management process for an existing firm. It is, however, quite obvious that environmental analysis is the cornerstone of new business opportunity analysis too. Indeed, today a much more greater emphasis is given than in the past to the fact that environmental analysis is an essential prerequisite for strategic management decision-making.

For instance, in his recent editions of Marketing Management, Philip Kotler, the world-renowned professor and author, describes Marketing Environment Audit as the first component of a Marketing Audit, whereas in the earlier editions of this book, the definition of Marketing Audit does not have any reference to the environment.

It is now unquestionably accepted that the prospects of a business depend not only on its resources but also on the environment. An analysis of the strengths, weaknesses, opportunities and threats (SWOT) is very essential for the business policy formulation. Just as the life and success of an individual depend on his innate capability, including physiological factors, traits and skills, to cope with the environment, the survival and success of a business firm depend on its innate strength - the resources as its command, including physical resources, financial resources, skill and organization - and its adaptability to the environment. Every business enterprise, thus, consists of a set of internal factors and is confronted with a set of external factors.

The internal factors are generally regarded as controllable factors because the company has control over these factors; it can alter or modify such factors as its personnel, physical facilities, organization and functional means, such as the marketing mix, to suit the environment. The external factors, on the other hand, are by and large, beyond the control of a company. The external or environmental factors such as the economic factors, socio-cultural factors, government and legal factors, demographic factors, geophysical factors etc. are, therefore, generally regarded as uncontrollable factors. As the environmental factors are beyond the control of a firm, its success will depend to a very large extent on its adaptability to the environment, i.e. its ability to properly design and adjust the internal (the controllable) variables to take advantage of the opportunities and to combat the threats in the environment. The business environment comprises a microenvironment and a macro environment.

MICRO ENVIRONMENT

"The micro environment consists of the factors in the company's immediate environment" that effect the performance of the company. These include the suppliers, marketing intermediaries, competitors, customers, and publics. "The macro environment consists of the larger societal forces that affect all the actors in the company's micro environment namely, the demographic, economic, natural, technological, political and cultural forces". It is quite obvious that the micro environmental factors are more intimately linked with the company than the macro factors. The micro forces need not necessarily affect all the firms in a particular industry in the same way. Some of the micro factors may be particular to a firm. For example, a firm, which depends on a supplier, may have a supplier environment, which is entirely different from that of a firm whose supply source is different. When competing firms in an industry have the same microelements, the relative success of the firms depends on their relative effectiveness in dealing with these elements.

- Suppliers: An important force in the microenvironment of a company is the supplier, i.e., those who supply the inputs like raw materials and components to the company. The importance of reliable source/sources of supply to the smooth functioning of the business is obvious. Uncertainty regarding the supply or other supply constraints often compels companies to maintain high inventories causing cost increases. It has been pointed out that factories in India maintain indigenous stocks of 3-4 months and imported stocks of 9 months as against an average of a few hours to two weeks in Japan. Because of the sensitivity of the supply, many companies give high importance to vendor development. Vertical integration, where feasible, helps solve the supply problem. It is very risky to depend on a single because a strike, lock out or any other production problem with that supplier may seriously affect the company. Similarly, a change in the attitude or behavior of the supplier may also affect the company. Hence, multiple sources of supply often help reduce such risks. The supply management assumes more importance in a scarcity environment. "Company purchasing agents are learning how to "wine and dine" suppliers to obtain favorable treatment during periods of shortages. In other words, the purchasing department might have to "market" itself to suppliers".

- Customers: As it is often, exhorted, the major task of a business is to create and sustain customers. A business exists only due to its customers. Monitoring the customer sensitivity is, therefore, a prerequisite for the business success. A company may have different categories of consumers like individuals, households, industries and other commercial establishments, and government and other institutions. For example, the customers of a tyre company may include individual automobile owners, automobile manufacturers, public sector transport undertakings and other transport operators. Depending on a single customer is often too risky because it may place the company in a poor bargaining position, apart from the risks of losing business consequent to the winding up of business by the customer or due to the customer's switching over the competitors of the company. The choice of the customer segments should be made by considering a number of factors including the relative profitability, dependability, stability of demand, growth prospects and the extent of competition.
- Competitors: A firm's competitors include not only the other firms, which market the same or similar products, but also all those who compete for the discretionary income of the consumers. For example, the competition for a company's televisions may come not only from other T.V. manufacturers but also from two-wheelers, refrigerators, cooking ranges, stereo sets and so on and from firms offering savings and investment schemes like banks, Unit Trust of India, companies accepting public deposits or issuing shares or debentures etc. This competition among these products may be described as desire competition as the primary task here is to influence the basic desire of the consumer. Such desire competition is generally very high in countries characterized by limited

disposable incomes and many unsatisfied desires (and, of course, with many alternatives for spending/investing the disposable income). If the consumer decides to spend his discretionary income on recreation (or recreation cum education) he will still confronted with a number of alternatives choose from like T.V., stereo, two-in-one, three -in-one etc. The competition among such alternatives, which satisfy a particular category of desire, is called generic competition. If the consumer decides to go in for a T.V. the next question is which form of the T.V. - black and white or colour, with remote-control or without it etc. In other words, there is a product form competition. Finally the consumer encounters the brand competition i.e., the competition between the different brands of the same product form. An implication of these different demands is that a marketer should strive to create primary and selective demand for his products.

- Marketing Intermediaries: The immediate environment of a company may consist of a number of marketing intermediaries which are "firms that aid the company in promoting, selling and distributing its goods to final buyers". The marketing intermediaries include middlemen such as agents and merchants who "help the company find customers or close sales with them", physical distribution firms which "assist the company in stocking and moving goods form their origin to their destination" such as warehouses and transportation firms; marketing service agencies which "assist the company in targeting and promoting its products to the right markets" such as advertising agencies, marketing research firms, media firms and consulting firms; and financial intermediaries which finance marketing activities and insure business risks. Marketing intermediaries are vital links between the company and the final consumers. A dislocation or disturbance of this link, or a wrong choice of the link, may cost the company very heavily. Retail chemists and druggists in India once decided to boycott the products of a leading company on some issue such as poor retail margin. This move for collective boycott was, however, objected to by the MRTP commission; but for this company would, perhaps, have been in trouble.
- Democratic: A company may encounter certain publics in its environment. "A public is any group that has an actual or

potential interest in or impact on an organization's ability to achieve its interests. Media publics, citizens action publics and local publics are some examples. For example, one of the leading companies in India was frequently under attack by the media public, particularly by a leading daily, which was allegedly bent on bringing down the share prices of the company by tarnishing its image. Such exposures or campaigns by the media might even influence the government decisions affecting the company. The local public also affects many companies. Environmental pollution is an issue often taken up by a number of local publics. Actions by local publics on the issue have caused some companies to suspend operations and/or take pollution abatement measures.

GROWTH OF CONSUMER PUBLIC IS AN IMPORTANT DEVELOPMENT AFFECTING BUSINESS

It is wrong to think that all public are threats to business. Some of the actions of the publics may cause problems for the companies. However, some publics are an opportunity for the business. Some businessmen, for example, regard consumerism as an opportunity for the business. The media public may be used to disseminate useful information. Similarly, fruitful cooperation between a company and the local publics may be established for the mutual benefit of the company and the local community.

Macro Environment

As stated earlier, a company and the forces in its microenvironment operate in a larger macro environment of forces that shape opportunities and pose threat to the company. The macro forces are, generally, more uncontrollable than the micro forces.

ECONOMIC ENVIRONMENT

Economic conditions, economic policies and the economic system are the important external factors that constitute the economic environment of a business. The economic conditions of a country-for example, the nature of the economy, the stage of development of the economy, economic resources, the level of income, the distribution of income and assets, etc- are among the very important determinants of business strategies.

In a developing country, the low income may be the reason for the very low demand for a product. The sale of a product for which the demand is income elastic naturally increases with an increase in income.

But a firm is unable to increase the purchasing power of the people to generate a higher demand for its product. Hence, it may have to reduce the price of the product to increase the sales. The reduction in the cost of production may have to be effected to facilitate price reduction. It may even be necessary to invent or develop a new low-cost product to suit the low-income market. Thus Colgate designed a simple, hand-driven, inexpensive ($10) washing machine for low-income buyers in less developed countries. Similarly, the National Cash Register Company took an innovative step backward by developing a crank-operated cash register that would sell at half the cost of a modern cash register and this was well received in a number of developing countries.

In countries where investment and income are steadily and rapidly rising, business prospects are generally bright, and further investments are encouraged. There are a number of economists and businessmen who feel that the developed countries are no longer worthwhile propositions for investment because these economies have reached more or less saturation levels in certain respects. In developed economies, replacement demand accounts for a considerable part of the total demand for many consumer durables whereas the replacement demand is negligible in the developing economies.

The economic policy of the government, needless to say, has a very great impact on business. Some types or categories of business are favorably affected by government policy, some adversely affected, while it is neutral in respect of others. For example, a restrictive import policy, or a policy of protecting the home industries, may greatly help the import-competing industries. Similarly, an industry that falls within the priority sector in terms of the government policy may get a number of incentives and other positive support from the government, whereas those industries which are regarded as inessential may have the odds against them.

In India, the government's concern about the concentration of economic power restricted the role of the large industrial houses and foreign concerns to the core sector, the heavy investment sector, the export sector and backward regions. The monetary and fiscal policies, by the incentives and disincentives they offer and by their neutrality, also affect the business in different ways. An industrial undertaking may be able to take advantage of external economies by locating itself in a large city; but the Government of India's policy was to discourage industrial location in such places and constrain or persuade industries undertaking, a backward area location may have many disadvantages. However, the incentives available for units located in these backward areas many compensate them for these disadvantages, at least to some extent.

According to the industrial policy of the Government of India until July 1991, the development of 17 of the most important industries were reserved for the state. In the development of another 12 major industries, the state was to play a dominant role. In the remaining industries, co-operative enterprises, joint sector enterprises and small scale units were to get preferential treatment over large entrepreneurs in the private sector. The government policy, thus limited the scope of private business. However, the new policy ushered in since July 1991 has wide opened many of the industries for the private sector. The scope of international business depends, to a large extent, on the economic system. At one end, there are the free market economies or capitalist economies, and at the other end are the centrally planned economies or communist countries. In between these two are the mixed economies. Within the mixed economic system itself, there are wide variations. The freedom of private enterprise is the greatest in the free market economy, which is characterized by the following assumptions:

i. The factors of production (labor, land, capital) are privately owned, and production occurs at the initiative of the private enterprise.

ii. Income is received in monetary form by the sale of services of the factors of production and from the profits of the private enterprise.

iii. Members of the free market economy have freedom of choice in so far as consumption, occupation, savings and investment are concerned.

iv. The free market economy is not planned controlled or regulated by the government.

The government satisfies community or collective wants, but does not compete with private firms, nor does it tell the people where to work or what to produce. The completely free market economy, however, is an abstract system rather than a real one. Today, even the so-called market economies are subject to a number of government regulations. Countries like the United States, Japan, Australia, Canada and member countries of the EEC are regarded as market economies. The communist countries have, by and large, a centrally planned economic system. Under the rule of a communist or authoritarian socialist government, the state owns all the means of production, determines the goals of production and controls the economy according to a central master plan. There is hardly any consumer sovereignty in a centrally planned economy, unlike in the free market economy. The consumption pattern in a centrally planned economy is dictated by the state.

China, East Germany Soviet Union, Czechoslovakia, Hungary, Poland etc., had centrally planned economies. However, recently several of these countries have discarded communist system and have moved towards the market economy. In between the capitalist system and the centrally planned system falls the system of the mixed economy, under which both the public and private sectors co-exist, as in India. The extent of state participation varies widely between the mixed economies. However, in many mixed economies, the strategic and other nationally very important industries are fully owned or dominated by the state. The economic system, thus, is a very important determinant of the scope of private business. The economic system and policy are, therefore, very important external constraints on business.

POLITICAL AND LEGAL ENVIRONMENT

Political and government environment has close relationship with the economic system and economic policy. For example, the communist countries had a centrally planned economic system. In most countries, apart from those laws that control investment and related matters, there are a number of laws that regulate the conduct of the business. These laws cover such matters as standards of products, packaging, promotion etc. In many countries, with a view to protecting consumer interests, regulations have become stronger. Regulations to protect the purity of the environment and preserve the ecological balance have assumed great importance in many countries.

Some governments specify certain standards for the products (including packaging) to be marketed in the country; some even prohibit the marketing of certain products. In most nations, promotional activities are subject to various types of controls. Media advertising is not permitted in Libya. Several European countries restrain the use of children in commercial advertisements. In a number of countries, including India, the advertisement of alcoholic liquor is prohibited. Advertisements, including packaging, of cigarettes must carry the statutory warning that "cigarette smoking is injurious to health". Similarly, advertisements of baby food must necessarily inform the potential buyer that breast-feeding in the best. In countries like Germany, product comparison advertisements and the use of superlatives like 'best' or 'excellent' in advertisements is not allowed In the United States, the Federal Trade Commission is empowered to require a company to provide the quality, performance or comparative prices of its products.

"What is being asked of the drug industry and of American business in general is a fuller disclosure of the relevant facts about products. For drugs, food additives, some cosmetic preparations, and so forth, a full disclosure requires more knowledge of the long-range side effects of materials ingested into the complex human body. For American industry as a whole, greater candour has been called for under such legislation as Truth in Lending and Fair Packaging Act, under administrative decrees such as the warning requirement on cigarette packages and advertising, under the threats of private damage suits using the common-law concepts of warranty, and under voluntary programmes such as unit pricing and listing nutritional content of foods. The increasing complexity of products and the variety of product choices suggest further moves away from 'caveat emptor' or 'let the buyer beware' doctrines, moves which on the whole should prove a welcome although sometimes inconvenient challenge for business".

There are a host of statutory controls on business in India. If the MRTP companies wanted to expand their business substantially, they had to convince the government that such expansion was in the public interest. Indeed, the "Government in India has an all-pervasive and predominantly restrictive influence over various aspects of business, e.g, industrial licensing which decides location, capacity and process; import licensing for machinery and materials; size and price of capital issue; loan finance; pricing; managerial remuneration; expansion plans; distribution restrictions and a host of other enactments. Therefore, a considerable part of attention of a Chief Executive and his senior colleagues has to be devoted to a continuous dialogue with various government agencies to ensure growth and profitability within the framework of controls and restraints".

Many countries today have laws to regulate competition in the public interest. Elimination of unfair competition and dilution of monopoly power are the important objectives of these regulations. In India, the monopolistic undertakings, dominants undertakings and large industrial houses are subject to a number of regulations which prevent the concentration of economic power to the common detriment. The MRTP Act also controls monopolistic, restrictive and unfair trade practices which are prejudicial to public interest. Such regulations brighten the prospects of small and new firms. They also increase the scope of some of the existing firms to venture into new areas of business. The special privileges available to the small scale sector have also contributed to the phenomenal success of the Nirma.

Certain changes in government policies such as the industrial policy, fiscal policy, tariff policy etc. may have profound impact on business. Some policy developments create opportunities as well as threats. In other words, a development which brightens the prospects of some enterprises may pose a threat to some others. For example, the industrial policy liberalizations in India, particularly around the mid-eighties have opened up new opportunities and threats. They have provided a lot of opportunities to a large number of enterprises to diversify and to make their product mix better. But they have also given rise to serious threat to many existing products by way of increased competitions; many seller's markets have given way to buyer's markets. Even products which were seldom advertised have come to be promoted very heavily. This battle for the market has provided a splendid opportunity for the advertising industry. Advertising billing has been increasing substantially. That an estimated cost savings of about Rs. 200 crores per year have accrued to the Reliance Industries as a result of the changes in duties on some of the material inputs used by them is just an indication of the tremendous impact the fiscal and tariff policies can have on the business.

SOCIO-CULTURAL ENVIRONMENT

The socio-cultural fabric is an important environmental factor that must be analysed during formulation of business strategies. The cost of ignoring the customs, traditions, taboos, tastes and preferences, etc., of people could be very high. The buying and consumption habits of the people, their language, beliefs and values, customs and traditions, tastes and preferences, education are all factors that affect business. For a business to be successful, its strategy should be the one that is appropriate in the socio-cultural environment. The marketing mix will have to be so designed as best to suit the environmental characteristics of the market. In Thailand, Helene Curtis switched to black shampoo because Thai women felt that it made their hair look glossier. Nestle, a Swiss multinational company, today brews more than forty varieties of instant coffee to satisfy different national tastes.

Even when people of different cultures use the same basic product, the mode of consumption, conditions of use, purpose of use or the perceptions of the product attributes may vary so much so that the product attributes method of presentation, positioning, or method of promoting the product may have to be varied to suit the characteristics of different markets. For example, the two most important foreign markets for Indian shrimp are the U.S and Japan. The product attributes for the success of the product in these two markets differ. In the U.S. market, correct weight and bacteriological factors are more important rather than eye appeal, colour, uniformity of size and arrangement of the shrimp which are very important in Japan. Similarly, the mode of consumption of tuna, another seafood export from India, differs between the U.S. and European countries. Tuna fish sandwiches, an American favourite which accounts for about 80 per cent of American tuna consumption, have little appeal in high tuna consumption European countries where people eat it right from the can. A very interesting example is that of the Vicks Vaporub, the popular pain balm, which is used as a mosquito repellant in some of the tropical areas.

The differences in languages sometimes pose a serious problem, even necessitating a change in the brand name. Preett was, perhaps, a good brand name in India, but it did not suit in the overseas market; and hence it was appropriate to adopt 'Prestige' for the overseas markets. Chevrolet's brand name 'Nova' in Spanish means "it doesn't go". In Japanese, General Motors' "Body by Fisher" translates as corpse by Fisher". In Japanese, again, 3M's slogan "sticks like crazy "translates as "sticks foolishly". In some languages, Pepsi-Cola's slogan "come alive" translates as "come out of the grave". The values and beliefs associated with colour vary significantly between different cultures. Blue, considered feminine and warm in Holland, is regarded as masculine and cold in Sweden. Green is a favourite colour in the Muslim world; but in Malaysia, it is associated with illness. White indicates death and mourning in China and Korea; but in some countries, it expresses happiness and is the colour of the wedding dress of the bride. Red is a popular colour in the communist countries; but many African countries have a national distaste for red colour.

Social inertia and associated factors come in the way of the promotion of certain products, services or ideas. We come across such social stigmas in the marketing of family planning ideas, use of bio-gas for cooking, etc. In such circumstances, the success of marketing depends upon success in changing social attitudes or value systems. There are also a number of demographic factors, such as the age, and sex composition of population, family size, habitat, religion, etc., which influence the business. While dealing with the social environment, we must also consider the social environment of the business which encompasses its social responsibility and the alertness or vigilance of the consumers and of society at large. The societal environment has assumed great importance in recent years.

As Barker observes, business "traditionally has been held responsible for quantities for the supply of goods and jobs, for costs, prices, wages, hours of works, and for standards of living. Today, however, business is being asked to take a responsibility for the quality of life in our society. The expectation is that business- in addition to its traditional accountability for economic performance and results - will concern itself with the health of the society, that it will come up with the cures for the ills that currently beset us and, indeed, will find ways of anticipating and preventing future problems in these areas". As Stern succinctly points out, the "more educated the society becomes, the more interdependent it becomes, and the more discretionary the use of its resources, the more marketing will become enmeshed in social issues. Marketing personnel are at interface between company and society. In this position, they have the responsibility not merely for designing a competitive marketing strategy, but for sensitizing business to the social, as well as the product demand of society".

DEMOGRAPHIC ENVIRONMENT

Demographic factors like the size, growth rate, age composition, sex composition, etc. of the population, family size, economic stratification of the population, educational levels, languages, caste, religion etc. Are all factors that are relevant to business? Demographic factors such as size of the population, population growth rate, age composition, life expectancy, family size, spatial dispersal, occupational status, employment pattern etc, affect the demand for goods and services. Markets with growing population and income are growth markets. But the decline in the birth rates in countries like the United States have affected the demand for baby products. Johnson and Johnson have overcome this problem by repositioning their products like baby shampoo and baby soap, promoting them also to the adult segment, particularly to the females.

A rapidly increasing population indicates a growing demand for many products. High population growth rate also indicates an enormous increase in labour supply. When the Western countries experienced the industrial revolution, they had the problem of labour supply, for the population growth rate was comparatively low. Labour shortage and rising wages encouraged the growth of labour-saving technologies and automation. But most developing countries of today are experiencing a population explosion and a situation of labour surplus. The governments of developing countries, therefore, encourage labour intensive methods of production. Capital intensive methods, automation and even rationalization are apposed by labour and many sociologists, politicians and economists in these countries. The population growth rate, thus, is an important environmental factor which affects business. Cheap labour and a growing market have encouraged many multinational corporations to invest in developing countries. The occupational and spatial mobilities of population have implications for business. If labour is easily mobile between different occupations and regions, its supply will be relatively smooth, and this will affect the wage rate. If labour is highly heterogeneous in respect of language, caste and religion, ethnicity, etc., personnel management is likely to become a more complex task. The heterogeneous population with its varied tastes, preferences, beliefs, temperaments, etc. gives rise to differing demand patterns and calls for different marketing strategies. References to a number of demographic factors that have business implications have already been made under "socio-cultural environment"

NATURAL ENVIRONMENT

Geographical and ecological factors, such as natural resource endowments, weather and climatic conditions, topographical factors, locational aspects in the global context, port facilities, etc., are all relevant to business. Differences in geographical conditions between markets may sometimes call for changes in the marketing mix. Geographical and ecological factors also influence the location of certain industries. For example, industries with high material index tend to be located near the raw material sources. Climatic and weather conditions affect the location of certain industries like the cotton textile industry. Topographical factors may, affect the demand pattern. For example, in hilly areas with a difficult terrain, jeeps may be in greater demand than cars. Ecological factors have recently assumed great importance. The depletion of natural resources, environmental pollution and the disturbance of the ecological balance has caused great concern. Government policies aimed at the preservation of environmental purity and ecological balance, conservation of non-replenishale resources, etc., have resulted in additional responsibilities and problems for business, and some of these have the effect of increasing the cost of production and marketing. Externalities have become an important problem the business has to confront with.

PHYSICAL AND TECHNOLOGICAL ENVIRONMENT

Physical Factors, such as geographical factors, weather and climatic conditions may call for modifications in the product, etc., to suit the environment because these environmental factors are uncontrollable. For example, Esso adapted its gasoline formulations to suit the weather conditions prevailing in different markets. Business prospects depend also on the availability of certain physical facilities. Some products, like many consumer durables, have certain use facility characteristics. The sale of television sets, for example, is limited by the extent of the coverage of the telecasting. Similarly, the demand for refrigerators and other electrical appliances is affected by the extent of electrification and the reliability of power supply. The demand for LPG gas stoves is affected by the rate of growth of gas connections.

Technological factors sometimes pose problems. A firm, which is unable to cope with the technological changes, may not survive. Further, the differing technological environment of different markets or countires may call for product modifications. For example, many appliances and instruments in the U.S.A. are designed for 110 volts but this needs to be converted into 240 volts in countries which have that power system. Technological developments may increase the demand for some existing products. For example, voltage stabilisers help increase the sale of electrical appliances in markets characterised by frequent voltage fluctuations I power supply.

However, the introduction of TV's, Fridges etc, with in built voltage stabilizer adversely affects the demand for voltage stabilizers. Advances in the technologies of food processing and preservation, packaging etc., have facilitated product improvements and introduction of new products and have considerably improved the marketability of products. The television has added a new dimension to product promotion. The advent of TV and VCP/VCR has, however, adversely affected the cinema theatres.

The fast changes in technologies also create problems for enterprises as they render plants and products obsolete quickly. Product-market-technology matrix generally has a much shorter life today than in the past. It is particularly so in the international marketing context. It may be interesting to note that almost half of Hindustan Lever's 1980 export business did not exist in 1987. In fact, as much as a third of the company's 1987 turnover was from products and markets, which were under three years of age.

INTERNATIONAL ENVIRONMENT

The international environment is very important from the point of view of certain categories of business. It is particularly important for industries directly depending upon imports or exports and import-competing industries. For example, a recession in foreign markets, or the adoption of protectionist policies by foreign nations, may create difficulties for industries depending upon exports. On the other hand, a boom in the export market or a relaxation of the protectionist policies may help the export-oriented industries. A liberalization of imports may help some industries which use imported items, but may adversely affect import-competing industries.

It has been observed that major international developments have their spread effects on domestic business. The Great Depression in the United States sent its shock waves to a number of other countries. Oil price hikes have seriously affected a number of economies. These hikes have increased the cost of production and the prices of certain products, such as fertilizers, synthetic fibres, etc. The high oil price has led to an increase in the demand for automobile models that economise energy consumption. The demand for natural fibres increased because of the oil crisis. The oil crisis also prompted some companies to resort to demarketing. "Demarketing refers to the process of cutting consumer demand for a product back to level that can be supplied by the firm". Some oil companies-the Indian Oil Corporation, for example-have publicized tips o how to cut oil consumption. When the fertilizer price shot up following the oil crisis, some fertilizer companies appealed to the farmers to use fertilizers only for important and remunerative crops. The importance of natural manure like compost as a substitute for chemical fertilizers was also emphasized.

The oil crisis led to a reorientation of the Government of India's energy policy. Such developments affect the demand, consumption and investment pattern. A good export market enables a firm to develop a more profitable product mix and to consolidate its position in the domestic market. Many companies now plan production capacities and investment taking into account also the foreign markets. Export marketing facilitates the attainment of optimum capacity utilization; a company may be able to mitigate the effects of domestic recession by exporting. However, a company which depends on the export market to a considerable extent has also to face the impact of adverse developments in foreign markets.

SUMMARY

International business is a necessity in today's world. The gains for greater awareness and knowledge of international business fare immense for nations, multi-national enterprises, trading companies, exporters and even individuals. To go global, the first step would be to understand the international business environment. International business is nothing but extending the areas of activities of business across the boundaries. We have discussed about the importance of understanding international business environment in detail. The concepts of microenvironment and macro environment with reference to the political, legal, economical and cultural background are also discussed. Understanding international business environment requires greater research and information. The fulfillment of this research could happen with greater understanding of the framework for analyzing the international business environment.

Note: MICROS Systems is a designer, manufacturer and marketer of enterprise information solutions for the global hospitality and specialty retail industries. Its offerings include software, hardware, and services comprising enterprise systems integration, consulting and support. The company operates in the US, Europe, Pacific Rim and Latin America. It is headquartered in Columbia, Maryland and employs 4,619 people. For a very good case study regarding this topic, reader can visit company's website www.micros.com

Bibliography

A. Balsa and T.G. McGuire, "Prejudice, Clinical Uncertainty, and Stereotyping as Sources of Health Disparities," *Journal of Health Eco-nomics*, January, 2003.

A. Birritteri, "Realizing the Benefits of an All-inclusive Employee Base," *New Jersey Business,* November, 2005.

A. Findler, P Healy, and K. Zernike, "President of Harvard Resigns, Ending Stormy 5-Year Tenure," *The New York Times,* February, 2006.

A. Mehrabian, *Silent Messages*, Belmont, CA: Wadsworth, 1971.

A.A. Cannella and D.C. Hambrick, "Executive Departure and Acquisition Performance," *Strategic Management Journal*, 1993.

A.G. Schick, L.A. Gordon, and S. Haka, "Information Overload: A Temporal Approach," *Accounting, Organizations & Society*, 1990.

A.K. Dixit and B.J. Nalebuff, *Thinking Strategically*, London: W.W. Norton, 1991.

A.M. Brandenburger and B.J. Nalebuff, "The Right Game: Using Game Theory to Shape Strategy," *Harvard Business Review,* July-August 1995.

B. Barney, "Company Resources and Sustained Competitive Advantage," *Journal of Management*, 1991.

B. Nussbaum, "Get Creative! How to Build Creative Companies," *Business Week,* August, 2005.

C. Goforth, "Still Recruiting Staff," *Akron Beacon Journal,* July, 2001.

C. Smith, "Finding The 'Right People' Just Got Easier," *Franchising World*, November, 2005.

C.E. Shannon and W. Weaver, *The Mathematical Theory of Communication*, Urbana: University of Illinois Press, 1949.

C.H. St. John and J.S. Harrison, "Manufacturing-Based Relatedness, Synergy, and Coordination," *Strategic Management Journal*, 1999.

C.N. Macrae and G.V Bodenhausen, "Social Cognition: Thinking Categorically about Others," *Annual Review of Psychology*, 2000.

C.W.L. Hill, "Differentiation versus Low Cost or Differentiation and Low Cost: A Contingency Framework," *Academy of Management* Review, 1988.

C.W.L. Hill, "The Role of Headquarters in the Multidivisional Firm," in *Fundamental Issues in Strategy Research,* ed. R. Rumelt, D.J. Teece, and D. Schendel, Cambridge, MA: Harvard Business School Press, 1994

D. Brown, "Success Begins in the Middle," *Canadian HR Reporter,* June, 2003.

D. Goleman, R. Boyatzis, and A. McKee, *Primal Leaders*, Boston: Harvard Business School Press, 2002.

D. Hamermesh and J.E. Biddle, "Beauty and the Labor Market," *American Economic Review*, 1994.

D. Stonehouse, "E-mail," *Sun Herald*, Sydney, June, 2005.

D. Tannen, *That's Not What I Meant!*, New York: Ballantine, 1987.

D. Woodruff, "Crossing Culture Divide Early Clears Merger Paths," *The Asian Wall Street Journal,* May, 2001.

D.A. Harrison et al., "Time, Teams, and Task Performance: Changing Effects of Surface- and Deep-Level Diversity on Group Functioning," *Academy of Management Journal*, 2002.

D.B. Simmons, "The Nature of the Organizational Grapevine," *Supervisory Management,* November, 1985.

D.C. Bamlund, *Communication Styles of Japanese and Americans: Images and Realities*, Belmont, CA: Wadsworth, 1988.

D.C. Thomas and K. Inkson, *Cultural Intelligence: People Skills for Global Business*, San Francisco: Berrett-Koehler, 2004.

D.D. Dawley and W.P. Anthony, "User Perceptions of E-Mail at Work," *Journal of Business and Technical Communication*, April 2003.

D.D. Steiner and J.S. Rain, "Immediate and Delayed Primacy and Recency Effects in Performance Evaluation," *Journal of Applied Psychology*, 1989.

D.J. Ravenscraft and F.M. Scherer, *Mergers, Selloffs, and Economic Efficiency*, Washington, DC: Brookings Institution, 1987.

D.J. Teece, "Economies of Scope and the Scope of the Enterprise," *Journal of Economic Behavior and Organization*, 1980.

D.M. Kreps, *Game Theory and Economic Modeling*, Oxford: Oxford University Press, 1990.

E. Silverman, "Making Your Mark," *Human Resource* Executive, November, 2004.

F. Russo, "My Kingdom for a Door," *Time Magazine,* October, 2000.

F.L. Schmidt and R.D. Zimmerman, "A Counterintuitive Hypothesis about Employment Interview Validity and Some Supporting Evidence," *Journal of Applied Psychology,* 2004.

G. Evans and D. Johnson, "Stress and Open-Office Noise," *Journal of Applied Psychology*, 2000.

G. Hertel, S. Geister, and U Konradt, "Managing Virtual Teams: A Review of Current Empirical Research," *Human Resource Management Review*, 2005.

G. Hitt and J.D. McKinnon, "Cheney Takes Blame for Shooting but Defends How It Was Disclosed," *The Wall Street Journal,* February, 2006.

G.H. Harel, A. Arditi-Vogel, and T. Janz, "Comparing the Validity and Utility of Behavior Description Interview versus Assessment Center Ratings," *Journal of Managerial Psychology*, 2003.

H. Lee, "Behavioral Strategies for Dealing with Flaming in an Online Forum," *The Sociological Quarterly*, 2005.

H. Mintzberg, *The Nature of Managerial Work*, New York: Harper & Row, 1973.

H.H. Kelley, "The Process of Causal Attribution," *Ameri-can Psychologist*, 1973.

I. Teotonio, "Rescuers Pull 'Victims' from Rubble," *Toronto Star,* April, 2005.

J. Davidson, "Fighting Information Overload," *Office Solutions*, 2006.

J. Larson, "Temps Are Here to Stay," *American Demographics*, February, 1996.

J. Pellet, "Driving Diversity," *Chief Executive,* May, 2004.

J. Pfeffer, *New Directions in Organizational Theory*, New York: Oxford University Press, 1997.

J.A. Breaugh, *Recruitment: Science and Practice*, Boston: PWS-Kent, 1992.

J.A. Breaugh, *Recruitment: Science and Practice*, Boston: PWS-Kent, 1992.

J.G. Miller, "Living Systems: The Organization," *Behavioral Science*, 1972.

J.M. Feldman "Beyond Attribution Theory: Cognitive Processes in Performance Appraisal," *Journal of Applied Psychology*, 1981.

J.P. Walsh, "Top Management Turnover Following Mergers and Acquisitions," *Strategic Management Journal,* 1988.

J.R. Kelly and S.G. Barsade, "Mood and Emotions in Small Groups and Work Teams," *Organizational Behavior and Human Decision Processes*, September 2001.

K. Griffiths, "KPMG Sacks 670 Employees by E-Mail," *The Independent*, London, November , 2002.

K. Tyler, "Train for Smarter Hiring," *HR Magazine,* May, 2005.

K..M. Jackson, "Buzzword Backlash Looks to Purge Jibba-Jabba from Corporate-Speak," *Boston Globe,* April, 2005.

K.J. Dunham, "Career Journal: The Jungle," *The Wall Street Journal,* October, 2003.

K.J. Krone, EM. Jablin, and L.L. Putnam, "Communication Theory and Organizational Communication: Multiple Perspectives," in *Handbook of Organizational Communication: An Interdisciplinary Perspective,* ed. F. M. Jablin et al., Newbury Park, CA: Sage, 1987.

K.N. Wexley and G.P. Latham, *Developing and Training Human Resources in Organizations,* 2nd ed., New York: HarperCollins, 1991.

L.Z. Tiedens and A.R. Fragale, "Power Moves: Complementarity in Dominant and Submissive Nonverbal Behavior," *Journal of Personal-ity and Social Psychology*, 2003.

L.Z. Tiedens and A.R. Fragale, "Power Moves: Complementarity in Dominant and Submissive Nonverbal Behavior," *Journal of Per-sonality and Social Psychology*, 2003.

M. Brandel, "Global CIO," *Computer world,* November, 2005.

M. Fujio, "Silence during Intercultural Communication: A Case Study," *Corporate Communications*, 2004.

M. McLuhan, *Understanding Media: The Extensions of Man*, New York: M-Graw-Hill, 1964.

M.E. Porter, "What Is Strategy?" *Harvard Business Review,* February, 2000.

M.E. Porter, *Competitive Advantage* (New York: Free Press, 1985); and M.E. Porter, *Competitive Strategy*, New York: Free Press, 1980.

M.J. Frank, "Justifiable Discrimination in the News and Entertainment Industries: Does Title VII Need a Race or Color BFOQ?" *University of San Francisco Law Review*, Spring, 2001.

N.R. Lockwood, "Workplace Diversity: Leveraging the Power of Difference for Competitive Advantage," *HR Magazine,* June, 2005.

P. Drucker, *Peter Drucker on the Profession of Management*, Boston: Harvard Business School Press, 1998.

P. Ekman and E. Rosenberg, *What the Face Reveals: Basic and Applied Studies of Spontaneous Expression Using the Facial Action Coding System*, Oxford, England: Oxford University Press, 1997.

P. Harris and R. Moran, *Managing Cultural Differences*, Houston: Gulf, 1987.

P. Tripp-Knowles, "A Review of the Literature on Barriers Encoun-tered by Women in Science Academia," *Resources for Feminist Research*, Spring/Summer 1995.

P. Winkielman and K. C. Berridge, "Unconscious Emotion," *Current Directions in Psychological Science*, 2004.

P.J. Taylor and J.L. Pierce, "Effects of Introducing a Performance Management System and Employees' Subsequent Attitudes and Efforts," *Public Personnel Management*, Fall 1999.

P.P. Wernimont and J.P. Campbell, "Signs, Samples, and Criteria," *Journal of Applied Psychology*, October, 1968.

R. Mullins, "Verizon Goes to Great Lengths," *Tampa Tribune,* February, 2006.

R. Reed and R.J. DeFillippi, "Causal Ambiguity, Barriers to Imitation, and Sustainable Competitive Advantage," *Academy of Management Review*, 1990.

R. Winters, "Harvard's Crimson Face," *Time,* January, 2005.

R.C. Lee, "Keeping Up with Growth," *Houston Chronicle,* August, 2005.

R.D. McPhee, "Vertical Communication Chains," *Management Communication*, 1988.

R.E. Rice, "Task Analyzability, Use of New Media, and Effectiveness: A Multi-Site Exploration of Media Richness," *Organization Science*, 1992.

R.F. Mager and P. Pipe, *Analyzing Performance Problems*, Belmont, CA: Lake Publishing, 1984.

R.L. Daft and R.H. Lengel, "Information Richness: A New Approach to Managerial Behavior and Organization Design," *Research in Organizational behavior*, 1984.

R.P. Rumelt, *Strategy, Structure, and Economic Performance*, Cambridge, MA: Harvard Business School Press, 1974.

R.S. Kaplan and D.P. Norton, *The Balanced Scorecard: Translating Strategy into Action*, Boston: Harvard Business School Press, 1996.

S. Ohtaki, T. Ohtaki, and M.D. Fetters, "Doctor-Patient Communica-tion: A Comparison of the USA and Japan," *Family Practice*, June 2003.

S. Scherreik, "How Efficient Is That Company?" *Business-Week,* December,2003.

S. Theil, "The New Old Age," *Newsweek.* January, 2006.

S.E. Jackson and R.S. Schuler, "Human Resource Planning," *American Psychologist*, 1990.

T. Copeland, T. Koller, and J. Murrin, *Valuation: Measuring and Mananing the Value of Companies*, New York: Wiley, 2000.

T. Koski, "Reflections on Information Glut and Other Issues in Knowledge Productivity," *Futures*, August 2001.

T. Matthews, "Ohio-Area Companies Turn to 'Evaluation Hiring' to Pick Best Employees," *Columbus Dispatch,* May, 2005.

T. Weiss, *Coaching Competencies and Corporate Leadership,* Boca Raton, FL: St. Lucie Press, 2003.

V. Gait, "Kid-Glove Approach Woos New Grads," *Globe & Mail,* March, 2005.

W.C. Kirn and R. Maugborgne, *Blue Ocean Strategy*, Boston: Harvard Business School Press, 2005.

Williamson, *Markets and Hierarchies*, New York: Free Press, 1988.

Index